SUCCESS

AFTER

COLLEGE

D1736350

EVERYTHING
YOU
NEED
TO
KNOW
TO
SUCCEED
AFTER
COLLEGE

EDITED BY GAYLE KIMBALL

EQUALITY=PRESS

To our college students and new hires who keep us current and to Jed Kimball-Hait who likes to see his name in his mom's books.

FIRST EDITION, FIRST PRINTING
Copyright 1993
by Equality Press and Gayle Kimball

ISBN 0-938795-24-4 (pbk.)
Library of Congress Catalog Card Number 93-070405
Everything You Need To Know To Succeed After College.
Edited by Gayle Kimball.
Self-help.

Questions regarding the content of this book should be addressed to:

Equality Press
42 Ranchita Way, Suite 4
Chico, CA 95928

The Talent:

Cover Design: Joe Martin
Text Design: Masa Uehara
Drawings: Kelly Lynn Baylor
Electronic Prepress: Joe Martin, Tzantarng Lee
Copyeditor: Phyllis Mannion
Photographers (in the order their photograph is displayed): Will Gibson, Faith Hayden, Expressly Portraits, Nancy Felling, Jamey Stillings, Jeff Teeter, Alain Tomatis, Nils Vidstrand, Erin Pekins, Wentling's Stuido, Ces Greene, Mercedes Maharis

Thanks to:

Lou Bentley, Greg Berryman, Jeff Baylor, Dolores Blalock, Steve Flowers, Les Hait, Brad Glanville, Wendy Lew Hoffman, Greg Kimball, Laura Rubio, and to these people who critiqued the entire manuscript: Kelly Lynn Baylor, Laura Curtin, Holly Etzel, Kathleen Gakle, Kriste K. Johnson, Kimmy Forssell, Melissa Mead, and Virginia Peters. Thanks to the authors for responding graciously to multiple requests for chapter revisions.

Your Success Team

1. Judith Eberhart
2. Colette Fleuridas
3. Pat Hanson
4. Matthews Jackson
5. Madelyn Jennings
6. Gayle Kimball
7. Francis Lee
8. Barbara Polland
9. Don Sabo
10. Taryn Sievers
11. Jacqueline Sheehan
12. Susan Suntree

TABLE OF CONTENTS

Introduction   viiii

1 How to Succeed in your Career   1
MADELYN JENNINGS, business executive; MATTHEWS
JACKSON, college administrator; GAYLE KIMBALL, professor
at California State University, Chico; DR. SYLVIA LOPEZ
ROMANO, college administrator; SUSAN SUNTREE, college
instructor and author; DR. MOON JEE YOO-MADRIGAL,
college instructor

2 Successful Financial Planning   45
TARYN SIEVERS, stockbroker, with a section by LES HAIT,
attorney

3 Understanding Men   71
DR. DON SABO, professor

4 Understanding Women   95
DR. COLETTE FLEURIDAS, professor and counselor

5 Secrets to Satisfying Sexuality   123
DR. PAT HANSON, professor and sex educator

6 How to succeed in Love   147
DR. GAYLE KIMBALL, author

7 How to Succeed in a Dual-Earner Family   185
DR. GAYLE KIMBALL, employed mother

8 How to be a Successful Parent   211
DR. BARBARA POLLAND,
professor, author, and psychotherapist

9 Taking Care of Yourself Successfully   229
JUDITH EBERHART, counselor, college instructor, and fitness
instructor

10 Using the Power of Your Mind for Success   249
REVERND MICHAEL FRANCIS LEE, minister

11 Successful Life Planning   271
DR. JACQUELINE SHEEHAN, psychologist

Final Words   291

➣ Introduction ➣

Greetings from our generation—most of the authors are in our thirties and forties—to readers who are launching your careers and families. We're concerned that the rug was pulled out from under many of you when the economy became shaky, many top government leaders in the 1980s were poor role models, some of you were latchkey children, and many of you experienced the divorce of your parents. Unfortunately, social institutions haven't responded to these concerns with comprehensive and visionary guidance. Our intent is to share what we've learned through our studies and experiences.

Many of us are professors and counselors who talk with young adults daily. Most of us work in California colleges, while Don Sabo teaches in New York, Taryn Sievers is a stockbroker in Oakland, Francis Lee is a minister in Paradise (yes!), California, Les Hait is an attorney, and Madelyn Jennings is a vice-president of personnel for Gannett, in Virginia. This book is a step in the direction of providing you with the information and resources you need to achieve your goals.

Each chapter starts with an affirmation because we have discovered the power of our thoughts to generate results. We include suggestions for journal topics to encourage your inner exploration. Additional readings about topics that are especially useful are marked by a drawing of a pointing hand. You will find a summary of key points at the end of each chapter to highlight important principles to apply to your life.

We notice that our college students expect to do it all. They plan to combine career and family, without realistic expectations of the strains of role juggling in a society which lags behind in equitable accommodation to employed parents and their children, to women, to people of color and those with alternative life-styles. We urge you to practice life-style activism and challenge the media claims that the baby bust generation is a silent one without unifying causes. We are encouraged by a 1992 survey of more than 200,000 college freshmen and women, conducted by UCLA researchers, which indicated increased desire to "influence social values," and do volunteer work.

Your Journal

We strongly suggest that you write in a journal as you read, responding to the questions raised in each chapter to explore and clarify your thoughts, values, and planning process. An avid journal writer since she was fourteen, poet Susan Wooldridge suggests that you use a small, plain loose-leaf notebook so you can insert pages and carry it with you. She recommends that you avoid a fancy book that might suggest you need to write perfectly and would attract curiosity from others. Use a pen you like to write with, include drawings, paste in useful tidbits and photographs, and give yourself permission to write quickly, sleepily, imperfectly. No one is going to evaluate your work!

It's a means to clarify your thinking and discover your inner self. Susan either ignores or addresses her inner critic, depending on her mood. Your journal never gets tired of you and permits you to be totally self-centered. For more ideas,☛ see Lucia Capacchione's *The Creative Journal* (Swallow Press at Ohio University Press).

━━━━━━━━━━━━━ **Personal Reflections** ━━━━━━━━━━━━━

Start your journal with an assessment of where you are now, then move on to what you most want to learn from reading this book, your immediate goals, and your goals for five years from now. What are your present strengths? What new knowledge and skills do you need to achieve your goals? How can you obtain these skills? In what areas would you most like to grow and develop? What kinds of social change would you most like to bring about? What chapter do you intend to read first? Why?

Some readers report feeling inadequate and overwhelmed at the thought of trying to be successful in all the areas covered in the book. Concentrate on one goal at a time, put less important goals on the back burner, acknowledge your positive traits, recognize that our aim is to grow rather than be perfect, and take time to watch the daisies. Making mistakes is inevitable for every human; unpleasant experiences can be our best lessons. People who have easy lives may not have the same opportunities to develop strength and depth. You may discover that what seems painful in the short-term often turns out to be for the best in the long-term. One step at a time is fine, and so are two steps forward and one step backward. Be kind to yourself, remembering that fact that the authors have made mistakes and learned from them provides useful knowledge for this book.

We would like the book to be interactive. Please write to us with your questions and comments. This edition includes reader questions and comments and we will provide updates in the next edition. We'll try to respond to you personally, too. Write to the editor, Dr. Gayle Kimball, CSUC-445, Chico, CA 95929. Tell us if there are other topics that you would like to see addressed and share with us what works for you in creating your successes. Enjoy your reading, journal writing, and action! Your panel of advisers wants to hear about your journey of inner exploration.

✪Next... Our guess is that the first issue you would like discussed is career success. So, in the first chapter, a panel of experts describes skills and information you need to do well on the job.

"My talents and abilities are recognized and encouraged by myself and my colleagues."

1

HOW TO SUCCEED IN YOUR CAREER

MADELYN JENNINGS

GAYLE KIMBALL

VINCENT PETKUS

MATTHEWS JACKSON

SYLVIA LOPEZ ROMANO

ARTHUR SANCHEZ

MOON JEE YOO-MADRIGAL

SUSAN SUNTREE

Chapter Goals

In Part 1, a panel of advisers tell how to interview for and get the right job and how to succeed in your career. In Part 2, they explain how to get past the glass ceiling for women and people of color (this is useful for all readers interested in understanding the diverse workforce) and in Part 3, they discuss how to develop effective written and oral communication skills.

Part 1—A Good Start

In this tight market, who's getting the jobs?

Madelyn P. Jennings is vice-president of personnel for Gannett in Arlington, Virginia. Gannett is a leader in the communications industry and publishes *USA TODAY.*

There's no question that it's tough to find a job in the 1990s. Company recruiters are no longer competing for scarce interview schedules at colleges and universities. M.B.A.'s graduating from big-name schools are no longer deciding which of several top dollar offers from Wall Street firms to accept. Businesses that were hiring aggressively in the 1980s are staying flat, or are laying people off. Over one-fourth of adults under 35 lived with their parents in 1992, indicating that it's harder to find a good job today than it was a generation ago. There are jobs out there, however. They may not be investment banker jobs starting at $75,000, but jobs that will give new grads a foot in the door.

Where are these jobs? They're in non glamorous industries—selling office equipment rather than junk bonds, starting on the line in a small manufacturing firm rather than in a training program for General Motors. They're in smaller towns—Peoria rather than Chicago, Ithaca rather than New York, Salinas rather than L.A. Small firms and startup companies are creating jobs while the giants are downsizing. Also some companies are relocating to other states where they will need to hire new employees. Demographic and political trends show that jobs will be available in areas like environmental science, health care, geriatrics, and recreation as the baby boomers and their parents age—rather than aerospace, nuclear engineering or middle management. The service sector is growing more than manufacturing.

Who's getting these jobs? People with lots of hustle who master the art of networking, who follow up on every lead, who are flexible about what they do and where they live, and who (nicely) don't take "no" as final. Successful job seekers do not sit at home waiting for the phone to ring. They contact potential employers every day, researching routes other than sending out resumes and reading ads in newspapers and journals. If you have friends in college, advise them to participate in a cooperative internship program in their field to establish contacts.

What sets someone aside when applying for a job with many applicants? First impressions are powerful. A good impression will follow the applicant through the process and a poor one is almost impossible to overcome. It starts with your first contact with the company whether by mail, telephone, or in person. Is your resume concise and explicit, with no typos, with a professional layout on quality paper? ☛ Refer to Martin John Yate's *Resumes That Knock 'Em Dead* (Bob Adams, Boston) and Yana Parker's *Damn Good Resume Guide* (Ten Speed Press). On the phone, do you sound upbeat yet professional? Are you on time for appointments and dressed appropriately? (No rundown heels, wild ties, strong perfume.) Are you unfailingly polite to the receptionist and the secretary and not just to the decision maker?

Companies look for an applicant who's done homework about the company, has thought of every conceivable question an interviewer might ask and has role-played the answers with her roommate. Hiring managers look for someone who's enthusiastic and can explain what he can contribute rather than asking solely about salary, training programs, and chances for advancement.

═══════════ **Personal Reflections** ═══════════

1. Visualize your ideal job. What do you value most about it: How interesting? Opportunities for advancement? How much good can you do? Salary? Prestige? Does it live up to your family's goals for you? Flexibility and benefits? Opportunity to travel? Fit with future family plans?

2. How close does your current job come to your ideal? What is your five-year plan for your career path?

3. Brainstorm every idea you and your friends can think of to help get the job you really want. Make a list of the skills you can bring to a job.

4. How much time do you want to devote to your job?

5. How far are you willing to move to get a good job? How would you create a social network in a new area?

6. What new skills and experience do you need to reach your goals?

How do I conduct a successful job interview?

Before the Interview:

Research the Company

♦ Check libraries/databases for the last six months' of clips. In the business reference section of the library, research the backgrounds of individual executives and other pertinent data.

♦ Read the annual report, recruiting brochure, quarterly reports; find out who's on the board. How are they organized? Does the chairperson's letter tell you something about their plans and style?

♦ Figure out what kinds of jobs you're interested in and what kinds of jobs they have; don't ask for a job in strategic planning if they don't have a strategic planning department.

♦ Check your college placement office for information about graduates who are with the company and call them. Ask about workplace culture, mission, style, and the glass ceiling for women and people of color.

Plan Ahead

♦ Think through how your course work and work experience can be applied to company needs and devise illustrations to prove the point.

♦ Look for companies that are healthy financially and where you can grow, e.g., don't get stuck as a paralegal in a law firm if you are interested in promotional opportunities up the ladder.

♦ Get to know successful people (your parents' friends, favorite faculty members, employers). Study how they make decisions and what they look for in hiring people.

♦ Think about how to differentiate yourself from other candidates. Ask yourself, "Why should this company hire ME?" Identify skills you've learned in various activities in addition to your academic training.

♦ Gayle Kimball (G.K.) makes the next three suggestions: Madelyn Jennings is "M.J." Videotape yourself doing a practice interview session with a friend. Start by shaking hands firmly and introducing yourself, then answer the question, "Tell me something about yourself." Reply in terms of the strengths you bring to a job. Watch for repetitive speech patterns (you know, totally, umm, yeah, OK, like). Be aware of hand gestures and posture, as 80 percent of communication is nonverbal.

♦ Consider taking lessons in the Alexander Technique which teaches how to move with ease and balance as you walk, sit, and stand, and identifies habits which interfere with natural poise and coordination. (☞ To locate a teacher in your area, write to NAST, P.O. Box 3992, Champaign, IL 61826-3992.) Lean forward to show interest and direct your head, neck, and physical energy upward, rather than slumping in your chair. A reader states that she has not hired people simply because they slouched during the interview.

♦ Spend time before the interview visualizing yourself as articulate, poised, centered, confident, knowledgeable, and making a positive impression. An interesting study observed athletes who practiced before an event, those who did not practice, and those who simply visualized how they would perform. The last group did as well as the first, and better than the second, indicating that imagining a desired result can help make it happen.

♦ Start now to build an affordable dress-for-success wardrobe by shopping for wool, silk, and linen classics at second-hand clothing and thrift stores. They can be altered to fit. Avoid fashion fads and buy classics, using a coordinated color plan.

During the Interview:

♦ Always arrive ten minutes early. Wear business attire appropriate to the position for which you're interviewing.

♦ Bring extra copies of your resume to help you fill out the application quickly, neatly, and accurately, and to provide if needed.

♦ Bring anything else you've done to show the caliber of your work.

♦ Don't smoke or chew gum.

♦ If interviewed at lunch, don't order alcohol. Do order food that's easy to eat (no finger foods) and eat a moderate amount.

♦ Listen carefully to questions. Don't interrupt the interviewer. Don't rush too quickly to an answer: It's fine to pause to organize your thoughts.

♦ Never use clichés, such as "I like working with people."

♦ Make sure you pronounce and spell the company name and the interviewer's name correctly.

♦ Breathe deeply from your abdominal area, thinking of your breath expanding your lower ribs around to your back.

♦ (G.K.) Women should avoid tag questions (don't you think? isn't it?) and questioning inflections which weaken declarative statements, along with slang, head cocking, rapid speech, squirming, giggling and other mannerisms which present a childlike image. Speak slowly to signal that what you have to say is worth hearing. Avoid formfitting or short clothes, slingback high heels, heavy make-up and any other distractions from your mind and personality. Create a professional rather than a sexy image. Men should not interrupt the interviewer, should listen carefully to what he or she has to say, and ask questions about the workplace culture.

♦ Shake hands before and after the interview. Refer to the interviewer by name as you answer his or her questions. At the end of the interview, say what you liked about the interview and what impresses you about the company. Summarize your strong points in a follow-up letter to the interviewer.

In the first 10 minutes don't ask:
♦ I don't know much about this company—what does it do?
♦ What's the salary? Are salary advances available?
♦ How good are benefits here?
♦ Is overtime common?
♦ How soon will I be promoted? (Remember, you're interviewing for *this* job, not the next one!)
♦ What jobs do you have available?

Do ask:
♦ Can you tell me about your workplace culture—what's important here?

♦ What is the background of the top people of this company? What were their career paths?

♦ Why is the position open? Who held it before and is that person still here?

♦ What are the two or three key business issues facing this employer in the next year or two?

♦ How would you describe a typical day on the job?

♦ How would you describe a successful manager here?

♦ May I talk to someone on the staff whose background is similar to mine?

♦ Can I see a copy of the position description for this job? If there isn't one, can you describe the four or five major job responsibilities?

♦ How is performance measured? How will I know when I'm performing up to expectations? (Get a copy of the performance appraisal form when you're hired so you'll know the standards.)

♦ What do you think the company will be like five years from now? What changes do you anticipate?

♦ What do you think are the areas in which my education and experience fit the job?

(If they offer you a clerical job, find out if there are any sales openings. Sales is a surer way to the top.)

Typical Interview Questions

Questions aren't hard if you anticipate them. The questions are followed by what the interviewer is really trying to find out. ☞ See Martin John Yate's *Knock 'Em Dead with Great Answers to Tough Interview Questions* (Bob Adams, Boston) and H. Anthony Nedley's *Sweaty Palms: The Neglected Art of Being Interviewed* (Ten Speed Press).

Why are you interested in us and in this job?
Are you motivated enough to have done some research on us and on this job? Do you want this job with this company or just any job?

Why should we hire you? What will you do for us?
Have you learned enough about us and yourself to be able to sell your strengths/experience in relation to our needs?

What adjectives would your prior faculty advisor or boss use to describe you?

Are you candid, but able to put a positive spin on possible negatives?

Why did you choose your college and major?
Are you self-directed and know what you want or do you just go with the flow?

Do you think your grades are a good indication of your academic achievement?
Do you accept responsibility for your actions—can you succeed in different situations?

Describe a failure in your life and how you handled it.
Are you human? Do you learn from your mistakes or just explain them away?

Would you rather work alone or as part of a team?
Are you savvy enough to know the right answer is, "It depends."

Was there one key thing you have learned on any of the jobs you've held?
Can you handle failure and grow? Can you handle success without it going to your head?

For any jobs you've had, describe the best and the worst bosses (or teachers).
What are you like to manage? Do you describe best boss in terms of how he/she contributed to your success and worst boss in terms of what you learned, not how he/she made you fail?

What accomplishments (at work or otherwise) make you proud?
What motivates you? What are your values?

How would you describe your management style?
How do you go about getting things done?

What do you read aside from classwork?
How broad are your interests and intellectual curiosity?

Where do you see yourself in five years?

Are you realistic about goals, yet motivated to succeed and willing to take responsibility for your growth?

What question should I have asked you that you're glad I didn't ask?

Can I get you to tell me what you're least confident about?

Close the interview with information you think hasn't come out—make your own sales pitch! Ask for the job. This shows a take-charge, assertive candidate.

(G.K.) Follow-up with calls. I got several jobs because I conducted a polite campaign of phoning regularly. I made it so clear I was enthusiastic about the job, they finally gave it to me. It's often true that the squeaky wheel gets oiled.

I've gotten the job; what should I do/not do?

You should do the job well. Work hard and be creative. Don't worry about someone else's bigger office or better sales territory. Don't begin yet to plot what your next job will be. In the first year just hunker down and do your job and more. Stay a little later, volunteer for special projects, and think about a better way to do a task. Polish the gem that is your current job rather than mining for the elusive diamond that's your next job.

Find opportunities to learn more about your company by:
- networking
- mentoring
- volunteering for projects
- accepting task force assignments
- studying the annual report and any other publications and speeches by leaders of your organization.

Continue to network. It's probably what got you the job in the first place and it works throughout your career. Network inside the company—if you're in sales, make some friends on the production side. Network outside the company—join professional organizations and get to know people doing similar work in other companies.

(G.K.) Study the culture of their workplace to learn its informal rules, taboos, and expectations for behavior and performance, as if you were an anthropologist studying a foreign culture. Interview successful people about what they and others did to excel. The interview process should be repeated periodically and a "kitchen cabinet" of a few close advisers established.

(M.J.) Learn the "sports" of the company. If it's stock market, know how the market closed yesterday. If it's jogging, try jogging. Learn to do and speak their informal language.

Throughout your career, look for ways you can help others with information, contacts, and friendly advice. It's how you grow. Should you need to move on by choice or because of one of those infamous downsizings, it will be these contacts that will give you the support and the leads you'll need to find that next job.

(G.K.) You will inevitably run into difficult people who play power games. Try disarming them by finding a point of agreement or getting them to buy into your success by asking their advice. Some may want the satisfaction of getting you upset, angry, or hurt (any negative reaction to their verbal blows) because they like to feel up to your down. Don't give them the reward of seeing you upset; don't reinforce bad behavior, using psychological behavior modification principles of rewarding good behavior to enforce it and ignoring bad behavior to eliminate it. Some power-hungry people will try to intimidate or threaten you. Be firm and they will back down.

If you feel overwhelmed, say, "I'd like some time to think about this; I'll get back to you," and leave or hang up the phone. Use assertiveness techniques (many books and workshops are available) by firmly repeating what you want, such as, "I expect courtesy from a colleague." Use direct eye contact and confident body language: Practice in front of a mirror. Many power games go on in the workplace when people are competing for advancement; you will probably be tested, subtly or not so subtly. The process is like the hazing and initiation rituals involved in pledging a sorority or fraternity.

Ignoring unacceptable behavior will sometimes be enough to discourage it, while at other times it has to be confronted. If someone is harassing you in any way, record their objectionable behaviors with specific times, places, and quotes. When a pattern is established, confront the harasser with a copy of your record. Tell him or her what you find objectionable, that you want it to stop, and that if the behavior does stop, you will forgive and forget. However, if he or she chooses to continue, you will pass the documentation on to the boss, the local media, or the court. Sexual harassment, including a hostile work environment, is a violation of federal law. Both men and women are protected against gender discrimination on the job. Start with the problem person, then follow the chain of command, telling the offender what you intend to do.

Just because someone is nice and jovial does not mean he or she is trustworthy. Put any important agreement into writing, signed by both parties. Even if someone is totally honest, he/she can forget or misunderstand, so this is very important to do. Also keep a paper trail, copies of memos written by and to you, as even well-meaning people often remember the same thing differently.

Many readers commented that they do not like the idea of playing games. You at least need to be aware that others play them, understand the rules of the work game, and then make an informed decision about how you intend to be successful in your job. Once you're in a power position you might be able to change the way the work game is played. The rules are described in the section on how women can get past the glass ceiling.

A reader asked about office romances. Think about what could happen if you break-up; is the possibility of revenge worth the risk? Women are still suspect for sleeping their way to the top; is this an inference people could use against either of you? It is a good idea when starting anything new not to talk about it, so that it cannot be sabotaged by people who might feel jealous or competitive. Do not make an office romance public knowledge if your work situation is such that one of you could be suspect for favoring the other or if you do not want to become the center of gossip.

(M.J.) Become a "pro" at your job. Get a reputation for quick responsiveness and real results. Use a "tickler" file system so that projects get proper follow-up and stay on target. Be a manager your people say is good. Get the reputation as a leader whose people are very competent (select them well!) and give 120 percent.

Look for opportunities to expand your contributions in your current job. If in a staff job, try to get some line experience, and vice versa, if you want to move up the ladder. If you miss out on a promotion, ask your boss what was missing in your background and how you can get that experience. Use the "not ready now" assessment to your own learning advantage. This could also provide an opportunity for you to discuss your career path with your supervisor. Make sure (after you establish your track record) that your boss knows what you see as your career path and put this in writing.

Be willing to take risks. It's OK to fail if you learn something in the process. Go for promotions offered, even if you think you're not ready. None of us is ever totally ready for promotions when they come. You won't get promoted just for being there. Do your current job very well if you expect to be promoted. "No job too big, no job too small" is a terrific attitude.

(G.K.) These same principles apply to graduate students; you need to find trusted mentors, network to gain informal information sources and support, find informants to explain the particular university culture, and apply time management techniques efficiently. In my Ph.D. program, we saved time by forming a study group and giving each other summaries of research about topics to be covered on our comprehensive examination. We investigated the types of questions asked on previous exams so we could focus our studies. I learned the hard way that you should thoroughly screen the professors you select to be on your dissertation committee; learn about their interests, possible biases, and how fair and helpful they were to previous students.

Graduate school is a tremendous amount of work, so develop social support systems such as taking turns cooking dinner with other students. You can rotate eating dinner at each others' homes and talk about university politics and your studies. Get loans and finish your degree as fast as possible rather than trying to work and study, taking years to complete your degree.

➤ What do employers wish new job entrants already knew?

Gayle Kimball is an author and professor.

I asked business persons around the country to comment on what skills new college graduates lack. They said that recent graduates frequently have unrealistic expectations about assuming managerial positions as an entry level employee. "You have to earn your spurs," said an Atlanta employee of a chemical company. Think about your goals for your career, apart from your parents' expectations for you.

An unrealistic but common assumption is that the work world is fair, that if you do a good job you will be recognized. In fact, this is only half of the avenue to success. The other half is knowing how to work with other people, acquiring mentors, being likable, promoting yourself, and being a good team member.

A high performer in a consulting firm, Kathy relates,

> I wish I had known how important it is to have the political skills to establish positive relationships at work. Employers aren't going to take care of you; you have to watch out for yourself and not think that just because you do a good job the employer is going to watch out for your future.

In her firm, promotion decisions are "very much dependent upon personal likes and dislikes," such as the vice-president who expects rising stars to work out with him at his health club, something her family responsibilities do not allow her to do.

Business people frequently mention that new graduates are unprepared for the team efforts utilized by many workplaces. Join a club, team, or service group and analyze the techniques of respected leaders. Negotiation skills are essential, learning how to give and take, ☞ as described in Roger Fisher and William Ury's *Getting to Yes* (Penguin) and Herb Cohen's *You Can Negotiate Anything* (L. Stuart). Being part of a team means that work cannot be put off till the last minute: Drafts may need to be circulated for feedback and clerical workers often will not accept typing assignments at the last minute. Planning ahead is critical because work is dynamic and subject to crises that require changes, unlike college assignments with set due dates.

Working as a team requires effective communication skills. Active listening, described in Chapter 6, can be practiced with family members, roommates, and friends. It's important to know when to speak up, when to be silent, and when to ask questions. Another frequent criticism is that recent graduates do not know how to deliver effective oral presentations and written reports. These should be "short, sweet, and to the point," suggested Corning's Tom Blumer (vice president of technology and manufacturing). Make a point of getting first drafts of a project critiqued and save time for many revisions.

When giving presentations, use visual aids such as charts or overhead projectors, slides, video, etc. Change the pace frequently. If appropriate, as people are entering the room, play taped music to get them in the mood you want to set. After making a presentation, seek out feedback as to what worked and what did not. Videotape yourself making a presentation and then critique it with colleagues.

Consider joining the Toastmasters' Club. (More suggestions are provided in Part 3.)

Seek out evaluations of your work in other areas as well, and practice doing active listening rather than becoming defensive, interrupting, or providing excuses. Thank the critic for taking the time to suggest improvements. Learn to "take the heat," to listen well to criticism without viewing it as a personal attack. If some of the criticism is mistaken, provide proof in writing, along with appreciation for the feedback.

I'd like to own a business. What should I think about?

Vincent A. Petkus is co-owner of an automotive repair and sales company in Chico, California.

Running your own business takes a commitment second only to child rearing. It taxes your ability, your energy, and your moral judgments, and your decisions affect your employees and your family as well as yourself. You will probably work more hours than any of your employees and earn less than in your previous job. Cash flow will be a constant concern. The most appealing aspect is the freedom to put your ideas into action. As I have watched my brothers and others run their businesses, I see that money, though important, is not the primary benefit; rather, it is gaining patience and knowledge.

The common mistakes I see new business owners make are lack of knowledge, planning, and capital. Not having enough resources to meet demands will tax your well-being. An owner has to be prepared for worst case scenarios such as a lawsuit. Be well-informed about the product or service you provide and surround yourself with experts. If you do not know much about finances, hire an accountant; bring in a consultant to help you improve your management practices.

A business owner is faced with paperwork and costs to meet government regulations concerning employee benefits, safety, and taxes; as well as the cost of utilities, equipment, building rental, training for employees, and health insurance. The paychecks our employees take home are less than half the costs we incur by employing them, with insurance and payments to the federal and state governments. The majority of new businesses are not successful and most do not make a profit their first year; to beat the odds, be better informed and backed by more capital than the failures who do not do enough homework. There are people, however, who even though they fail in their first venture pick themselves up to become giants in their field.

☞ Resources: the U.S. Small Business Administration (1-800-368-5855); the Service Corps of Retired Executives (1-800-368-5855) provides free advice; the *Encyclopedia of Small Business Resources* by David Gumpert and Jeffrey Timmons (Harper & Row); *Small Business: An Information Sourcebook* by Cynthia Ryans (Orynx Press); and the *Small Business Success* magazine (1-800-848-8000 outside of California and 1-800-237-4769 in California.)

I know that time is my most precious resource. How can I make the most of it to get everything done?

Gayle Kimball

Professionals average over 50 hours of work each week. Combined with family responsibilities, this requires efficient time management and organizational skills. The most important principle is to conquer procrastination by dividing work into small units that can be accomplished easily and regularly. This builds a momentum of success—in contrast to the depressing effect of avoiding a task. For example, when I correct student papers, I divide them into piles of five papers. When I finish a pile, I take a short break to do something different, then return to the next pile energized and not feeling overwhelmed by the large stack because I know my next task is only five papers. I also do easy tasks first to energize myself.

How to Get Many Things Done

1. Make lists and **prioritize** for each day, week, and month. Carry a calendar with you. Ask yourself how you really want to use your time. Stick to priorities; delegate or say no to items low on your list. Ask yourself, "Do I live to work or work to live?"

2. Make your work **environment pleasing** to your senses: display pictures and photographs, drink herb tea, eat unbuttered popcorn, put fresh flowers in a vase, listen to calming music, and take short breaks in dim light to breathe deeply and to move your body. Practice relaxing each muscle and repeat affirmations, such as " I am relaxed," "I have all the time in the world," "Let go and let good," or "I am attuned to creative guidance from my higher self." Breathe from

your abdomen and think about relaxing.

3. Give yourself **rewards** for completing a major task—a concert, a weekend trip; even rewards as childlike as gold stars or crossing off items on your list can motivate task completion.

4. Break difficult and lengthy tasks into **small pieces** and accomplish some every day. Do quick tasks immediately: Do not put them in a catchall pile where they must be remembered and handled again. Have a color-coded filing system for quick access to information you need, including folders of "do now," and "do—no rush," "$," and "read." A file cabinet is a must.

5. Procrastination is depressing and robs you of energy, while achievement gives you energy. Once you get over the hump of starting, momentum is reinforcing. **Routines** help with getting started, such as working on project x for an hour every day, from eleven till noon. During this time it is not OK to answer the phone, clean up, or give in to other excuses.

6. **Delegate** and pay for help (such as domestic work or filing at work) whenever possible. This is good for the people involved in sharing responsibility too.

7. Try to avoid meetings by substituting shorter **telephone** conversations; also use the telephone to find information and shop by catalog.

8. Do **two simple things at once**, such as talking on the phone and going through mail. Always take reading with you to appointments where you will probably have to wait.

9. Save time by **concentrating on the task** at hand. If you are preoccupied with something else, write about it in your journal, or write a letter which you tear up. Always read with a pen in your hand, underlining or taking notes to prevent "spacing out" and having to reread the material. Ask yourself questions about the topic as you read. Skim rather than read word for word or sentence by sentence. If you're bored, give yourself a limit: "I'll concentrate for 20 more minutes and then I'll take a break."

10. **Prevent boredom** by approaching work from a different angle or learning new developments in your field. Keep up with newsletters and journals and general news magazines as a source of new ideas.

11. Keep your **energy level high**. Exercise regularly, get enough sleep, and eat nutritious meals; maintain your health, as described in Chapter 9. If you're an introvert, take time alone to recharge your

batteries. If you're an extrovert, plan social interactions. To identify your personality type, ☞ see *Please Understand Me* by David Kiersy and Marilyn Bates (Prometheus Nemesis Books). Keep your mind and spirit energetic by taking fun breaks, planning leisure activities to look forward to, and cultivating a support system of friends and family. Relaxation techniques are provided in ☞ *The Relaxation and Stress Reduction Workbook* by Davis, Eshelman, and McKay (Harbinger); and Burns' *Feeling Good Handbook* (William Morrow).

Part 2—The Glass Ceiling

What do women need to know to get past the glass ceiling at work?

(The "glass ceiling" is the barrier through which top management positions can be seen, but not reached by women and people of color.)

Madelyn Jennings warns, "If young women think that sex discrimination is a thing of the past, they're wrong." She suggests:

♦ If you suggest an idea which is then repeated by a man at a meeting, thank him for agreeing with you. Then **document your idea** on paper as the originator.

♦ **Choose your battles**. If you encounter sexist behavior coming from ignorance, explain that it needs changing. If it's part of company values, weigh the risks and rewards of fighting from within versus moving on. Magazines that list the best companies for women, include ☞ *Working Woman*, *Working Mother*, and *Business Week*. See also Gigi Ranno's *Careers and the College Grad* (Bob Adams).

♦ **Overcome the reputation** that women are less willing to take lateral job reassignments, downgrades, travel, and special assignments. Don't be reluctant to get off a career track to get some needed experience.

♦ If you get promoted and you think it's because you are the company token, **take the job** and prove them wrong.

♦ If you start or join an information network for women or person of color, be alert: If the network's role is to **spread knowledge** and information, it will be viewed constructively. If it's adversarial, you may get the wrong kind of attention.

♦ If you feel, after a fair amount of time, you've struck your head on the glass ceiling—tell them why and if no changes are forthcoming, quit. Of course, line up a better job first. It's a big world out there and you have many choices!

(G.K.) Male college graduates are likely to advance faster and earn more than female college graduates after five years on the job. The majority of women workers will experience sexual harassment. U.S. Labor Department reports in 1992 indicate little progress in breaking through the glass ceiling in upper management for women and people of color. Young men are just as discriminatory as older men, reveals a study of sexism in the court system by the U.S. Court of Appeals' district covering the nine Western states (60 percent of women lawyers surveyed had experienced sexual harassment on the job).

Change occurs slowly, and the work world is still shaped by men in a fraternity-type system. Men are considered the elite members within the hierarchical system based on male experiences, such as team sports and military service. Even traditional female jobs are usually managed by male administrators (elementary principals directing teachers, doctors directing nurses). The fraternity has its own vocabulary and traditions from which women are usually excluded. An explanation for the continuation of the glass ceiling is the "comfort factor," despite the fact that women are a large majority of the new job entrants and a large reservoir of the best and brightest talent. High level males do not want to adapt their fraternity to women, feeling uncomfortable swearing in front of women, socializing, or traveling with them.

A high-ranking manager, Elise, told me that when she was hired as a vice-president, the assumption was that she would not succeed. "I had to prove myself over and over again, every day," she said. She was put through tests to see if she would buckle under the strain. An example of a test by competitors was doing "in-runs," bypassing her by going directly to her staff (note the sports imagery). "I had to **be strong to be heard** in meetings; I just kept talking through interruptions and surprised them."

The career game involves "grandstanding," to let others know your effectiveness. At Elise's level, people are watching to see who is "up slope," who has plateaued, and who is "down-slope." She made the error of thinking that fairness is a guiding principle, when in fact one's skills as a negotiator determine salary and perks. She never had a female mentor, although she got advice from men as she progressed along her career path. Elise thinks it is important to have a **career plan** with a time-line attached to goals. One of the rules of the career game is not to stop at the job you have, but advance to more challenging jobs, so she looks for better job openings.

She also juggled the second shift of family responsibilities, admitting, "I do feel guilty about the time I spent away from my children, but I'm a better and happier person for having a career." She faced jealousy from her husband, explaining that "although he was proud of my career success at first, it shocked him that he couldn't stand my visibility." He had an affair and they divorced.

In order to climb the ladder to be able to implement change, women need to **learn how the fraternity system works**. In ☛ *Games Mother Never Taught You* (Warner), Betty Lehan Harragan explains that the rules are shaped by the military hierarchy (the chain of command means you do not go over your boss' head, line jobs are more valued than staff jobs), competitive team sports (the aim is to win, not have good relationships among all the teams; learn about football so when your boss says to be the quarterback on a task, you'll understand), and locker room language.

Moving toward equality on the job is not easy when the media give women confusing messages. Rent the videotapes *Pretty Woman* and *The Butcher's Wife* for evidence that the Cinderella myth is alive and well. See *Working Girl* to learn that clothes make the woman, sleeping with a powerful man is helpful, and women are competitors for male approval. See *Broadcast News*, *Crossing Delancey*, and *Fatal Attraction* for proof that career-focused women are neurotic, sexually frustrated, and would give it all up for a husband and baby.

Betty Friedan, author of the classic *The Feminine Mystique* (Norton) that galvanized the women's movement of the 1960s, warns of a new **"feminine mystique."** Women are to believe that the strains in balancing work and family are their fault, rather than caused by the lack of social accommodation to women's employment. As women make progress in the work world, a backlash is generated. Since men are taught that their identity stems from their work and that women are inferior, it follows that some men will be angry about women doing "male jobs" and thus threatening male status as superiors. The anger is often expressed in physical harassment in blue collar jobs and verbal harassment in white collar jobs.

For example, at my university, male department members referred to three female job applicants with a vulgar term for female genitals, c— 1, c—2, and c— 3. In another department, a professor said about his female colleagues, "We were fine until the bitches entered our department." (Readers in their twenties felt that younger men would not have this same resentment about integrating women. What do you think?) If a group of female (or ethnic) faculty are seen talking together, this often invokes jokes about plotting a revolution, indicating tacit recognition of women's lack of power.

Three authors in their twenties explain the backlash against women's gains via media efforts to keep women preoccupied with their appearance, rather than pushing for political and social change. ☞ Must reading is Susan Faludi's *Backlash* (Crown) and Naomi Wolf's *The Beauty Myth* (Anchor). The personal is political; the ideology used to keep women subordinate has changed throughout the centuries from selecting Biblical passages written by Paul out of context, to putting them on a pedestal, to Freudian psychology, to unhealthy preoccupation with appearance beginning in elementary school—but the intent remains the same. Young adults need to realize that the struggle for equality is not over.

In ☞ *Feminist Fatale* (Donald Fine), Paula Kamen focuses on young women's attitudes. As she traveled around the country, she found that one of the main issues for people in their twenties is how to balance work and family. Like their mothers, women in their twenties blame problems on their own inadequacies instead of looking for social solutions, Ms. Kamen reports. Women and men agree that mothers, not fathers, should slow down their careers to care for children. Most women have an "I'm not a feminist but..." attitude because of the lack of ongoing consciousness-raising for young people about sexism.

Women need to **strategize about long-term goals** for their careers and plan how to achieve them, rather than waiting for Prince Charming to sweep them off their feet. Women are taught to have less sense of control over their lives than men, so this requires rethinking role-socialization. Succeeding at work requires learning to strategize, as if preparing to win a military battle, certainly not a concept comfortable to most women. If a private goes into battle alone, he or she will lose. The soldier needs allies and to be represented by generals.

Susanne, an attorney, suggests that you find out who is influential and why and form an alliance with a powerful person to fight for you on the front line. This person will be flattered by your respect and become personally involved, buying into your progress when advising you. For example, Susanne gave her proxy in a vote to a man she was having some difficulties with, telling him she agreed with his viewpoints. "Massaging his ego" worked, she said, for "he has been like sugar ever since." Young women readers expressed concern about "brown-nosing." You can hold true to your principles and still curry favor with someone you do not especially like in order to achieve a useful goal.

Political skills need to be learned in order to advance your career. Power has to do with creating "networks of mutual obligation." Marie, a human resources manager, suggests that women identify the business problems that colleagues face, help them "resource it," and then ask them for information when needed, rather than working alone. Politicians frequently use this "you scratch my back, I'll scratch yours" technique to get legislation passed. Executives report the importance of getting others invested in an idea early in the campaign to sell it.

Politics is about power. Powerful people are likely to touch, take up space, monologue, and make declarative statements. Women managers warn of being invisible in a male-dominated workplace and advise, "Let them know you're there or they'll never see you." "Don't sit back and be the smiley one." Subordinates allow themselves to be touched, they take up little space, they allow others to enter their space (as by being cornered or standing too close or leaning over them), they allow themselves to be interrupted, they disclose personal experiences and feelings, they smile a lot, they are overly friendly and try to make the superiors feel important by minimizing their own abilities.

Experiment with not behaving like a subordinate. The difficulty is that women who act assertively may be viewed as abrasive, unfeminine, self-promoting, and hard to get along with. Some women consider themselves bicultural, shifting their behavior at work and in social situations.

Being ladylike can get in the way; sometimes it is necessary to be impolite, for example, by interrupting monologers. Experiment with the power game, as if you were playing chess. Try assuming the power behaviors listed above in a setting other than work, so you can really experiment. To prevent being interrupted, lead up to the point you are making rather than making it first. Avoid unnecessary apologies, take the initiative to shake hands or speak, lower your voice tone, make declarative statements rather than using the female speech pattern of adding tag questions. Sit on a table rather than stand looking up to someone tall, take space by spreading out papers, and look colleagues in the eye rather than looking away.

Personal Reflections
---

1. How do you take or give away your power?
2. What role do you want to assume in workplace politics?
3. What would you do if someone tried to use power games to dominate you?
4. How important is work success to you?
5. How do you feel about "schmoozing?"

On the job, women need to learn to **speak in business language**—action rather than feelings, just as men need to do the reverse off the job. For example, when Myra became affirmative action officer at an Indianapolis bank, she faced some resentful men. She did not speak to them in terms of fairness and morality, but explained that the work force is becoming increasingly diverse, thus, they need to learn how to best utilize their labor pool to insure their continuing success as managers. When she found out her boss' boss was referring to her as "that little girl in personnel," she did not discuss her hurt feelings but rather how his comment interfered with getting her work done well for the organization. She used the language of team playing and the bottom line. Further, she took the initiative by inviting colleagues to lunch to discuss business politics.

The game requires some **emotional detachment**, which boys learn by playing sports where rules and winning are more important than the feelings of the players. Boys also learn a put-down humor, which combined with fear of being a sissy, teaches them to armor themselves emotionally. They are taught, "no pain, no gain." Girls, however, are likely to stop playing a game if feelings get hurt, forgetting about the rules, explains ☞ Carol Gilligan in *In a Different Voice* (Harvard University Press). She believes that the origin of this gender difference is that boys are taught to detach from their primary parent—their mother, while girls are encouraged to stay connected, leading to different moral development. (As is usual in social science,☛ Carol Tavris disagrees with these conclusions, as she explains in *The Mismeasure of Women* (Simon & Schuster).

Women need to be aware of **gender differences in negotiation styles**. Men are likely to make firm demands and few concessions, while women are likely to look for areas of agreement and use logic to support their ideas. A laboratory study found that men tend to think of negotiation as "a sporting event in which the other person is an opponent to be beaten," while women tend to think about a convivial relationship between the negotiators. A New York attorney was turned down as partner in her law firm because she was considered unloyal and soft due to her cordial dealings with opposing teams of attorneys. No one gave her this feedback until her rejection: A mentor could have bridged this lack of communication between the male and female cultures.

However, women are taught skills they can use to advantage, as evidenced by a study of persuasion styles which shows that the female style is more effective in getting people to change their minds: It involves agreeing with their partners to achieve a win-win solution and trying to relieve tensions. ☛ See Norma Carr-Ruffino, *The Promotable Woman* (Wadsworth).

A reaction has set in to women becoming male clones or finding their identity in male approval. There is growing interest in an androgynous management style, utilizing the strengths of both genders. Madelyn Jennings observes, "The new generation of women is learning to be her own person. I feel deeply that the white male, in dealing with the female professional, sorely needs his consciousness raised as to the lessening importance of the old formula."

Promote yourself. Let others know of your achievements and your creative thinking. Simply tell people you're enthusiastic about the job or hard working, whatever image you want to create. You'll hear what you say repeated. In laboratory studies, college women pay themselves less than men for equal work and join men in rating what men do higher than women doing the same task. This bias is the outcome of sexist socialization of girls to have less self-esteem and to base their success on their appearance and how much people like them rather than what they do. It is naive to think that working hard and doing a good job will speak for themselves.

This process of self-promotion may require overcoming female socialization not to outshine males, not to be too assertive, not to take risks, to doubt one's leadership ability, to wait for a male protector or initiator, and to regard success as unfeminine. Even high-achieving women may feel they are impostors who doubt their abilities or explain away their success as luck, while men are more likely to credit their success to their own efforts and their failures to bad luck.

Women may sabotage their own advancement by being perfectionists, self-effacing, or not delegating work. A positive step is to repeat a **directional statement**, such as "I am capable," and use other techniques designed to transform negative thinking patterns (see Chapter 10). At the same time, women need to seek out honest criticism of their work and style, as they may be viewed as not tough enough to handle a frank review.

To counter the anxiety of performing in a male-defined work world, it is necessary to take time to **recharge emotional batteries**. Women professionals I interviewed do this by talking with family members and friends, exercising, making love, meditating, being in a therapy or support group, reading for fun, and engaging in hobbies like gardening—doing rigorous pruning when angry! I find a foot pounding activity like jogging or aerobics is a must to relieve tension, perhaps like a child having a temper tantrum. These enjoyable activities should be scheduled on a daily basis. These women also compartmentalize, forget about work at home and about home at work, give up feeling indispensable, are clear about their priorities, and set reasonable goals.

Women professionals often have to unlearn the workaholism and perfectionism they developed to prove their abilities. Learning to **say no** is crucial, because one of women's main problems is having too much to do. Studies show that the most effective coping techniques involve making change—such as sharing family work, rather than managing feelings that surround the situation by thinking things could be worse.

Workers who experience sex discrimination on the job have **legal protection**: the Equal Pay Act of 1963, Title VII of the Civil Rights Act of 1964—enforced by the Equal Employment Opportunity Commission (Title VII was proposed by a legislator as a failed ploy to prevent the passage of the bill); the Pregnancy Discrimination Act of 1978 (passed by Congress to overturn a ruling by the Supreme Court that pregnancy discrimination was not gender related and therefore not covered by Title VII); Affirmative Action; and the Civil Rights Act of 1991. This law extends the right to sue for monetary damage and ask for a jury trial, and directs the court to judge a discrimination case through the eyes of a "reasonable woman." Sexual harassment is defined as unwanted sexual attention and includes a hostile work environment, such as display of degrading posters; it is a violation of Title VII, and grounds to sue an employer. An organization ☛ called "9 to 5" provides information about sex discrimination on the job; their phone number is 1-800-522-0925. To discuss a possible suit, contact the federal government's Equal Employment Opportunity Commission.

Employers should be encouraged to provide manager training programs for a diverse work force, as done by Corning, Gannett, and IBM; to establish formal networks of information and mentoring for women and people of color; and to establish family support programs such as family leave, flexible work hours, and assistance with dependent care. ☛ For current information about employer programs, contact Catalyst (250 Park Ave, South, NY, NY 10003), Wider Opportunities for Women (1325 G St. N.W.,LL, Washington D.C. 20005) and, for family-friendly policies, the Families and Work Institute (212) 465-2044, or the Conference Board, also in New York City. *Working Woman* and *Working Mother* magazines provide useful current updates, as does the *Working Woman* weekly television show hosted by Kathleen Matthews.

How can African Americans get past the glass ceiling?

Matthews Jackson is vice-president of educational and student services at Butte College in Oroville, California.

The question addresses the reality that little has changed in the relationships among whites and African Americans; whites largely own and run America's businesses and African Americans work for them. For the most part, historic attitudes and stereotypes persist, so how can African Americans develop successful strategies to move into positions of power within these institutions?

Whites have historically had an attitude of racial superiority, consistent with the fact that they owned not only the land and the businesses of America (having conquered the Native Americans), but also the vast majority of African Americans. Those they did not own they exercised legal dominion over. African Americans, therefore, struggled not only with the legal system which bound them to inferior status, but also the psychological trauma of being oppressed, the destruction of their self-esteem, and their ability to feel powerful enough to control their environment

The reality is that people who have power do not usually give it up or share it voluntarily, and people who do not have power or, who do not feel they are powerful, have very little success at acquiring power or the feeling of self-worth which comes with it.

During the 1960s and 1970s, as a consequence of the Civil Rights Act of 1964, more African Americans were granted access to higher education and subsequently were hired, primarily in middle management, in both the public and private sectors. Unfortunately, much of the employment was symbolic, and few African Americans are involved at corporate conference tables in significant decision-making roles. Sam Greenlee's film, *The Spook Who Sat by the Door,* poignantly captures this plight of African Americans in the corporate world.

Here are some suggestions for getting past the invisible barrier to success. Remember that African Americans have been fighting this battle for several hundred years; change is not easy, but once won, it can be long-lasting.

Probably the single, most significant characteristic held in common by African Americans who have gotten past the glass ceiling is their unbridled belief in themselves, **confidence** borne of the knowledge that they are valuable as human beings and capable as managers and workers. Usually, this self-esteem is engendered in individuals long before they ever get into the work realm, by parents, a mentor, a teacher who has convinced the person of his/her own personal worth and dignity.

However, for African Americans, there is a delicate balancing act. Our sense of confidence is frequently labeled as arrogant (code for not knowing our place). So while we must convey a strong message of self-assurance, we must at the same time possess a dignity and presence which can only be construed as confidence. If we expect others to be comfortable with us, we must be comfortable with our own personhood first.

Few successful African American business persons would argue that their success is the consequence of some innate ability. Even the most gifted of us know that there is absolutely no substitute for **preparation**. Few acquire success by being average; indeed, the

Willie Mays complex is still at work. In order to climb the ladder of success, African Americans must usually prove that they are not only equal to their white peers, but must frequently outperform them simply for the privilege of working.

Preparation includes understanding the culture and values of the employing organization. It means being conscious of office politics. Acquiring an influential, in-house mentor who is willing to serve as your guide is a critical factor in succeeding and being accepted in the organization. Preparation also means cultivating an area of expertise within the organization which is perceived as valuable. You must not, however, be perceived as so narrow in your abilities that you are thought to be capable only in that one area. Cultivate a generalist's knowledge of the entire company; know enough about the total operation to be an articulate spokesperson.

If you aspire to the pinnacles of decision-making, you must be willing to spend whatever time the task demands. Just being a nine-to-fiver is not enough. Dedication to the task, thoroughness in preparation, and performance, combined with loyalty and dedication, are the keys to success. If you envision yourself in a position of power, you must creatively set the stage by **giving 110 percent.**

Value the art of creating a **base of support** within the organization: Be expert, hard working, likable, and worthy of respect. Because there probably are not many African Americans on the management team, it is important to create a niche for yourself. In this regard, playing up or playing down your color should be avoided. You and they must feel comfortable that you are there because you merit it. Bring attention to yourself through the good quality of your work.

To become powerful in the corporation, you must have a vision of yourself in the decision-making role. However, vision without a plan or a strategy, may just mean dreams deferred. Develop a **plan for success**. The plan should include both short-term and long-term goals and each step should be attainable. The plan should include strategies and activities which heighten your profile and present you in a positive manner. One of the greatest barriers to success is the failure to **be self-analytical**. Make constant assessments of your strengths and weaknesses and develop a self-improvement plan. Be honest in your self-examination, then play up your strengths and shore up your weaknesses.

Be altruistic by making personal sacrifices for the good of your organization and, most importantly, no matter how good and capable you are, **be humble**. Don't be afraid to blow your own horn when necessary, but remember it is best when someone else blows it for you. While I mention humbleness only briefly, I cannot overemphasize its importance. A mentor once told me that all great leaders have one characteristic in common—humility, an inner peace borne out of such a strong sense of your own worth that you don't need to think of yourself first. Humbleness causes us to listen to the ideas of others and to respect those ideas. It means to acknowledge that you are not always right and that you are willing to compromise and share power for the common good.

Successfully shattering the glass ceiling is possible; there is an exponential growth of African Americans in corporate decision-making roles. It is a part of the evolution from slavery to emancipation to civil rights to economic success. See yourself as a player in this transition. Cultivate strong self-esteem, be diligent about your preparation, have a vision, prepare a plan, be self-critical, demonstrate humility, be a team player, and you will acquire success. Do not use your blackness as an excuse for failing or a reason for succeeding. You are, first and foremost, a valuable person.

SUGGESTED READINGS

"Guide to Power in the Workplace," *Essence*, March 1993: 71-101.
"Skills for the New World Order" and "Employability—The Fifth Basic Skill," *Chronicle Guidance Publications*, January, 1993: 21-24.
Thomas Dye. *The Politics of Equality*. Indianapolis, IN: Bobbs-Merrill, 1971.

How can Latinos and Latinas get past the glass ceiling?

Sylvia Lopez Romano, Ed.D., is a student affairs administrator at California State University, Chico. Arthur R. Sanchez, Ph.D., a psychology professor at CSUC, writes the second half of this section.

My career in higher education administration spans eighteen

years; during this time I have learned the hard way. I believe I have some insights to share with other Latino/as aspiring to career success.

At age sixteen, I dropped out of high school, married, and raised five children. This was culturally acceptable, for it wasn't expected that a Mexicana would do anything else but marry and have children. Latinas were subordinate to their mates and their families. I never dreamed of returning to school until my last child entered school and my husband and I decided that my becoming a teacher would be a positive move for our family. The cultural norms dictated that what was good for the family should be good for me.

Going back to school opened up a whole new world. I earned two B.A.'s, an M.A., teaching and administration credentials, and an Ed.D. These accomplishments by a dropout and teen parent followed a nontraditional avenue to success. Juggling a household of five children, a foster child, a husband, full-time employment, and college classes, taught me that **organization and follow-through** are essential for success in any venture. I worked hard to achieve quality in my tasks. Latinos should recognize their **life experiences** as opportunities to learn.

The most important strategy for success is to know your **personal definition of success**. This definition determines your happiness and your self-esteem. Do not allow society, family, or friends to define your view of success, which I personally gauge by my internal feeling of peace. Other strategies for success include obtaining skills in organization, planning, goal-setting, timing, and producing quality work, as well as striving for mental and physical well-being. I bought into the supermom, superwife, superemployee syndrome, as a result of cultural norms placed upon women—especially Latinas. We are schooled in the caretaker role, as caregivers for our children, spouse, and aging parents.

Balancing work and family requires mental and physical well-being. Developing **self-esteem** requires determining your own goals and priorities. This may feel like going against the family or cultural group, but if you remain true to yourself, your contributions will reflect the positive energy you gain.

As a Latino/a, you bring a valuable perspective to Anglo-dominated spheres of influence. Surround yourself with bright, energetic, and positive individuals to gain the **emotional support** to keep you energetic and able to combat oppressive behavior at the workplace. You can test new ideas and practice strategies with your colleagues.

A mentor once admonished me for working hard. She insisted that working hard did not pay off; rather, **working smart** is vital. My cultural heritage led me to believe that hard work resulted in promotion and acknowledgments. What I learned is that without the support of decision makers, hard work does not result in advancement. Time spent with your supervisor discussing projects will benefit you later.

We need a **new paradigm;** Latinos need to begin to think like winners. Shift your thinking from being oppressed to being a survivor, a talented individual. The world is yours for the taking with proven methods for success.

(A.S.) As I reflect on my experiences as a Latino educator and advocate, I realize the influence and continual impact my ethnic identity has on my professional development. I am the fourth of six generations of my family who have lived in California. I am the first to receive a doctorate degree and some of my male cousins and I are the first ones in my family to receive a college degree. Although a number of women in our families have enjoyed a variety of successes, none has received degrees in higher education. I believe the men who succeeded in higher education, like myself, have benefited from traditional Mexican values which reinforced independence among males, a natural fit with dominant Euro-American values.

However, success in my family does not automatically infer a college degree or independence. Although my parents are not formally educated, I have a great deal of respect for the knowledge, wit, and wisdom they demonstrate. My appreciation of them has contributed to my ability to **keep perspective** in an effort to maintain close family ties, interdependence, and affiliation.

It is important to realize that not all Latinos are alike. Any Latino who endeavors to succeed will have to deal with balancing two sets of cultural values, often in opposition. The way we accommodate the two sets of values constitutes our differences. For me, surviving high school required embracing Euro-American values over traditional Mexican values. I remember the stress when members of my own culture rejected me as an outsider and prejudiced whites also saw me as an outsider. In college I shifted toward a balance of commitment to both sets of cultural values. I believe the acculturative process provides those who survive the stress with a set of **principles** that enhance success in any arena.

The ability to satisfy the needs of employers whose principles generally reinforce independence can be balanced with the Latino's need for affiliation, respect, and personalism. The ability to successfully communicate and move between different cultural environments, without compromising the inherent value of either, speaks to the strength of the Latino. Success and self-esteem for the Latino build on the support of **social networks** such as the family and a feeling of pride in one's heritage. Latinos should keep sight of the balance our presence provides the work environment.

How can Asian Americans get past the glass ceiling?

Moon Jee Yoo-Madrigal, Ph.D., is an instructor
at California State University, Chico.

A new awareness of our diversity as a people is occurring in the 1990s. (In this section, the term "Asians" is used interchangeably with the term "Asian Americans" and includes the various Asian groups in America.) Asian Americans are the fastest growing minority group in the United States. This growth is primarily due to the 1965 immigration law which repealed racially biased immigration quotas and, for the first time, opened America's door to a large contingent of Asian immigrants.

Asian Americans are celebrated as America's "model minority." The success stories about Asian Americans have made headlines and most present a glowing report on the stunning achievements of Asian Americans in academia. According to Ronald Takaki, the exaggerated publicity about the "success" of Asian Americans has created a new myth. The model minority myth masks the complexity of Asians in America and different realities they face. Although Asian Americans come from sharply distinct backgrounds, they find their diversity as individuals is denied. Many feel forced to conform to the "model minority" mold and want more freedom to be their individual selves.

Consider the perception that Asian Americans are better off than the white majority. The recent U.S. Census shows that, as a group, Asian Americans have the highest family income of all racial groups. But, when the U.S. Civil Rights Commission adjusted income levels to account for such cultural factors as family-member labor, it showed that Asian Americans earn less than Blacks and Hispanics.

Asian groups who are poor are rendered invisible: To be invisible is to be without service programs.

Asian Americans report that they are often stereotyped as passive and lacking the aggressiveness required in management. This passive label confuses timidity with good manners. Asians are just as aggressive as anyone else, although most just do not show it so overtly to outside groups. Asian cultural norms place a higher value on the group than the individual, a good characteristic for a manager.

Asian American women must deal with stereotypes attached to their gender as well as their race. The news media portray Asian women as the most desirable of all ethnic groups. The exotic dragonlady Suzy Wong, or the docile Madam Butterfly, to today's plethora of Asian American TV anchorwomen such as Connie Chung, who have given society a new image. By and large, Asian American women are seen as attractive, exceedingly feminine and above all, exotic. This stereotype is pejorative as it makes it harder to be taken seriously in the working world. Stereotypes keep us from seeing the truth. Asian women must challenge the sexualization of their roles as decorative Geishas.

Asian Americans are not raised the same way as our friends from different ethnic groups. Asians, by tradition, teach their children the development of virtue, humbleness, modesty before superiors, and self-control. Asians may look at the world order differently from their Western counterparts. Our culture emphasizes a contextual, indirect, inner-directed, and self-reliant work style. In contrast, Western culture emphasizes control, hierarchy, aggression, and a work ethic that is oriented towards a win-lose outcome. All of these so-called successful white male qualities are considered by Asians as poor taste and immature, an assertion of individuality over the group. To Asians, taking a lot of risks and a lot of criticism, asserting one's point of view, and talking about one's self are qualities to avoid. The workplace needs to adapt to **cultural pluralism** and empowerment as alternatives to assimilation or conformity to Anglo values.

Yet we must learn to **advertise ourselves**, and know our own strengths. Instead of reacting to outside pressures and influences, we need to take risks, be spontaneous, and more assertive. Cultural emphasis on reserved behavior may deaden creativity and individuality.

It is important to **cultivate mentors** and develop informal and formal networks of support. **Do your homework**. Read your company's policies. Do you merit a raise or a new title under their qualifications?

Ask other employees how they rose through the ranks.

Try to work it out. You will get results if you can solve a problem internally. If you cannot talk to your supervisor, see your personnel department, union representative, or equal employment opportunity officer.

Don't be reluctant to seek legal remedies. Opportunities for the promotion of Asian Americans could get lost in the competition because of our reluctance to utilize legal rights.

Go through the right channels. Before suing your company, you must file a charge of discrimination with the Equal Employment Opportunity Commission (EEOC). If you choose to file suit, your employer cannot fire you in retaliation. The attorney you hire should be a specialist in employment law. For referrals, consult the local chapter of the American Bar Association or the American Civil Liberties Union. To find out the statute of limitations in your area, contact the nearest EEOC office.

Contact the **Asian American organizations** listed here closest to your home: the Asian American Law Caucus, Asian Americans for Equality, the Chinese American Legal Defense, the Japanese American Citizen's League, the Violence Against Asians Task force, Chinese Affirmative Action, or the Korean American coalition.

Asian Americans are contradicting the stereotype of the hard working, uncomplaining minority by protesting the discriminatory practices in the nation's colleges and in the job market. We need not be afraid of telling the truth.

SUGGESTED READINGS

Shirley Hune, "Shifting Paradigms: An Overview of Asian Pacific American Future," and Elaine Kim, "Policy for Women," and other periodicals are available from LEAP (Leadership Education for Asian Pacifics), 327 E. Second St., Suite 226, Los Angeles, CA 90012-4210.

Ronald Takaki. *Strangers from a Different Shore : A History of Asian Americans*. New York: Penguin Books, 1989.

Part 3 —Communication Skills

> ## How can I write and speak effectively?

Susan Suntree, M.A., a poet, playwright, and essayist, teaches at East Los Angeles College

This part of the chapter describes how to say what you mean in a way that prompts people to read your work or listen to you attentively. Successful written and spoken communication begins with cultivating your ability to listen closely to your own inner voice and to pay careful attention to others.

For many people, writing and giving speeches makes them most uncomfortable, as was found in a study of successful men by Adele Scheele, described in *Skills for Success* (Ballentine). Yet all of us spend many of our waking hours communicating with our families, room-mates, coworkers, friends, and ourselves. These everyday conversations provide us with a basis for developing our abilities to speak and write well. Writers at all levels of experience and sophistication report having the same experience—writing flows from an inner resource that we all share. The source of our daily conversations, endless inner babble, and illuminating inspirations is also the source of writing.

According to Carol Lem, a Master English instructor at East Los Angeles College, daily reading and writing practice, like a journal, promote the continued development of good writing and keep you connected with yourself, the source of writing material. Most of our time in college is spent taking in information. We must make time to reflect on what we've learned. This is the beginning of knowing how to think independently as well as creatively. Each of us shapes a philosophy of life: Reading your journals can reveal the direction yours is taking.

> ## What can I do about writer's block?

Most people don't realize that writer's block, like stage fright, is common to professional as well as occasional writers. Knowing that having trouble starting is an utterly ordinary experience, so common as to be expected, takes some of the romance out of the suffering.

The key is to have techniques you can turn to when the golden trumpet of inspiration isn't blasting down your resistance. Technique saves the day. A method to rely on, like good tools, is essential. Never underestimate the value of good tools.

Tool 1: A comfortable, well-lighted **place to work**. Do you like where you are sitting? Does your desk or table top look appealing, do you have good pencils or pens and paper at hand, a picture or object you like? Do you have a dictionary and grammar handbook close by? Your work station talks back to you, either supporting your endeavor or contributing to your unhappiness in being there. Is your chair comfortable, supporting your back, allowing your forearms to extend parallel to the floor when your fingers touch the keyboard of your computer or typewriter?

Tool 2: **Adequate light**. An incandescent 100-watt or color-corrected, fluorescent light bulb of similar brightness is a requirement. Close the curtains behind your desk if the glare on your monitor screen is causing eyestrain. This can make you irresistibly sleepy.

Tool 3: **Privacy**. To finish your task and gain the satisfaction that comes from writing even a short piece, you need to be able to concentrate fully, let go of daily cares, and drift down into the richness of your life. Interruptions from friends and family destroy the concentration that is required. Examine your schedule and environment to find a time and a place to call yours. Can you create a space in your closet, attic, or garage? Go to the library, if necessary, to get that first draft finished. If you insist on having uninterrupted time to work, you'll find your writing is better, finished more quickly, and that the activity of writing itself is more satisfying.

Caution: Television and most vocal music attract the mind to listen. To hear your inner voice requires your complete, relaxed but alert, attention. Your best work will mirror the inner conversation that flourishes in quietness.

Try this: Having created a quiet, well-lighted space, pick up a pen or turn on your computer.

1. At the top of the page, write a noun that relates to your subject.

2. Pause, close your eyes, and for a few seconds, feel the energy of your attention collect and drift down inside your body.

3. Feel your breath enter and leave your chest; watch the darkness behind your eyes. Let go of everything for just a moment. Be patient.

4. When you feel relaxed and alert, open your eyes, and begin

writing whatever comes to mind as you look at your topic. Be merely a scribe; write what comes to you like toast popping from the toaster.

5. Pay attention. Feel how the words inside you flow steadily when you are prepared for them and then get out of the way.

Practice this for awhile. Whenever you have writer's block, this exercise will divert the stream around the boulder of inertia and fear.

There is another person you now must take care of—your inner teenager. If there is a choice between sitting at even the most inviting desk and going out to play, most of us would much rather play. Paradoxically, the lively, cunning, inventive part of ourselves that does our best writing is the first one out the door. This creative aspect of ourselves sometimes needs to be enticed to sit still and go to work. Provide treats such as tea, gum, chips, and other immediate rewards. Promise yourself good times to come when the job is finished. Be specific about it. Recognize and treat well this part of yourself. NEVER break your promise. You will notice your resistance to writing becoming more manageable.

Most of all, treat writing like a practice. Just do it. When you decide to write, keep watching your fears and resistance as you go ahead and keep your commitment to write. Don't wait for times to get better: Now is the time. Put your pen to paper or fingertips to keys, and proceed.

How do I organize my writing?

If you haven't cultivated a method for organizing your writing, try the following steps, then change them to fit your own temperament and circumstances. This process breaks down the procedure of writing into small jobs so you can say to yourself, "Right now, all I have to do is just this one task."

Suntree's Seven Writing Steps

Step 1—Prepare. Remember the prescription: Saturation, Inspiration, Creation. Soak yourself in the issue; read, discuss, take notes, calculate. Take notes on index cards with a numbered code for each source (so you don't have to rewrite the source on each card). Use different color cards for different themes. Do not put different topics on one piece of paper as they are too hard to organize. When you think you can't absorb another thread of information, let go of it for awhile. This allows your subconscious mind to take over.

Step 2—Prewrite. Record your topic at the top of the page. Try stream of consciousness: Occasionally glance back at the topic while you continue to write everything you can about the subject. Don't censor, don't worry about grammar or spelling, and don't stop until everything that comes to you is written. Expect to be surprised. We write to find out what we think.

Try clustering: Write your topic in the center of a sheet of paper. Now write in a random pattern around the topic the thoughts that come to mind about it. Free associate all you want.

Step 3—Make a List. Examine your prewriting for main points. Circle and collect them into a list. Choose the most compelling points. These are the bases of your thesis or the central idea you will present about your topic. Turn your final list of main points into a sentence or thesis statement. Revise your list of main points, examining it for order of importance and how each relates to the next. Under each main point, list the evidence, descriptions, and examples that support it. Refer to your prewriting for ideas. Notice how you've told yourself what you want to write about this topic; you haven't had to abstractly think it up.

Take a break. Pet the cat. Exercise briskly.

Step 4—Draft 1. Review your list and tinker with it. Write your thesis at the top of the page. Starting with the first main point, turn your list into paragraphs, point by point. Write your conclusion. Go back and write your introduction last. How can you introduce someone or something you don't know? It is usually easiest to place the thesis at the end of the introduction so you can lead the reader from the catchy opening, through the topic and its general importance, to the points you will address.

Step 5—Draft 2. Rewrite your rough draft. Add transitions. Have it read by a friend or two. Make improvements. Take a break.

Step 6—Draft 3. Read your work aloud to anyone who will listen and give you an honest response. If no one is available, read it to a parrot, mirror, or preferably a tape recorder. Listen to the feedback thoughtfully. Choose what is useful and make improvements.

Step 7—Final Draft. Type or print your final copy. Use your computer's spellcheck. Proofread carefully and make corrections. Check spelling and punctuation; look for missing words or repeated phrases. Try reading your piece backwards by uncovering it word by word and line by line using a blank sheet of paper. Feel proud of your work.

How can I write well?

Stanley Oropesa, Dean's Lecturer in the UCLA Writing Program, offers the following tips about style:

1. **Less is more**. Be as direct and honest as possible. This will give your work elegance and impact. Two popular words—*it* and *there*—signal that your style might be too wordy or flabby. Likewise, eliminate weak passive verbs: *is, are, were, have been.*

2. **Try role playing**. Assume the voice or style of a close friend, teacher, boss, or colleague. Write your ideas as s/he might express them. Use writing in another person's voice as a way to find your own. If you are having trouble, write as if you are the instructor or manager.

Virginia Stout, a Master English teacher at Antelope Valley High School, suggests to writers:

-Keep your audience in mind. Choose words and expressions they will understand.

-Stay focused on your subject.

-Be concise. Shorter is usually better.

-Use specific language and examples; use humor.

-Proofread carefully and have your work checked by someone with an eye for details.

How do I go about writing a speech?

The classical pattern, adopted by many essay and report writers, was created by the ancient Greeks who highly valued a good speech. The basic rule is to state what you are going to say, say it, and restate what you've just said. When writing a speech, consider the following steps:

1. Survey the topic to be discussed. **Narrow your subject** so you can be thorough and specific. Start with your own interest in the subject.

2. **Define the purpose** of the speech. How do you want the audience to respond? Do you want them to be entertained, take action, or better understand a situation? What are your personal goals in giving the speech?

3. **Analyze your audience**. Tailor your word choice, jokes, anecdotes, and examples to their interests and to suit the occasion. Successful speakers seek ways to connect personally with their audiences by finding common concerns and addressing them. For example, if you are addressing a city council, find out the personal interests of the council members, and relate your issue to those subjects. This creates a win-win strategy that allows people to want to see things your way because they see that you treat their views as important.

4. **Gather your materials**, do research. Remember to begin with your own knowledge and experience.

5. **Make an outline.** Study other people's speeches, in a library, for ideas about organization.

6. **Pay special attention to your introduction** which must attract the audience's attention, reveal the general subject, and present the particular angle that you are going to discuss. Many speakers like to begin with a brief, often humorous, anecdote to lead into the speech.

7. **Practice** your delivery. Practice a lot, using your friends and family as audiences. Overrehearse your opening lines. Use a tape or video recorder. Time your speech. Practice so that nervousness doesn't speed you up beyond 150 words per minute. Use the active form of verbs so that when you "lay it down, it stays down!" as the prince of hipsters, Lord Buckley, used to say,

8. Deliver your speech. **Talk to people, not to your notes**. Try to deliver the speech using an outline. Don't read your speech. Make contact with your audience. Before you begin, breathe, feel your feet on the ground, relax your belly, breathe, look at your audience, and begin.

9. Prepare for a question-and-answer session if one is to follow your speech. **Anticipate questions** and be prepared to answer them. Always repeat the question for all in the audience to hear before you answer it.

Tips for Speech Giving

1. Keep breathing, keep relaxing your belly and feeling your feet on the ground.

2. Be brief. An average speech is 13-20 minutes long.

3. Highlight your notes or outline.

4. Pick a couple of people in the audience to talk to, especially at the beginning of your speech.

5. Pay attention to your posture. Don't lean on the podium or stand on one foot.

6. You don't have to deliver the perfect speech. If you are human, your audience can identify with you.

7. Don't apologize for anything. Just notice what has happened—an awkward pronunciation, a dropped note card—take care of it, and go on.

What can I do about stage fright?

Stage fright is normal. Everyone, including professional actors and public speakers, feels it. Pay attention to your body when it strikes. Become familiar with the sensations. As you watch it and experience it, carry on with whatever you are doing. Stage fright can turn into high energy that will illuminate your performance. If possible, go to the site of your speech, and rehearse there.

Some Olympic track athletes use visualization to improve their races. You can use it to quiet your nerves and build confidence. Sit in a quiet place, close your eyes, and visualize the day leading up to your speech. See yourself walk from your chair to the podium. Continue to visualize yourself going through your speech calmly and enjoyably. Feel the power and pleasure of the event. Breathe. Visualize varying conditions, especially ones you may fear, and see a calm, positive outcome.

What should I understand about gender differences in speech?

Men and women use language differently, for different reasons, and often mean different things even when they use the same words. Sometimes it seems like English plus estrogen creates a different language than English plus testosterone! In her book *You Just Don't Understand,* linguist Deborah Tannen shows that, for men, talk is generally used to achieve or negotiate status. Men often don't listen sympathetically, but rather to learn what kind of advice is needed. Talking to create and maintain intimacy isn't widely practiced by men. Women, on the other hand, use communication to make a personal connection or to encourage intimacy.

Tannen studied the way children communicate. She found that when boys talk together, they face away from one another. They usually talk about objective things like sports. Boys play games that focus on winners and losers. They also tell jokes and brag about their accomplishments. Girls face one another, maintain eye contact, and tend to talk about personal issues and other relationship-oriented topics. Girls play games, like hopscotch or house, that emphasize cooperation and imagination. Bragging is avoided.

Ms. Tannen sees these patterns persisting into adulthood. Men see conversation as an attempt at domination and fear being pushed around. Women, who are used to a lifetime of intimate sharing, interpret men's unwillingness to chat or to listen without giving advice as an attempt to push them away. Men tend to make declarative statements: "This is how it is." Women tend to add approval-seeking questions to the end of their statements or to qualify them: "In my opinion, this is how it is, isn't it?"

Tannen believes that women are caught in a dilemma. In the business world, men often interpret women's lack of bragging as a lack of confidence. According to several studies, men talk more than women do and regularly interrupt women much more often than women interrupt men. This places a double pressure on women. On the one hand, if a woman talks as much and interrupts as frequently as a man, and focuses on objective topics like a man, she is discounted as a "shrew" or unfeminine. On the other hand, if a woman maintains the feminine model, she is dismissed as lacking the necessary toughness or confidence.

To improve communication skills, men and women can learn from one another. Men can practice active, sympathetic listening by really paying attention to what is being said and by realizing that the speaker primarily wants to be heard. Restate what you have heard so the speaker can verify that you've understood his/her points. People who want advice usually ask for it. Men can also learn the lesson extolled by Benjamin Franklin who, after observing the impact of his communication style, began to qualify his statements with such phrases as "in my opinion," which he felt left more room for the other person to respond.

Women can learn from men to speak their opinions without overly weighing them with qualifications and approval-seeking questions. With more women assuming leadership positions at every level of our culture, men and women need to be aware of differing communication styles so that they don't let our playground acculturation create problems in our adult lives. Communication is how we present ourselves in the workplace, so it is worth honing our skills as speakers and writers.

SUGGESTED READINGS

J.J. Gibbs. *Dancing With Your Books: The Zen Way of Studying.* New York: Plume, 1990.

Natalie Goldberg. *Writing Down the Bones.* Boston: Shambhala, 1986.

Ed McMahon. *The Art of Public Speaking.* New York: G.P. Putnam, 1986.

Deena Metzger. *Writing for Your Life: A Guide and Companion to the Inner World.* San Francisco: Harper Collins, 1992.

Deborah Tannen. *You Just Don't Understand: Women and Men in Conversation.* New York: Morrow, 1990.

Floyd Watkins and William Dillingham, eds. *Practical English Handbook.* Boston: Houghton Mifflin, 1992.

The most important points for me to apply from this chapter

1. Do your homework and overprepare for job interviews.

2. Learn from videotaped sessions how to improve making a presentation.

3. Approach a new job as an anthropologist learning about a new culture, interviewing informants.

4. Learn the unspoken rules of the work game. Where and how do colleagues exchange useful information?

5. Strategically develop power networks to share information and support. Encourage higher-ups to feel ownership in your success by asking for their advice and acting on it.

6. Develop oral and written communication skills by having experts critique your work, reading, frequent practice, and taking classes.

7. Work with concentration and efficiency, but prevent burnout.

Make your work environment pleasurable. Schedule in regular time to play, relax, and recharge your batteries.

8. Be aware that this is a workaholic culture. Aim for balance. Think about what you would like engraved on your tombstone: You accumulated possessions or you loved deeply and made a positive difference?

9. Draw on the strengths of your ethnic background and realize the value of cultural diversity.

SUGGESTED READINGS

Richard Bolles. *What Color is Your Parachute?* Berkeley, CA: Ten Speed Press, 1991.

Betty Lehan Harragan. *Games Mother Never Taught You.* New York: Warner Books, 1989.

Tom Jackson. *Guerrilla Tactics in the Job Market.* New York: Bantam, 1991.

Miguela Rivera. *The Minority Career Book.* Boston: Bob Adams, 1991. (See the magazine *Equal Opportunity* (516) 273-8919.)

Robert Wegmann, Robert Chapman, and Miriam Johnson. *Work in the New Economy.* Alexandria, VA: American Association for Counseling and Development, 1989.

✪Next... One of the byproducts of a career is earning enough money to invest and multiply. The next chapter provides information you need to make wise choices about financial management. Chapter advisers are a stockbroker, attorney, and business owner.

2

*"Learn to seize
good fortune,
for good fortune
is always
there."*

SUCCESSFUL

FINANCIAL

PLANNING

TARYN A. SIEVERS

WITH LES HAIT

46

Money means different things to different people, including freedom, power, control, or security. Whatever it means to you, it is important to view money as a tool that will help get you where you want to be financially when you want to be there.

This chapter explores money: how to get it, how to keep it, and how to invest it. We all would like to win millions in the lottery, but because few of us do, learning about money, its terminology, and the risks and rewards associated with different investment possi-bilities can be invaluable for a secure financial future. You work hard for your money, so it is important to know how to make your money work hard for you.

The key to being successful with money is planning. First, you need to establish a money plan with a goal, well-thought-out steps toward achieving that goal, and a time frame in which you want to reach it. You might think of your money plan as you would a trip. Set a goal. Determine how and when you want to get there and use your money as a roadmap to reach that goal.

What you need to know about you and your money:

Five questions to ask yourself

1. What is your comfort zone?

Consider if your current financial situation is comfortable. Think in terms of the amount of debt you owe, the amount of credit you have, how much money you have saved, and how much money you are currently saving on a regular basis.

Ideally, you want to have no debt, though it isn't always possible. You want to keep the amount of debt you owe to a minimum. The amount of interest you pay when you owe money can be be incredibly high. Interest on consumer debt (i.e., credit cards, automobile loans, student loans) is no longer a tax deductible item.

High amounts of debt can cripple even the best money plan. Make a list of all your debts (liabilities) and all your assets. Calculate the amount of interest you are paying annually on the money you owe, and then subtract the amount of interest on your debts from the earnings on your savings. You may want to consider paying off some of the debt with some of your savings.

Another way to ease your debt crunch is to consider consolidating your loans. Perhaps you can consolidate your credit card debt to one card with a lower interest rate. Many student loan institutions allow this too. Most student loan programs will defer payments for the following reasons: unemployment, illness/disability, rehabilitation, graduate fellowships, active military duty, volunteering with a tax-exempt organization, parental leave, medical internship or residency, and being a full-time teacher in a teacher shortage area. Each situation has certain limits for the deferment of payments.

Debt has its advantages too. In our society, the extension of credit by financial institutions to consumers has become essential. You will need to establish credit at some point, if you haven't already, so that you can finance an automobile or a home. If you haven't established credit, it may be a good idea to purchase something on credit just to establish a good payment record, then pay off the balance as soon as you can.

Your savings method should be regular and routine. Select a time that you regularly put money into savings, i.e., $50 each paycheck, or a percentage of your income on the first of the month. Think of it as paying yourself first. It is important to get into the habit of saving.

2. What are your liquidity needs?

Liquidity refers to the accessibility of your money. The more liquid your money is, the more accessible it is. But the more accessible it is, the lower return you will earn. For example, the most liquid you can be is to have cash in your hand, but cash does not earn interest at all. Next, would be checking accounts and savings accounts which are very accessible but earn a very low rate of interest. In 1993, passbook savings accounts pay 3.25 percent and checking accounts usually pay less, depending on the balance you keep in your checking account.

You want to keep enough money liquid so you have a cushion in case an emergency comes up, but you don't want to have too much liquid and earn only a low rate of interest on your money when other investments could give you a higher return.

You may ask just how much money should be liquid. The answer depends on your situation. As a rule of thumb, it is wise to keep between two and six months living expenses liquid. You may need more or less depending on your employment situation, plans for a major purchase, medical problems, etc.

3. What is your risk comfort level?

On a scale of one to ten, if one is having your money beneath your mattress, and ten is gambling in Las Vegas monthly, where are you on the scale? Knowing what kinds of risks you are willing to take with your money is important. Generally, the more risk you take, the higher potential return you can get, but you also take the chance of losing a portion or all of your money. Different investments have varying degrees of risk and return possibilities. Knowing your own risk level and the risks associated with different investments can be helpful in deciding how to invest your money.

4. What is your time frame?

As we begin to accumulate assets, we often associate a time frame with these assets or monies. This time frame is helpful in the decision-making process of deciding how the asset or money should be invested. For example, suppose your employer contributes to a retirement account for you, giving you a choice as to how that money is invested. If you have 30 years until retirement, you might consider this a long-term investment and your investment choice would probably be different than it would be for money you were going to use in the next few months. Money invested for the long term often is invested in more growth oriented vehicles that fluctuate in value (widely sometimes) such as stock, but over time, the returns tend to be better than in shorter term investment vehicles like savings accounts.

5. What are your performance expectations for your investment choices?

It is important to have realistic expectations of what kind of return you can earn on a specific investment. We know that, typically, the more risk you take, the higher the potential return on your investment. For example, if you put $1,000 in a savings account for one year at 1993's 3.25 percent interest rate, you would earn $32.50. Essentially, your $1,000 is not at risk at all because your $1,000 will always be $1,000 and you are simply earning interest on it. If you invested $1,000 in stocks or bonds, you would not know the return until the end of the year because no one can guarantee the return on these types of investments. In this case, your $1,000 could fluctuate in value because the stock and bond markets fluctuate daily. Historically, the returns on stock have outperformed other investments. Since 1926, stocks have consistently provided the highest total returns of any financial asset class.

How do I know where to invest?

Today, there are so many different types of investments to choose from it can be confusing and difficult to know what is best suited to you. Learning the basic types of investment vehicles and terminology can be invaluable. Set aside some money each month and start investing! Some funds have a minimum investment of as low as $500.

Simply put, there are two things you can do with your investment money: Loan it out or buy something. When you loan out your money, you get interest. This type of investment is a debt instrument. When you buy something, you hope the value of what you purchased increases. This is owning an equity.

Think of a debt instrument as an I.O.U. If you loaned a friend money for a certain period of time at a set rate of interest, s/he would pay you the interest and the money at the end of the period. This is how bonds work. Often, debt instruments are called fixed income investments because they provide dependable income.

Equity is ownership. When you purchase stock, you are buying a slice of the company. If you own AT&T stock, you are a part owner of American Telephone & Telegraph Company. If the company does well and makes money, the value of the AT&T stock will go up and so will the value of your shares. If you buy gold, and the value of gold increases, so will the value of your gold. Of course, values can drop too although with investments such as land or gold, there will always be some value attached to the asset. There are no guarantees or fixed income rates on equities. However, some equities pay dividends, which are distributions of the corporate profits. But there is also no limit to the upside of equities. If you own shares in a company that continues to excel, your shares can continue to increase in value indefinitely.

Ten Basic Investment Vehicles

Money Markets

These investment pools invest in short-term debt instruments to banks, governments and major corporations. They are perfectly liquid in that you can get your money at any time with no penalty. They pay a slightly lower rate than certificates of deposit and usually more than passbook savings. Often they provide check-writing privileges and should be used as a place to keep reserve cash. Money market rates are very sensitive to interest rate fluctuations. In 1980 they paid 14 percent, while in early 1993 the rates were around 3 percent.

U.S. Treasury Securities

World-wide, these are considered the safest investments. When you buy them, you are essentially loaning money to the U.S. Government. They are direct obligations of the U.S. Treasury. (This is what the federal government issues to finance the deficit.) There are three types:

♦ Treasury bills—Mature in one year or less and come in $10,000 minimum denominations. These are purchased at a discount and mature at $10,000. (Early 1993 rates were 3.2 percent for one-year bills, 6.4 percent for 10-year bills, and 7.3 percent for 30-year bills.)

♦ Treasury notes—Mature in 2-10 years, come in $1,000 minimum denominations and pay interest semi-annually.

♦ Treasury bonds—Mature in 10-30 years, come in $1,000 minimum denominations, and pay interest semiannually.

Series EE savings bonds are issued by the U.S. Government and are purchased at 50 percent of face value. The 1993 rate was 5.04 percent. If you hold the bonds 5 years or more, you will earn 6 percent retroactive to the purchase date. These bonds have a maturity of 12 years, but you can redeem them 6 months after purchase. For up-to-date rate information, call 1-800-US Bonds.

Due to the risk-free nature of these securities, the interest rate is usually low. All interest earned on U.S. Treasury securities is free of state and local taxes and there are other special tax-free features for those intending to use the money for a college education.

Certificates of Deposit (CD)

These are issued by banks, like I.O.U.'s to the bank. You loan money to the bank for a set period of time at a set rate of interest. The longer the term of the CD you buy, the higher the rate you will get. Amounts up to $100,000 are insured by a government agency. Interest rates are usually slightly higher than those for treasury securities. If you have to cash in a certificate of deposit early, you are charged a penalty. (A one-year interest rate in 1993 was 3.5 percent.)

Corporate Bonds

These are I.O.U.s issued by corporations. Basically you are loaning money to a corporation for a set period of time at a set rate of interest. Minimum investment is $1,000 and interest is paid semiannually. Maturity dates range from 1-30 years. Like other fixed income investments, the longer the term, the higher the rate. Two agencies, Moody's and Standard & Poor, determine the credit worthiness of the corporation and assign ratings to the bonds (aaa, aa, a, bbb, bb, b, ccc, and so on, with aaa being the highest). Bonds with higher ratings are considered more secure and pay lower interest rates than lower quality bonds. Very low-rated bonds are considered "junk bonds" and are a risky investment.

Municipal Bonds

Municipal bonds are similar to corporate bonds except they are issued by states, cities, counties, and other municipalities. The interest earned on municipal bonds is entirely tax-free (both federal and state) forever. This holds great appeal for many investors. The interest rate is lower because of the tax-free nature of the bonds. Generally, the higher the tax bracket you are in, the more beneficial tax-free bonds are to you.

Annuities

Created by insurance companies, this investment option provides tax-deferred compounding. You can purchase an annuity with a lump sum payment or with many payments over time. You can choose to have a fixed rate of interest or a variable rate. In both cases, while your money is accumulating or compounding, you pay no tax on its earnings. It is similar to an IRA in that way. However, if you withdraw the funds before the age of 59-1/2, the IRS imposes a 10 percent penalty, plus taxes. This is for retirement money.

Here is an example of tax-deferred compounding. If you were to put $20,000 in a regular, taxable investment earning 8 percent for 20 years, and were in the 33 percent tax bracket, at the end of 20 years you would have $56,825. Had you put $20,000 in an annuity paying 8 percent, you would have $93,219!

Common Stock

Stock is ownership in a company. The value of the stock is directly related to the success of the company. The stock market fluctuates daily, as does the value of your stock. There is no maturity date on stock; you can buy and sell it whenever you like.

Over the last 60 years, the average share of stock listed on the New York Stock Exchange has appreciated at a compound annual rate of about 10 percent. If you figure in the 1929 market crash, the annual rate of return comes to about 10 percent and if you had purchased stock immediately after the crash, your return would be about 14 percent.

Choosing individual stocks involves considering the amount you are going to invest, the risk you are prepared to take, how much time you are willing to be in the market, and how closely you want to follow the market. Use common sense when selecting a stock. You want a good company, with good management, that makes good products that have a growing demand for them. The company should have its financial house in order, be adaptable to change, and be futuristic in its planning. You might want to consider the social impact of the product or service and select companies that have good environmental practices and fair employment standards.

Mutual Funds

The second way to invest in the stock market without having to select different stocks yourself is by investing in mutual funds. A stock mutual fund is like a basket of different stocks. By buying into a mutual fund, you own a little bit of different stocks for a small amount of money (usually the minimum is $500 to $1,000). Professional managers manage mutual funds so you don't have to decide what and when to buy or sell. You are automatically diversified so your risk is spread out. If you are in a fund with 100 stocks in it, and one falls in price drastically, it is unlikely that the other 99 will fall at the same time. Dividends are paid quarterly and you can either choose to receive or reinvest them.

There are also bond mutual funds, stock and bond funds, gold funds, utility funds, foreign stock funds, and socially responsible funds, to name a few of the many kinds available. You might want to ask your broker about these mutual funds which select only from companies which do not pollute, are good corporate citizens, etc. Currently, there are over 18,000 mutual funds listed. There are many ways mutual funds structure their fees. Ask your investment advisor or broker about "loads" (sales charges) and "management fees."

Gold

Investing in gold can be done by buying gold coins, gold bars, or stock in gold mine companies. Gold is basically an inflation hedge. When inflation is high, gold prices go up. In politically and economically unstable societies, it has historically been a way to maintain wealth. The problem with gold is it doesn't pay dividends or interest and it may cost you money for storage and insurance.

Collectibles

Antiques, art, rare stamps, and coins are examples. Since the market for collectibles is "thin," meaning there probably are not hoards of people waiting around for you to sell your stamp collection, the value of what you own may not match the price you get. Most collectibles are traded through dealers or auctions, and transaction costs can be expensive. Appreciation is possible, but from an investment standpoint, there are better alternatives.

Is it time for me to become a homeowner?

Although many factors enter into the decision about buying your first home, you may first want to ask yourself, "Do I want to buy a home at all?" Consider if you really want to take on the responsibility of owning property, if you are secure enough in your career and income to make mortgage payments, and if you are going to remain in the same geographical area long enough to enjoy your home.

Once you decide that you are ready to purchase your own home, there are many more decisions to make involving how to buy it and how to finance it. After you have chosen the house you wish to purchase, you will need to speak with a loan representative to discuss the financing.

It is important to consider carefully what kind of a loan representative you select. Basically, there are two types: direct lenders and mortgage brokers. A direct lender is a loan representative who works for a bank or savings and loan. When you deal with a direct lender, the representative has more control over your loan in terms of helping you qualify, negotiating, and the time frame in which your loan is processed. Another advantage is that you have recourse if there is an error or a discrepancy in your loan package. A mortgage broker can shop for a loan for you among many different sources but the ultimate lenders may not be reputable institutions. Often in this case, you have little or no recourse if something goes awry with the financing. Your real estate agent can recommend lenders for you. It is wise to meet with several and then select the one you feel has experience, is trustworthy, and with whom you feel comfortable working.

How much of a down payment will I need?

Generally, lenders prefer that you invest 10-20 percent of the value of the house as a down payment. The larger the down payment, the lower your monthly mortgage payments will be. Lenders use "debt ratios" to determine the kind of a loan for which you can qualify. Most lenders insist that the total house payments, property taxes, insurance costs, and other recurring consumer debt payments totalled do not exceed 36 percent of your gross income. For example, if your house payment, with taxes and insurance, is estimated to be $1,000 a month and you have a $400 a month car payment, most lenders would require your monthly gross income to be $3,888 ($1,400 divided by .36 equals $3,888). Lenders also look at your job stability, the type of work you do, its upward mobility potential, and your credit rating.

Many lenders offer "first-time-buyer programs" that allow you to put down as little as 5 percent of the purchase price. Ask about these. Also, VA loans are still available. VA loans require no down payments and are available to people who have served in the U.S. military.

If your parents or relatives want to help you with a down payment, it is a good idea to have them gift it to you and keep the funds in a "seasoned" account. A seasoned account is one where money is given to you and you keep it for approximately three months to show financial stability. Lenders like to see this.

What type of mortgage is best for me?

There are many flavors of mortgages. The two basic types are fixed and adjustable. A fixed mortgage is when your interest rate is fixed for the term of the loan and your monthly payments are always the same. The most popular type is a 30-year fixed mortgage. Fixed mortgages are most suited to homeowners who think they will own the property for several years and who like knowing that their payment will always be the same. If you purchased a $150,000 home and put 10 percent as a down payment ($15,000), you would need a $135,000 mortgage or loan. At an 8 percent interest rate, your payment would be $990 a month, your property taxes would be approximately 1.25 percent of the purchase price or $156 a month, and your hazard insurance would be approximately .3 percent of the loan amount or $33 a month.

Another type of fixed mortgage is a 15-year loan. This is often recommended if you plan to own the property for most or all of the fifteen years. This type of loan is beneficial because you end up paying less interest on the loan because you are paying down the principal balance much quicker. The monthly payment on a 15-year loan is higher than on a 30-year loan. Using the example of a $135,000 loan amount, the monthly payment would be $1,290.

Adjustable rate mortgages are loans with interest rates that vary. Interest rates can be adjusted monthly, semiannually, or annually. The interest rates on adjustable mortgages are usually lower than fixed mortgages, often 1-3 percent points lower. The risk is when interest rates increase, so does your monthly mortgage payment. Often, adjustable rates are recommended to those homeowners who do not mind fluctuating monthly payments and those who do not expect to own the property for very long.

The fees you pay when you finance a home are called "points." One point is one percent of the loan amount. If you are charged one point on a $135,000 loan amount, your loan fee would be $1,350. Banks have sales where they reduce point charges, so watch for these. There are other fees associated with purchasing a home too. These include the real estate brokerage fee, title insurance, and escrow fees.

What can I do now so that I can retire comfortably?

As part of your money plan, it makes sense to plan for retirement, no matter how old or young you are. Retirement plans still offer tax advantages that can help save you taxes now while providing a vehicle in which to save for your golden years. Various investment firms often have free booklets providing advice about how to plan for your retirement, and computer software programs such as "Retire ASAP" by Calypso Software and "Retirement Planning Kit" by T. Rowe Price are available. Also start planning for your children's college expenses as soon as you have babies, as you will not be able to use your paycheck to cover the costs.

A 401(k) is a retirement plan that your employer can offer you. It is called a 401(k) after the tax code that created the plan. These are very beneficial. In a 401(k) plan, you can choose to deduct from your paycheck a certain percentage of your income to be put in a retirement account for you. These contributions are pre-tax dollars, meaning you do not pay taxes on this part of your paycheck. You can often choose how you would like this money invested. Many companies offer investment selections like stocks, bonds, mutual funds, or annuities. Also, any interest, dividends, or appreciation this money may earn while it is in the 401(k) plan is not taxed. Better yet, some employers even match your contributions.

An IRA is an individual retirement account. It is also a tax sheltered account like the 401(k). You can set up IRAs at almost any type of financial institution. You can choose how you would like the IRA money invested, i.e., CDs, stock, bonds, etc. All interest, dividends, and appreciation are not taxed while they are in the IRA. Anyone who works can make a contribution to their IRA, but the deductibility of the contribution depends on a few factors. If you are not eligible for a 401(k) or another qualified retirement plan at work (or if one is not offered), you can deduct your IRA contribution of up to $2,000 a year, no matter what your income. If you are eligible for a 401(k) or some other retirement plan at work, you may be able to deduct the contribution depending on your adjusted gross income.

IRAs are a good way to save money on taxes. This example shows the power of tax-deferred compounding. Suppose Sam saves $2,000 a year for 40 years, earns 10 percent on it and is in the 28 percent tax bracket. At the end of 40 years, he has $324,512. If Sally puts $2,000 a year into an IRA (deductible contributions), and earns 10 percent for 40 years, she has $973,704! Every year, Sally's money is not taxed, while Sam's is , so he has less growth year after year.

What is an IRA rollover?

An IRA rollover is when you "roll" money from one type of qualified retirement plan to another. This usually happens in one of two ways. When you leave a job and you had money in some type of retirement plan with that employer, like a 401(k), often you will receive a distribution. This distribution is either a check (or stock) from the company that represents your share of retirement funds accumulated up to that point. You can then transfer your retirement distribution into an IRA rollover. This is not a taxable event if you do it properly. A new law went into effect in 1993 regarding these types of distributions. In order to avoid a new 20 percent IRS withholding tax, you have to direct your former employer to send the distribution amount to the financial institution where you have set up your IRA rollover. If you do not have your retirement distribution transferred but take the money yourself, the IRS will penalize you with 20 percent immediately.

In either case, if you don't put and keep that money in an IRA rollover, the IRS penalizes you 10 percent, the state penalizes you 2-5 percent, plus the entire distribution is considered taxable income, so you are taxed on it that tax year at your tax rate. Suppose you receive $10,000 in a retirement distribution upon termination and you choose not to roll over the distribution. You are penalized $1,000 by the IRS (10 percent), $250 by the state (2-5 percent), plus $2,800 in federal taxes (assuming a 28 percent federal tax bracket), plus approximately $800 for state taxes (assuming an 8 percent state tax rate). Penalties and taxes cost you $4,850 or 48.5 percent of your distribution in this example. Not rolling over a retirement distribution is extremely expensive and should be avoided. Once the money is in the IRA, you can invest it almost any way you choose.

Another instance when you may hear the term IRA rollover is when you take an already established IRA from one financial institution and move the money to another financial institution. For example, if you were to go to bank ABC where your $2,000 IRA is and get the check for the amount of the IRA, you have 60 days to deposit that $2,000 into another IRA at some other financial institution with no tax liability whatsoever. Again, you are simply rolling over retirement funds from one account to another. Normally, you would do this to get a higher rate of return or more investment choices.

How should I select a financial adviser?

In the past, we bought insurance from an insurance broker, certificates of deposit and savings instruments from a banker, stocks and bonds from a stockbroker, and mutual funds from mutual fund companies. Now, the deregulation of the investment industry has made it possible to purchase different types of investments from different investment advisors.

A stockbroker, assuming s/he is affiliated with a firm that is a member of the New York Stock Exchange, probably has the most investment options available to you. Stockbrokers earn commissions only when their clients make transactions. A financial planner is someone who charges a fee for making a "personal financial plan" for you or he/she charges per transaction, or both.

When selecting any type of financial adviser, you are placing a great deal of faith and trust in someone who is going to help you with decisions that will affect your financial future, your retirement, and perhaps the estate you wish to leave your children. You should interview financial advisers and ask yourself the following questions: Does s/he have the same basic investment philosophy as you do? For example, are you both conservatively oriented? Does he have expertise in the area in which you are interested? Does she appear to be concerned with your best interests? Do you honestly trust this person with your money and your financial future?

It is important to spend time choosing an adviser. Ask your friends, associates, and colleagues who they recommend for advice on financial matters. Go visit a few nominees, ask them questions, and get to know them before you select one.

How should I buy a vehicle?
Vincent A. Petkus

The majority of car purchases are made on a whim, on the basis of emotions; this error is costly. Do your homework. ☞Study *Consumer Reports*, AAA (American Automobile Association) reports, and automotive magazines. Before you go shopping for a car, define what you need, which may not necessarily be what you want. That is, don't purchase a two-door sport coupe if your family will need a four-door van in the next five years. Secondly, know what you can afford. Before shopping go to your bank or credit union for pre-approval for a loan. The least expensive loans are generally offered by credit unions. Sometimes manufacturers offer special first-time buyer programs or low interest incentive promotions. Decide on a realistic monthly amount you can afford to spend repaying a car loan and paying for insurance.

Demand dictates the price for a particular car or truck: The more popular a car is, the more difficult it is to "deal." The law of supply and demand means that cars in great demand may be sold for more than the sticker price and cars in greater supply can be sold below the sticker price, if you bargain well. Tell the salesperson what you want to pay and what you can pay elsewhere and refuse to play the game of haggling.

Be careful of sales pressure and tactics. Many dealerships employ pressure to purchase, using various sales strategies. The basic rule is, if you are not sure, wait before you decide to buy. Do not be intimidated, as there are many more cars and places to buy. It is nearly impossible to return a vehicle, so take your time; it's your money.

Another alternative to a dealer is a broker, much the same as a real estate or stock broker. He/she buys cars wholesale at discount and can sell them cheaper than a dealer because he/she does not have the high overhead of showrooms and multiple salespersons. The broker charges a percentage or a fee. The advantage of a broker is the lack of pressure to purchase a particular car or truck because brokers do not represent any auto manufacturers or have investments in vehicles that must be sold. Brokers merely take your order and quote you a price: Often the savings are quite substantial. Any repair shop can service a car under warranty except when the manufacturer is paying for a defect, in which case the car must be repaired by a factory-authorized dealer.

If you plan to buy a used car, common sense tells you that the older the car and the more mileage, the more likely you are to have problems. Buy from reputable dealers or independent car lots. Be aware that some sellers may alter a vehicle to influence its value, by masking engine problems or turning back the odometer. Check for wear on the driver's seat and on the tires in your detective work, if you suspect the odometer reading seems inaccurate. Low mileage cars should not have worn seats. Get a trusted mechanic to check out a car you are thinking of buying; he or she should be able to tell if the vehicle has been in an accident or has engine problems. To check for signs of an accident, look for repainting or missing emblems or trim.

Take your time; test drive the car the first thing in the morning before it has been warmed up. Get agreements in writing, including any warranty. Verbal agreements will not hold up in court. In summary, when buying a car, decide on the basis of your budget, your needs over the next five years, and careful research into types of vehicles, prices, and best loan sources. Expect to bargain unless you are buying a car in high demand.

The same principles apply to selecting the shop to repair and service your car. Ask acquaintances about their experiences, call AAA for their list of approved mechanics in your area. Select repair facilities that specialize in the vehicle you own. They generally see and repair the same problems and are very efficient. Certified technicians are best able to repair vehicles. Also get repair cost estimates in writing: When in doubt get a second opinion. If problems do arise, contact the shop first, so they can make you a satisfied customer; if not, contact AAA or consumer affairs for assistance. Safe driving!

How can I create a budget and stick to it?
Attorney Les Hait answers the next six questions.

If you have access to a computer, there are computer programs available to help you establish and stick with a budget. For example, ☛Intuit's program "Quicken" is a wonderful program for computerizing your checkbook and categorizing by expenditure all of the money you spend through your checking account. Another popular software program is ☛ Andrew Tobias' "Managing Your Money," (Meca Software), which also helps with investment, as does Reality Technologies' "Wealth Builder." The latter will set up budgets for you, so you can contrast how you expect to spend your money with how you actually spend it. It provides a very effective form of discipline.

Or you can simply take an hour or two each month to go through your spending to determine exactly how you spend your money. ☛Joe Dominguez has some excellent suggestions in his tape series and *Your Money or Your Life* (Viking) about how to control and budget your spending. He suggests that you compute the actual dollar amount you earn per hour. When you have the answer to that question, you can evaluate all your spending in terms of the time it takes you to replace that expenditure. If, for example, you are netting $10 an hour for your labor after taxes, and you want to buy a $50 pair of new jogging shoes, it will cost you five hours of your work to pay for those shoes. You then evaluate if the purchase is worthwhile for you.

As you begin to pay attention to and focus on your spending habits, you will find yourself spending less and saving more. As with anything else, the more concentrated focus you give to sticking to a budget (not as a matter of personal rigidity, but as a matter of self-affirmation), the more change there will be in your spending habits.

What is the best way to handle my income taxes?
Should I itemize my deductions?

If you have access to a computer, excellent tax preparation guides are available for IBM PC compatible computers and Apple Macintosh computers. ☛"Andrew Tobias' "Tax Cut" is available through Meca Software, Inc. (P.O. Box 912, Fairfield, Connecticut 06430). "MacInTax" and the related IBM program are available through Chipsoft, Inc. (6330 Nancy Ridge Drive, Suite 103, San Diego, California 92121). "Turbo Tax" by Chipsoft is a best-seller. The discounted price is substantially less than the list price in a computer store. ☛(See the January 1993 issues of *PC Magazine* for a personal finance survey and the magazine *Computerized Investing*'s annual guide to investing programs.) These computer programs have interview formats that walk you through the preparation of your tax returns. Each provides "hand-holding" type question-and-answer interviews and prints out the tax forms for you.

Generally, the single, best tax deduction available is home ownership, which includes a mobile home, a motor home, or a boat, as well as a regular home. The interest deductions from the home amount to a subsidy for home ownership. Often federally insured loan programs are available to allow buyers to purchase their first home with very little down payment. Many more people are probably capable of owning homes than do currently. It is often possible to buy a home, with one or more roommates, even while going to college, deducting the interest from earnings.

Yes, there is a "marriage penalty" for two-earner spouses. The two people, together, as husband and wife, generally pay more in taxes than if they are filing separately.

If you have access to the computer programs described above, it may be easier to prepare your own taxes than pay for the service because a knowledge of the basic tax laws assists you in your financial decisions. Adequate tax planning is one of the most important steps you can take, although it may be appropriate to hire a tax preparer at first or if your financial situation is complex.

Should I buy life insurance?

Life insurance is an appropriate investment for people who need to insure the financial safety of others. If a spouse or one or more children are financially dependent upon you, then it is prudent to have some life insurance available to help financially upon your death. If you are single, and have no dependents, then life insurance from the point of view of insuring your life, is probably not an appropriate idea.

There are a variety of life insurance programs which provide a method of tax-free compounding of your money over time. The advantage of investing in a life insurance policy can be that the compounding of the regular payments accumulates tax-free within the life insurance policy. There is a significant difference between accumulations that are taxed and accumulations that are tax-free, allowing for more rapid growth on the tax-free ones. Often funds can be obtained by borrowing from the life insurance policy. Consequently, it may be appropriate to purchase a life insurance policy as an investment, even if you are not currently married or involved in a relationship where others are dependent upon you.

When do I need to write a will? If I wish to do it myself, what do I need to do to make it legal?

You will need to make a will if you want to have a say in the management of your estate in the event of your death. Usually you will not need a will if you do not have any substantial estate or any children. A will can be used to make specific gifts of specific furnishings or jewelry to specific people that you wish to have them. A will can be used as a simple expression of what you want done with your estate.

☛ Nolo Press, of Berkeley, California publishes a number of excellent books about how to do your own will. They also have a computer program for the preparation of your will which can generate a will that is valid in all states.

You can make a "holographic will" on blank paper with no printing on it whatsoever, not even a motel's letterhead stationery. Nothing should be on the sheet of paper at the time you begin to use it as your last will. You can revoke all prior wills and codicils. You can write out your wishes in your own handwriting, not printing, and especially not typing. After you have written out what your desires are, expressing words of testamentary intent (such as "this is my last will and testament...") and after you have dated the document, make provisions as specifically as possible for which of your heirs receives which of your assets. Be sure that no witnesses to sign the will, because the entire holographic will must be in your own handwriting.

The will should be signed by yourself, preferably at the bottom, and dated. Keep the original in a safe place. You may wish to make copies of it available to your heirs or beneficiaries. Naturally, if your estate is complex, a simple holographic will is not sufficient to guide your heirs through all the legal technicalities and pitfalls that might occur.

An alternative to a will is a living trust which bypasses the probate process and the courts, saving money in legal proceedings, as well as time. Property can be transferred after death by showing the trust agreement and a house deed to a title company, for example. ☛ Nolo Press in Berkeley publishes a computer program to draw up a living trust and Denis Clifford's book *Plan Your Estate with a Living Trust* is helpful.

Knowing that half of the recent marriages end in divorce, what can I do to protect myself financially?

The rules about divorce are different for each state. They are complex and the subject of many books. Typically, the more money you make, and the more children you have, the greater amount you have to pay in child support if you are not awarded custody of the children. Similarly, you pay a greater amount in spousal support if your spouse is financially needy.

Regardless of whether or not you are married, if you have children, you are liable for their support even if you leave the state. In a bellwether state like California, family law is relatively gender-neutral in awarding child custody. Generally the better parent is awarded custody, regardless of gender, or custody is shared. The non-custodial parent normally is required to pay some child support. In California, child support is determined by computer-generated calculations (☛the most common software program is "Dissomaster"). Special child support rules apply when the regular custodial parent is on welfare.

The most common pitfalls I see in my divorce cases are that people believe they can "trust" their spouses to be fair. For example, one client had a child not of the marriage, and two children of the marriage, of whom she had custody. Her former spouse pleaded with her to be "fair" and allow him to have the children for several years. At the end of several years he repudiated the written agreement, declared in his court filings that she was a bad mother, and sought custody of all three children, plus child support for her child that was not even a child of his marriage. It is important to plan for what might go wrong and try and address it in any written agreements.

If I need a lawyer, what are guidelines for selecting her or him?

Probably the best guidelines for selecting a good lawyer are to shop around and to talk to people who have used the services of the lawyer you are considering. Interview two or three different lawyers even if this requires spending some money in consultation fees. You can sense who is competent, energetic, and knowledgeable about the area in question. Ask yourself who is more likely to be committed to pursuing your case.

The answers to these questions will give you a strong sense of who will have rapport with you so that the two of you can cooperate effectively, as a team, in handling your legal matters. It is important that the lawyer not adopt a "professional posture," where he or she tells you what to do. It is preferable that there be a sense of teamwork in handling your matter.

Taryn Sievers' Ten Steps to Creating Your Money Plan

1. Establish your financial and investment goals—both long-term and short-term. Write them down.

2. Start a savings method that you are comfortable with. It may be so much per week in dollars or a certain percentage a month.

3. Learn! Read personal investing magazines, newspapers and books to keep up on changes in investment strategies. Many local adult schools offer helpful investment classes.

4. Be patient.

5. Be realistic in your expectations.

6. Review and evaluate your financial goals and investment strategies at least annually to accommodate the changes in your life. April is a good time to do this because you are reviewing your tax and financial situation anyway.

7. Keep good records.

8. If you make a mistake, admit it. Be willing to cut your loss in a bad investment choice before it grows into a bigger loss.

9. Be open to new and different ideas and strategies, knowing that they may or may not fit your money plan.

10. Be reasonable. Your investments can increase and decrease in value depending on many factors: the economy, interest rates, the stock and bond markets, the political climate, the global economy, etc. Know the potential risks and the potential rewards associated with what you own.

═══════════════ **Personal Reflections** ═══════════════

1.Many of us have irrational attitudes about money. Write *money* in your journal and list your associations with it.

2. Describe your parents' and your partner's attitudes about money.

3. How do you feel about saving and spending? How would you like to act in regard to saving and spending?

4. Do you feel like you deserve abundance in your life?

5. How do you feel about owning a house? Describe your dream house, including its location.

6. If you had unlimited money, how would you spend it to create positive change?

7. If you were to write a will now, how would you give away your assets?

Les Hait reminds us that one of the major stumbling blocks to acquiring financial well-being is short-term thinking. Often we are urged by our emotions to select something that is only a short-term benefit. In order to progress financially we do need to do long-term thinking and planning. Most people tend to overestimate what they can accomplish in a year and tend to underestimate significantly what they can do in a decade. Many of us are victims of the "New Year syndrome" where we check in only once a year to see how we are doing financially. Far more appropriate is to measure our achievements monthly and weekly.

Ultimately, in order to obtain financial abundance, we need a plan that enables us to spend less than we earn and invest the difference. We then simply have to continue to invest those returns on an ongoing basis until a critical mass of investment funds have been accumulated to create financial independence or affluence. The critical point is to save money by spending less than we earn.

Practical Money-Saving Tips by Taryn Sievers

♦ When making large purchases, always comparison shop and research the purchase before you make it. For example, when considering the purchase of a car, review issues of *Consumer Reports* to compare brands, prices, and the history of the product. Wholesale stores often have less expensive household supplies than at grocery stores.

♦ If you are used car shopping, remember that many rental car companies sell their cars at good prices. It has been said prices are better on used cars in the classifieds, but shop around.

♦ Remember that certain products tend to go on sale at the same time every year, such as appliances in the spring. Try to buy at the end of the season; when stores are trying to decrease their inventory, they often lower their prices. (Buy summer clothes at the end of the summer for next year, buy skiing equipment at the end of the winter.)

♦ Utilize the newspaper ads. Often used items like furniture, appliances, and computer equipment can be purchased at substantial savings. Remember thrift shops, used record stores, and garage sales.

♦ Shop the market for credit cards. Credit cards either charge no annual fee and higher interest rates or an annual fee of between $25 and $100 and lower interest rates. Depending on whether you make monthly payments or pay off your balance every month, you may benefit more from one type of card than another. Some credit cards give you frequent flyer miles on various airlines and some will pay you a percentage of the amount you charged in a "cash back" at the end of the year.

♦ Stick to your list when you shop. For example, always take a grocery list when you go to the market: Studies have shown the list keepers spend less than those who go shopping and wing it. And never go shopping for food when you are hungry!

♦ Try to carry as little cash as you need. Often, the less cash you carry, the less you will spend.

♦ Borrow video tapes and books from the library for no charge.

♦ Buy used clothing. Do not buy clothes that need dry cleaning or shop just because you are bored or trying to fill up an empty emotional space. (Do volunteer work or exercise instead.)

♦ Take your lunch to work sometimes. Have a hot water pot at work to make drinks and soup.

♦ Join a carpool or use mass transit instead of driving to work, or if close enough, ride your bike.

♦ Lower the temperature gauge on your hot water heater to 120°, install a low-flow shower head, and use the washing machine and dishwasher only when full.

SUGGESTED READINGS

Joseph Dominquez and Vicki Robin. *Your Money or Your Life.*
New York: Viking, 1992.
(The New Road Map Foundation, P.O. Box 15981, Seattle, Washington 98115, has a six audio tape and workbook set by Joe Dominquez titled "Transforming Your Relationship With Money and Achieving Financial Independence.")

Jeffrey B. Little and Lucien Rhodes. *Understanding Wall Street.*
Cockeysville, MD.: Liberty Publishing, 1983.

Lois Engel and Brendan Boyd. *How to Buy Stocks.*
New York: Bantam Books, 1987.

Charles J. Givens. *Wealth Without Risk*
New York: Simon & Schuster, 1990.

68

Victoria Felton-Collins. *Couples and Money.*
New York: Bantam Books, 1992.

Periodicals:
Barron's
Businessweek
Forbes
Fortune
Investor's Daily
The Wall Street Journal

ABOUT THE AUTHORS

TARYN A. SIEVERS

I'm an associate vice president with Dean Witter Reynolds in Oakland, California. In addition to being an investment broker, I teach accredited courses on financial topics at University of California Berkeley Extension, and at five different adult school districts in the San Francisco Bay Area. I have a B.S. in business administration with an emphasis in finance, and a B.A. in journalism. My hobbies include skiing, running, traveling and cooking. My hope is that money and investing become a less intimidating topic for those of you who want successfully to manage your own finances.

VINCENT A. PETRUS

I am general manager of Chico Independent Auto.

LES HAIT

I specialize in divorce and personal injury cases, and research financial investing and peak performance psychology. My law degree is from the University of California at Berkeley. I like to jog, ski, and surf. I share in the care of my son, Jed, with my wife, Donna, and his mother.

Personal Reflections

1. In preparation for the next chapters about relationships, record your dreams. Can you identify themes and personal symbols that repeat? This is an efficient way to get to know yourself and what you bring to a partnership.

2. What else is on your mind right now?

3. How are you defining your own view of success?

✪Next... Now that you have thought about the knowledge needed to multiply your savings and provide financial stability, we'll turn to interpersonal skills. Understanding the other gender is the key to empathy and getting along harmoniously. The author of the next chapter, on understanding men, is a professor and an athlete.

3

UNDERSTANDING

MEN

DON SABO, PH.D.

Chapter Goals

In this chapter, we look at personal and social aspects of men's lives and gender identities. The main goal is to provide some answers to questions that women often raise about men's behavior and moods. We examine men's conformity to traditional masculinity and how many of the old, patriarchal scripts still get played out in social and sexual relationships. The chapter issues range from communication between the sexes to lovemaking, male anger, men's health, and men's involvement with work and family. Finally, men's responses to women's efforts to create gender equality are discussed and evaluated.

Why do men buy into gender stereotypes?

Understanding men and masculinity has always been a major fascination for me. I spent much of my adolescence wondering about what makes men and women think, feel, and behave in the ways they do. My curiosity about dating behavior, sexuality, men's violence, male psychology, and gender issues grew during the college years and, eventually, I devoted my doctoral work to the study of gender. My main research interests as a professional sociologist have focused on aspects of men's lives. This intellectual work has helped me deal with my own life as a working person, husband, father, friend, and political agent. I don't claim to have generated any "ultimate answers" to the man question, but I have made progress toward better understanding myself, other men, and women.

One of the great myths of sexist culture is that men and women are biologically programmed to enact their gender roles. The "anatomy is destiny" formula belies the fact that masculinity varies across persons, time, and cultures. Gender identity is largely learned and reconstructed as we move through life. The frameworks for masculine identity come mainly from outside the body, not inside. Masculinity gets imported into men's bodies and minds, takes hold, and then expresses itself in everyday feelings and behavior. Take time now to list in your journal the traits you associate with an admirable man. Think about what your list might look like if you grew up in a nonwestern country.

While growing up, boys internalize various cultural messages about traditional masculinity. We learn to behave "like men," which means not to behave like women. We're told: Don't be a sissy or a wimp. Keep a stiff upper lip. Big boys don't cry. Take it like a man. Be independent, try not to depend on others. Be tough and aggressive and keep your feelings to yourself. In fact, if you can hide your feelings even from yourself, so much the better. Strive for success and superiority over others. What other messages about masculinity do boys learn as children?

Each of these cultural messages gets conveyed in myriad ways and gradually becomes a bar in the cage that takes shape in a man's gender identity. By the end of adolescence, the cage of masculinity has become so formidable and rigid that, in effect, men have difficulty breaking out of it. Men buy into traditional gender stereotypes; therefore, it is difficult to break out of the psychosocial cage of learned masculinity.

Males also cling to traditional definitions of masculinity because they represent vehicles to power, achievement, and success. Men in positions of power in government, for example, still often posture themselves as tough and decisive warriors. In order to change George Bush's image of being an indecisive wimp in the 1988 election campaign, strategists emphasized his experiences as a World War II bomber pilot. Equations between strength, power, and success are prominent in media and fiction, with heroes ranging from Joe Montana, Jose Canseco, Michael Jordan, and Donald Trump, to the Terminator and Rambo.

Males gravitate toward these cultural equations of empowerment because, like most people in capitalist economies, they want to better themselves and climb the proverbial ladder of success. Indeed, traditionally "masculine" traits such as aggressiveness, goal-directedness, and ambition are very useful for advancing one's career and competing in the marketplace—for both men and women. ☛ For a discussion of how sports shapes traditional masculinity, see Michael Messner, *Power at Play: Sports and the Problem of Masculinity* (Beacon Press).

Finally, men tend to accept traditional definitions of masculinity because they tend to perceive masculinity in monolithic or all-or-nothing terms. Most men are not aware of alternative masculinities. They lack the vision and flexibility to step outside the masculine cage and construct an identity that incorporates both so-called masculine and feminine dimensions. Some men feel strange about choosing a career in a female-dominated and caring profession like nursing.

Other men may feel their manhood is threatened by the prospect of becoming a househusband and parent. The more hung up on traditionaly masculine expectations a man is, the more he tends to see women's and men's roles in black-white, either-or terms. Women, in contrast, are learning that to become liberated from outmoded gender expectations does not mean that they become like men. Gender liberation comes from becoming more flexible and integrating elements of "femininity" and "women's roles" into what is worthwhile in "masculinity" and "men's roles."

Why do men act like they have it all together?

The traditional script for masculinity says that men are supposed to have it all together. Men are supposed to be financially successful, sexually skilled, athletic, confident, resolute about not backing down from a fight or a tough problem, able to deal with life on their own, and capable always of saying the right thing (especially where women are concerned). Men are supposed to drive the right car, wear the right clothes, and listen to the right music. Most of all, men are supposed to be in control of themselves, their emotions, those around them, and their destinies. Being cool means being in control. The racial, ethnic, and social class trappings of coolness may be different, but the message is basically the same.

This image is, if you think about it, ridiculous in that only a handful of men ever meet most of the expectations. And yet, the traditional masculine ideal remains a blatant part of the culture portrayed in countless forms on Monday Night Football, beer ads, film and video, books and magazines. It is in the middle of this contradiction, however, that you can discover the "Catch 22" of masculinity. Traditional masculinity is basically not attainable. Fulfilling the masculine ideal is like climbing a mountain that has no summit: You never can get there.

The masculine ideal generally flows from the dominant culture and, through socialization, becomes part of individual identity. Boys compare themselves and others to the traits and achievements they believe are representative of all or most men. One consequence, therefore, is that when men identify too strongly with the traditional masculine ideal, they get sucked into feeling inadequate or inferior when they do not attain that ideal. They blame themselves for their own failures or inadequacies rather than trying to locate the sources of these feelings in the gender stereotypes and gender hierarchies that surround them.

Readers may be thinking that femininity is equally idealized in our culture and, therefore, just as unattainable. You are right. One difference is, however, that modern feminists have critically analyzed the myths and ideologies underpinning traditional femininity. They have exposed the illusions and pitfalls behind the platitudes and stereotypes. Today women feel like they can pursue alternative femininities (e.g., a career, political ambitions, sports) or mix aspects of traditional women's roles (e.g., motherhood) with the new, liberating identities they are constructing. In contrast, men have only begun to critique masculinity and to question whether the timeworn patriarchal formula for living makes any sense. Most men have not spent a lot of time thinking about gender stereotypes and sex inequality. Men are not critically conscious about gender although it may be in their personal and social interests to be so.

The women's movement and women's studies give women a vehicle for rethinking traditional gender roles, femininity, and sexuality. Men do not have the same kind of critique of traditional masculinity going for them on a large scale. A critique of masculinity asks why masculinity gets defined in such a way that it is unattainable? Whose interests does it serve? Aren't there healthier and saner ways to live than those prescribed by traditional masculine scripts?

Feminists emphasize that the masculine ideal serves the collective political and social interests of men by preserving their power and privilege over women. Masculine activities and interests are elevated while feminine pursuits and accomplishments are devalued. Men's studies scholars also point out that discourse about the masculine ideal helps groups of high-status and privileged men to manipulate groups of lower-status men. For example, military elites use idealized messages about manhood to recruit and motivate poor or working-class boys who end up fighting battles that mainly enrich the male elites who sit atop the economy. Do you remember the recruitment slogan "The Marine Corps Builds Men"? It may build men, but for what purpose and at whose risk and expense?

Recent critical analyses of the inter-male dominance hierarchies in sports provide another example. For the sake of winning, big time college football coaches use stirring messages about manliness to get players to deny pain and risk injury. While the coaches collect fat salaries and universities generate millions of dollars in television revenues, less than half of NCAA scholarship athletes in football and basketball graduate from college and many are left with arthritis and injured knees in their middle age. Men's studies scholars are asking who benefits from these relationships?

Why can't men be more open about their feelings?

Young boys are often taught to endure emotional grief, anxiety, feelings of inadequacy, or pain in stoic silence. Boys who are "too emotional" run the risk of being labeled "sissies," "wusses," or "queers." The suppression of emotions is a built-in requirement for many adult roles that men pursue. For a man in the role of lawyer, soldier, quarterback, manager, or machine operator, loss of emotional control is looked upon as hindering performance. Indeed, as women increasingly enter these occupational roles, they are discovering similar prohibitions on emotional expression.

Researchers have found that overly aggressive males have greater difficulty expressing emotions and empathizing with others. This suggests that boys' training for aggression also inhibits emotional responsiveness. Secondly, because male relationships are basically competitive, men learn to regard self-disclosures as a potential source of weakness and vulnerability. Another factor inhibiting male expressiveness is homophobia, or the fear that any displays of affection between men or lapses into "feminine" sentiment may be considered signs of homosexuality.

It is also important to realize that the prevailing image of male emotional inexpressiveness is itself a gender stereotype. The extent to which men bottle up or express emotions varies a great deal from individual to individual and across situations, ethnic groups, and cultures. Everybody has an emotional life, yet traditionally, men's roles have allowed fewer opportunities for the expression of emotions than women's roles. For example, I remember holding back tears in a movie theater with a date. I believed that the "boyfriend" was supposed to be stoic, unsentimental, and in control of his emotions. As a linebacker on high school and college football teams, I learned to be tough and to mercilessly beat up on other players. These were the rules to live by. Even though I experienced sadness, hurt, or compassion on the inside, I rarely showed these sentiments on the outside.

One result of tuning into traditional masculinity is that men are not only less likely to express emotions, but they are also less adept at recognizing, labeling, and experiencing an emotion when they are actually experiencing it. This lack of recognition can lead to confusion, anger, or brooding silences in a man. Women may view this as intentional withholding when, in fact, the man is truly not conscious of a set of feelings. As men increasingly participate in less rigid, more nurturing kinds of roles such as parenting and, as the masculine stereotype continues to wane, men may feel free to explore and express their feelings more openly.

======== **Personal Reflections** ========

Here is a fill-in-the-blank exercise that you might use to write about in your journal or to spark a not-so-everyday conversation with a friend.

1. I learned from my father that being a man means _____.
2. I learned from my mother that being a man means _____.
3. If I had to identify the feeling state that most dominates my day-to-day moods and personality it would be _____.
4. It's not easy to express my feelings around members of the opposite sex because _____.
5. It's not easy to express my feelings around my same-sex peers because _____.
6. During the last week I have experienced the following six emotions _____.
7. When I think about sexuality, I feel _____.
8. When I think about my career, I feel _____.
9. When I think about my love life, I feel _____.
10. For me, the most difficult aspect of being a man (or woman) is _____.

Why don't men listen to women?

In a sexist culture, women and femininity are systematically devalued while men and masculinity are valorized. Boys learn that men's opinions and positions are more important than women's. The cultural devaluation reflects and reproduces patterns of sex discrimination in which men are likely to occupy positions of respect and power. For example, sociologists have observed that members of minority groups are more attuned to the subtle movements and moods of the dominant groups. Under the institution of slavery, blacks paid more attention to the actions of whites, in part, because whites were in a position to hurt them or grant them favors. Whites, in contrast, were less perceptive about blacks because blacks resided in relatively lower social positions. Likewise, in the system of structured gender inequality, women have become more perceptive about men than vice versa.

Men's inattention to women in conversation may also be a form of dominance striving. The phrase "dominating a conversation" takes on new meaning in this context. By disregarding or squelching women's verbal input in certain social settings, men are able to carry out their agendas and maintain their status advantages. Men's domination of conversation and discourse is often also formally institutionalized. For example, the entire congressional subcommittee that was selected to hear Anita Hill's charges of sexual harassment against Judge Clarence Thomas was comprised entirely of men.

Sexual fantasy often comes between men and women and serves almost like a filter that blocks communication. A male may think about a woman's beautiful lips during a conversation and, as a result, is only dimly aware of what she is actually saying. This is not a biological occurrence. Within sexist culture, men are encouraged to perceive women as sexual objects. This way of seeing women gets reinforced daily by the media and, as a result, some men experience difficulty seeing women in more multidimensional, less objectified terms. Men lose because they misunderstand women's messages and fail to see women for who they really are. Like women, men lose out in the end because sexual fantasy and performance pressures usually create distance between the sexes rather than fostering communication, understanding, and empathy.

Do men want more than sex?

"Men have only one thing on their minds!" "Most men's brains are between their legs." These images of men constantly on the make are common enough to be cliché, and they distort what most men feel about their sexuality. Research shows that most males want relationships with women that combine affection and commitment with eroticism. Yet men often face pressure that gets translated into the "man-as-hunter/woman-as-prey" approach to sexual relationships. Within many male subcultures (e.g., peer groups, athletic teams, fraternities), men are encouraged to treat women as sexual objects. Males who get "too close" to women may be ridiculed as "pussywhipped" or "under the thumb" of a woman friend. Sex and love are seldom allowed to mix. A split emerges between men's inner needs and outer appearances, between their desire for the love of women and treatment of them as sex objects.

Most men do not really know what they want from their sexual lives. We seem torn between yearning for excitement and conquest and the longing for love and intimacy. On one side, we feel titillated by the glitter of contemporary cosmetics and corporate advertising. Blatantly sexual and slickly commercialized images of semiclad women in MTV videos or the latest edition of the *Victoria's Secret* catalog jolt our minds and bodies. We are sporadically turned on by the simple hedonism of the so-called sexual revolution and the sometimes sleek, sometimes sleazy veil of soft and hard core pornography. Many of us fantasize about pursuing eroticism without the work of commitment; some live the fantasy.

On the other side, more men are becoming aware of genuine needs for intimate relationships. We are beginning to recognize that being independent, always on the make, and emotionally controlled, are not meeting our human needs. Furthermore, the traditional masculine script is certainly not meeting women's needs, expectations, or satisfying their emotional needs. More men are exploring a definition of sexuality that can be a vehicle for expressing and experiencing love.

In our culture many men are suffering from "sexual schizophrenia." Their minds lead them toward eroticism while their hearts pull them toward emotional intimacy. Married men can get hung up on erotic fantasies about other women and feel sensually distanced from their spouses even though they love them. The "guys" nudge single men away from emotional commitment, and men usually have a lot of difficulty reading what it is women want from them. Men rarely ask women what women themselves want because to do so is to admit that they are not the hip, suave, cool, or "in control" kind of males that they are striving to be. One result is confusion. What men want rarely coincides with what they need. The immediate promises of eroticism end up being a distraction from getting in touch with their deeper emotional needs.

Male sexuality changes throughout the life cycle. We can rethink and reshape our sexuality by listening more closely to women's voices. We can pay less attention to what the guys say we ought to do (Get it on. Let her know who's boss.) and tune in to our own emotional and sensual needs. We can avoid the sexist trap of putting women down in order to raise our own self-esteem.

Here is an exercise to try in the privacy of your own room or in a small group. It's designed to give you insights into the ways women are often portrayed in the media. Get hold of a *Sports Illustrated* swimsuit issue. Randomly select pictures and then literally imitate the poses of the models. Do you feel like an athlete? Do you feel silly or competent, revealed or exposed, physically vulnerable or strong, sexually empowered or objectified? Write a journal entry on your experiences with these feminine poses. If you did the exercise in a small group setting, write about how you felt in front of others.

Why do men hurry through foreplay?

Our inner sense of "maleness" or "femaleness" influences the ways we see ourselves as sexual beings. As we develop, sexual identity emerges as an extension of an already formed gender identity, and sexual behavior becomes scripted by cultural meanings. This means that traditional male scripts that emphasize competition, winning, aggression, domination, and goal attainment, also shape men's lovemaking behavior. Taught to be "achievement machines," many males organize their energies and approach to life around a performance ethic that spills over into sexual relations. The goal-directedness and preoccupation with performance and technique enter into male scripts of lovemaking. Contemporary women seem to be telling men to pay less attention to actual intercourse and orgasm, and to get into the overall process. Put another way, making love isn't like running a 50-yard dash, but rather, a delightful jog in the park.

When intercourse becomes the chief goal of sex, it bolsters men's performance inclinations and limits their ability to enjoy other aspects of sexual experiences. It can also create problems for both men and their partners. Since coitus requires an erection, men are under pressure to get and maintain erections. If erections do not occur, or men ejaculate "too quickly," their self-esteem as lovers and men can be impaired. In fact, sex therapists tell us that men's preoccupation and anxieties about erectile potency, penis size, and performance can cause the very sexual dysfunctions they fear.

☞ There are two books that I always recommend to male friends who want to better understand men's changing sexual needs, fantasies, and experiences: Bernie Zilbergeld, *Male Sexuality,* (Bantam) and Michael Castleman, *Sexual Solutions: A Guide for Men and the Women Who Love Them* (Touchstone).

In the past men's perceptions of women's sexuality and lovemaking have been distorted by myths and misinformation. Prevailing nineteenth century medical opinion, for example, held that women were "naturally" passive and did not enjoy sex. This belief meant that, for many couples, the sex act got defined as a progression from male erection to male penetration to male ejaculation with very little sensitivity to women's sensual needs or orgasmic response. These erroneous attitudes toward female sexuality spilled over into the twentieth century. Indeed, it was not until the mid-1960s that sex researchers William Masters and Virginia Johnson established that most women achieve orgasm primarily through clitoral stimulation rather than from stimulation within the vagina.

Cultural myths about female sexuality flourished, in part, because women's opinions on sexual matters were seldom heard. It was male "experts" who discussed and defined "human" sexuality. Sigmund Freud went so far as to say that women who experienced clitoral orgasms were immature and frigid. Such notions placed expectations on men to prolong erections in order to stimulate orgasm without touching the clitoris. In the past, most males learned about women's sexuality from these "experts" or from other males. Boys gleaned "how-to" information from older boys or male peers who, in turn, got their insights from other males, the media, or pornography. *Penthouse Forum,* for example, is riddled with "myth-information" about women's sexual needs and practices; e.g., women enjoy pain during intercourse, women prefer giant penises, or most women use dildoes. Myths about men's sexuality are also prevalent. For example, "real" men are portrayed as being interested in having sex all the time, always ready for action. Penis size is also likely to be exaggerated, as is the role of penis in lovemaking.

In more recent decades, women have been more outspoken about their sexual preferences and desires. The publication of ☞ *The Hite Report* on female sexuality in 1976 created a good deal of controversy because it asked new questions about male sexual performance. While Shere Hite's study of female sexuality was criticized on methodological grounds, it was unique in that *women* were defining their own sexuality and discussing male sexual performance rather than male experts. Public and educational discussion of female sexuality became more common during the 1980s and many males began to listen to women's voices. Whereas Sigmund Freud had misguided earlier generations of males through the corridors of female sexuality, Shere Hite, Lonnie Barbach, Nancy Friday, and "Dr. Ruth" Westheimer were helping newer generations of men to better understand women's sexual makeup, fantasies, and needs.

Both females and males have much to gain from restructuring sexual relationships along egalitarian lines. The psychologist Abraham Maslow found that self-fulfilled persons made no distinctions between the roles of the two sexes in sex play, hence providing evidence for a positive interplay between gender equality and sexual adjustment. Egalitarianism is fostering greater communication between women and men which, in turn, may facilitate better understanding of one another's sensual desires and needs.

Why do some men take work so seriously and others not seriously enough?

The connections between masculinity and work are many and complex. Many of the personality characteristics believed to be essential for work within the capitalist economy are the same as those we attribute to masculinity. Competitiveness, aggressiveness, tough-mindedness, lack of concern for emotions, and goal-directedness are generally held to be prerequisites for success in the corporate-industrial setting.

Male socialization for work begins early in life, and associations between men's roles and employment are formed in boyhood. By the time adults begin asking, "What do you want to be when you grow up?" a boy has developed firm notions about adult gender roles. Soon he understands that it is important for his developing identity to be successful in his adult occupation. More directly, he begins to make connections between success and its perceived rewards such as recognition, approval, love, and money. In turn, he views domestic and family work as female and not his primary responsibility.

Men are apt to see work as a competitive struggle that pits them against a harsh and demanding array of social and economic circumstances. Indeed, this view represents the highly competitive realities of the modern workplace, with which most individuals, male and female, must contend. Yet, for men, the gender expectations seem to say that just "making a living" is not enough. In the race for success, the stakes are seen as being higher. The stress is on personal achievement, which is most often defined as obtaining top-level jobs and incomes.

The problem is, while male socialization entreats men to climb to the uppermost rungs of the socio-economic ladder, there is only room enough for a few at the top. The unequal distribution of wealth and opportunity in American society makes fulfilling stereotypically masculine levels of success less likely than most men realize. And so it may be wise for males to rethink the connections between success striving and traditional masculinity. There is danger in buying into the cultural equation which relates masculine adequacy to the size of a paycheck or the next promotion.

While some men seem to thrive on these expectations, for others the pressures and anxieties surrounding job and career become too much to bear. Some males resolve their fears and anxieties by toning down career aspirations or pulling away from the competitive game entirely. While the latter may be a healthy decision for some males, for others it can lead to maladaptive behaviors such as alcoholism, excessive drug use, addiction to television watching, or even suicide. A wise strategy, therefore, is for men to critically rethink the connections between masculinity, family, career, and becoming a "success" in life that is measured by more than professional or occupational outcome.

Why are some men allergic to housework?

Sociologist Arlie Hochschild found that many women are not only earning a paycheck, but doing most of the housework and child care as well. ☛ See *The Second Shift* (Viking). After returning home from work, they put in a "second shift" chasing after kids, driving, cooking, and cleaning. On average, women put in fifteen more hours than men each week, which adds up to an extra month of 24-hour-days each year.

While women's participation in the workplace rapidly expanded during the past century, men's contributions to housework and child care has increased at a snail's pace. Men's share of the housework increased from 20 percent to 30 percent between 1965 and 1981. While many men are devoting more time to household chores, women still bear the brunt of responsibility for these tasks. (☞ See John Robinson, "Who's Doing the Housework?" *American Demographics*, December, 1988.)

What kinds of benefits can men derive from taking on more responsibility for housework? In short, what's in it for men? First, by devoting more time to housework, men can enhance the overall financial status of their household. Economic realities in the 1980s and 1990s are such that both partners need to work outside the home. A man's investment in housework, therefore, can feed his partner's ability to succeed at work. Both spouses benefit.

Secondly, sharing housework responsibilities can lower the potential for resentments to develop within a relationship. Women resent getting stuck with most of the housework and, consciously or unconsciously, feelings of anger and resentment can build, creating tensions between spouses. ☞ *The Miller Lite Report on Sports and Fitness in the Lives of Working Women* (Sabo and Snyder, the Women's Sports Foundation, 1993) found that many white collar women were frustrated by the fact that their spouses had more time for sports and exercise because wives were doing more of the family work. Men who exploit their spouses are sometimes harried by guilt feelings that can lower self-esteem. By forging an equitable arrangement for tending to household chores, couples can demonstrate their love and support for one another on a daily basis. The subtle resentments and bad feelings that stem from inequality can be avoided, perhaps leading to better sex!

Finally, housework has been equated to femininity in patriarchal culture. Because it is considered "women's work," housework has gotten a bum rap in male subcultures. The moorings of these stereotypes are obviously grounded in the traditional division of labor between men and women. If you think about it, there is nothing inherently "masculine" or "feminine" about cooking dinner or vacuuming a rug. While it is true that housework is often a drag, I believe that many men are discovering that it can also be fulfilling.

Once men begin to drop the cultural assumption that housework is somehow unmanly, they can begin to explore its positive dimensions. Occasionally, I like washing dishes by hand. I define it as a zen-like activity and enjoy the feel of the hot water on my hands. I watch the cats play, eavesdrop on the kids, or just look out the window and muse. I also like blasting the stereo while dusting or cooking, occasionally breaking into dance. I also like my environment to be somewhat orderly and clean and, as a houseworker, I actively participate in shaping the environment that influences my moods and my family's. Doing housework also helps me get my mind off writing, teaching, and professional concerns. Best of all, doing my fair share of the housework allows me to actively nurture the family that, in turn, nurtures me.

Why do men get angry so often?

Scratch a man and very often he will bleed anger. Women wonder why men are often moody and periodically tend to blow up in their faces like miniature psychosocial volcanoes. Male anger is not some abstract entity. People often get burned by men's anger, some more seriously than others. Men act out their anger on one another in the form of fighting, ridicule, or cutthroat competition. Women are especially victimized by men's anger and violence in the form of rape, date rape, wife beating, assault, sexual harassment on the job, and verbal harassment. Women know that anger is a prerequisite for male violence. Most men, though they live with anger, have very little insight into its origins, presence, and movements within their bodies and minds. Men's anger, and the verbal and physical violence that tend to come with it, is a very complicated issue.

The traditional masculine stereotype calls on males to be aggressive and tough. Anger is basically a by-product of aggression and toughness and, ultimately, part of the inner terrain of traditional masculinity. Like gasoline in an engine, anger fuels male aggression and men's sense of power. Images of angry young men are compelling vehicles used by males to separate themselves from women and to measure their status in respect to other men. Males commonly "size up one another" by gauging who is capable of beating up whom. When athletes or fans get "psyched" or "pumped up" before a game, part of what is going on is that they are drumming up anger in order to attack opponents. In some men, anger becomes an inner sign that they are maintaining a gender identity that helps them to be strong, aggressive, independent, and fearless. In short, anger is an emotional verification that they are successfully conforming to the traditional masculine mandate.

Men's anger and violence derive, in part, from sex inequality. Men use the threat and/or application of violence to maintain their political power and economic advantage over women and lesser-status men. Male socialization reflects and reinforces this larger pattern of male dominance. As boys come to accept the male-dominated status quo, they internalize its cultural image of the prototypical man who is depicted as angry and violence-prone. Many male subcultures (e.g., athletic teams, fraternities, military troops, gangs) are vehicles for traditional masculine scripts and, as such, do much to equate demonstrations of violence and anger with manhood. Crosscultural studies show that sex segregation correlates with men's violence proneness; in societies with highly differentiated gender roles, outward displays of violence among men and in all-male settings are common. Similarly, studies of delinquent male gangs reveal the existence of a subculture of violence. It may be that when males are separated from females in same-sex subcultures, they are more apt to exaggerate physical superiority in order to prove their "manhood."

Why do men often take health risks?

My grandfather used to tell me with a wink in his eye, "Find out where you're going to die and stay the hell away from there." His counsel is not absurd when placed in the context of preventive health. Research shows that American women live longer than men. Data from the National Center for Health Statistics (1992) show that women outlived men by 6.8 years in 1989. Men's lower life expectancy has been shown to be related both to biological and psychosocial processes. Factors related to men's roles and traditional masculinity influence men's health and illness. The fact that men have always had higher rates of lung cancer than women, for example, is partly attributable to cigarette smoking. In the past, smoking was associated with rugged masculinity. So too, drinking alcohol has been traditionally surrounded by an aura of male *esprit d'corps*. Alcohol consumption has been shown to be a causal factor in illness such as cirrhosis of the liver, heart disease, lung cancer, and accidental death.

Boys' socialization for aggression and daring makes them prone to fatal accidents. Males are three times more likely than females to die from accidental causes (e.g., automobile and motorcycle accidents, drowning). The code of masculine bravado contributes to premature death in the form of homicides; men are four times as likely to die from homicide as women. Men are also more apt than women to commit suicide, though women attempt it more often than men. Men "succeed" at suicide because they ordinarily employ more lethal means than women do—a woman may take pills while a man uses a gun.

Researchers have also found that men are more apt than women to deny their feelings surrounding illness and death. One explanation is that gender stereotypes shape men's perceptions of illness. Because they are expected to be stoic, independent, and powerful, young men learn to suppress fears about weakness, death, and dying, and to regard asking for help or self-disclosure as expressions of "feminine" dependence. The following discussion of testicular cancer shows how men's denial around illness and death can produce negative consequences.

The epidemiological data on testicular cancer are sobering. Though relatively rare in the general population, it is the fourth most common cause of death among 15-35-year-old males, accounting for 14 percent of all cancer deaths for this age group. It is the most common form of cancer affecting 20-34-year-old white males. The incidence of testicular cancer is increasing, and about 5,900 new American cases were diagnosed in 1990. If detected early, the cure rate is high; delayed diagnosis is life-threatening. Regular testicular self-examination (TSE), therefore, is an effective preventive means for insuring early detection and successful treatment.

Denial appears to influence men's perceptions of testicular cancer and TSE. Studies show that most males are not aware of testicular cancer and, even among those who are aware, many are reluctant to examine their testicles as a preventive measure. Even when symptoms are recognized, men sometimes postpone seeking treatment. Moreover, men who are taught TSE are often initially receptive, but the practice of TSE decreases over time. Men's resistance to TSE has been linked to awkwardness about touching themselves, associating touching genitals with homosexuality or masturbation, or the idea that TSE is not a manly behavior. And finally, men's individual reluctance to discuss testicular cancer partly derives from the widespread cultural silence that envelopes it. The penis is a cultural and, in the context of gender oppression, a political symbol of male power, authority, and sexual dominance. Its symbolic efficacy, therefore, would be eroded or neutralized by the realities of testicular cancer.

In short, traditional masculinity can be hazardous to men's health. Men would do well to listen to grandaddy's counsel and rethink how traditional gender relations are putting their health and longevity at risk.

How are men responding to women's quests for equality?

Someone once said, "The fish are the last ones to discover the ocean." And so it is with men and patriarchy. Despite patriarchy's historical longevity and societal pervasiveness, men have failed to reckon with the fundamental realities of social grouping by sex. Women have been trying to get our attention for more than a century. Several waves of feminism have challenged North Americans to look critically at gender issues and eliminate some of the injustices that attend sex inequality.

Men are beginning to hear the din of women's heady protests, anger, political and cultural dreams, and messages from the heart. Some men seem intimidated by feminists or women who do not play traditionally feminine roles. While some men seem to be afraid of the changes they think that feminism represents, others are downright threatened and angry and are basically saying to feminists, Up yours! ☞ Susan Faludi discusses some men's antifeminist sentiment and resistance to women's quests for gender equality and change in her book *Backlash: The Undeclared War Against American Women* (Doubleday).

Other men have taken the feminist challenge to redress inequality and rethink gender issues seriously. A critical dialogue about men and masculinity has emerged during the last 10-15 years. It is critical because it problematizes men and masculinity, in that it is recognized that there is something rotten in the ways that manhood has been defined, the ways that men spend their lives, the ways that men relate to one another and to women and to the planet. Increasingly, men are beginning to rethink their identities, their sexuality, and the violence they act out toward women and toward one another. A new area of writing and research has emerged called "men's studies," that not only seeks to critique men's lives, but also to help men change themselves and to reweave the latticework of their relationships.

When I was a college student in the early 1970s, I was dissatisfied with many of the gender games I felt obligated to play out with my male friends and women. I never felt comfortable with the traditional male script—acting confident and cool with women when I felt insecure and vulnerable, being tough on the outside and never talking about the personal issues that churned on the inside. I didn't realize it at the time, but I was searching for alternatives to the old masculine script. I wanted a "new suit of clothes," so to speak, that I felt more comfortable wearing in daily life. I discovered that there were women on campus who also felt constrained and inhibited by the traditional gender scripts. Most of them considered themselves feminists in one way or another, and I began to seek out their company. I read feminist books and attended women's lectures. The discovery of feminists and feminisms helped me to rethink and rebuild my life and gender identity.

As a man interested in feminism during the early 1970s, I felt rather alone and a bit weird: There were not thousands of men signing up to join the women's movement! Eventually, however, more men began writing and talking about gender issues. Men's support groups began to sprout up and the new men's studies literature gave me more to read and think about. A pro-feminist men's movement emerged and I got involved. Today, there are tens of thousands of men who not only support gender equality but are committed to forging more healthful, humane, and nonsexist ways of being men.

The 1980s saw the growth of men's movements in the United States. The followers of Robert Bly's "mythopoetic men's movement," for example, use story-telling, myths and drumming in order to help men get in touch with the cultural and unconscious roots of masculinity. The National Organization for Men against Sexism (NOMAS) struggles against sexism and explores gender issues as varied as men's violence against women, men and spirituality, reproductive rights, men's health, men and pornography, homophobia, bisexuality, and gay rights. "Free Men" and "Men's Rights, Inc." are examples of men's organizations which focus on the oppressiveness of the male role, sometimes called "masculinists." There are also organizations that advocate for fathers' and gays' legal rights. Religious denominations have begun sponsoring men's weekends and support groups.

For an excellent introduction to the emerging area of men's studies, see a book of readings edited by ☞ Michael Kimmel and Michael Messner called *Men's Lives* (Macmillan). A national magazine that discusses pro-feminist alternatives for men is ☞ *Changing Men*, 306 N. Brooks Street, Madison, WI 53715. There are now two journals that publish scholarly work on men and masculinity: *Men's Studies Review*, 827 Delaware Street, Berkeley, CA 94710, and *The Journal of Men's Studies*, P.O. Box 32, Harriman, TN 37748-0032.

One of the most powerful lessons that I learned from feminism is that "the personal is political." This means that we cannot put up walls between our personal lives and what is happening in society, politics, or history. As regards gender issues, it means that we can better understand the personal world of our gender identity by exploring the social and historical contexts in which gender identity emerges, and vice versa. Many men who are involved with the men's movement stress the importance of exploring the inner roots of their masculinity and, in the process, transforming their identities. They're doing this important psychological work in support groups, men's conferences, men's weekend retreats, or in counseling settings. Other members of the men's movement emphasize the need for men to ally with women in order to secure pay equity in the workplace, better child care, an end to domestic violence and rape, and a more peaceful society.

Both these approaches to change are necessary. Yes, we need personal change but, without changing the political, economic, and cultural structures that surround us, the subjective gains and insights forged within individuals will erode and fade away. Personal change needs to be rooted in structure and buoyed up by institutional realities. Without a raft or boat or some structure to hang on to, even the best swimmer tires and slips beneath the waves.

SUGGESTED READINGS

Connell, R. W. *Gender and Power: Society, the Person and Sexual Politics.* Stanford, CA: Stanford University Press, 1987.

Craig, S. *Men, Masculinity, and the Media.* Newbury Park, CA: Sage Publications, 1992.

Franklin, C. W.   *Men and Society.* Chicago: Nelson-Hall, 1988.

Jackson, D. *Unmasking Masculinity: A Critical Autobiography.* London: Unwin Hyman, 1990.

Keen, S. *Fire in the Belly: On Being a Man.* New York: Bantam Books, 1991.

Messner, M., and Sabo, D. Sport, *Men, and the Gender Order: Critical Feminist Perspectives.* Champaign, IL: Human Kinetics Books, 1992.

Pleck, J. H. *The Myth of Masculinity.* Cambridge, MA: The MIT Press, 1987.

Sabo, D., and Runfola, R. *Jock: Sports and Male Identity.* Englewood Cliffs, NJ: Prentice Hall, 1980.

Sanday, P. *Female Power and Male Dominance: On the Origins of Sexual Inequality.* New York: Cambridge University Press, 1981.

Segal, Lynne. *Slow Motion: Changing Masculinities, Changing Men.* New Brunswick, NJ: Rutgers University Press, 1990.

Stoltenberg, J. *Refusing to Be a Man.* Portland, OR: Breitenbush Books, 1989.

Thorne-Finch, R. *Ending the Silence: The Origins and Treatment of Male Violence against Women.* Toronto: University of Toronto Press, 1992.

The most important points to apply

♦ Men's behavior is shaped mainly by social and cultural influences and not by physiological factors like brain differences, hormones, or instincts.

♦ Contrary to stereotypes, men do have feelings. The problem is that the masculine ideal encourages men to suppress and hide their emotions. This robs men of a wider range of emotional expression and can lead to moodiness, anger, or aggression.

♦ Traditional gender roles tend to block or complicate communication between the sexes.

♦ Men's sexual behaviors, attitudes, and fantasies are profoundly influenced by their gender identities. Males learn to be "masculine" before they learn about sexuality. Following the traditional masculine script distorts men's perceptions of women's sexual needs and can lead to problems of sexual adjustment for men as well.

♦ The traditional masculine ideal equates manly self-worth to success at work and career rather than to spending time nurturing his family.

♦ Anger is a very real part of many men's emotional lives. However, men's anger should not be understood as strictly personal in origin or consequence. Gender inequality, traditional masculine socialization, and sexism foster the development of aggression and violence proneness among men.

♦ Masculinity may be dangerous to men's health. Identification with the traditional male role increases men's health risks.

♦ There is no such thing as "masculinity." There are many different types of masculinities that exist in North American culture.

♦ Gender studies are no longer exclusively about women. The men's movement and the new men's studies literature are generating facts, ideas, and visions that can help men rethink and reshape their identities to fit the changing realities of the 1990s.

ABOUT THE AUTHOR

D O N S A B O, P H. D.

I am a sociology professor at D'Youville College in Buffalo, New York. My writing and research revolve around gender issues and the analysis of sport and society. I work hard to serve organizations such as the North American Society for the Sociology of Sport, the National Organization for Men against Sexism, and the Women's Sports Foundation. I like to says "A man's place is in the women's movement," and I take great satisfaction in working with women's organizations in order to make society a better place for both women and men. I co-edit the "SportsMen" column for *Changing Men,* a national pro-feminist magazine. I advocate for fairness, justice, and greater opportunities for women and racial/ethnic minorities.

I've been married for seventeen years and have three children— an adopted son Jeffrey, a biological daughter Natalie, and a foster daughter Tia. I try to influence my children's lives without telling them what to do. (This is no easy task!) My marital relationship with Linda is the most important thing in my life, though I've learned that marriage is filled with hardships and disappointments as well as good things like love and happiness. I love music and spend good time playing blues and boogie woogie on the keyboards. I'm committed to a regular fitness regimen. Whereas I used to think physical strength and fitness were "masculine" characteristics, I now advocate these goals for both women and men.

✪ Next... We have seen that the male role is an arduous one, This requires avoidance of behavior stereotyped as feminine, to be examined in the next chapter. The author is a therapist who teaches a psychology of women course.

"I am gaining a greater understanding of and respect for myself, my friends and romantic partners, and for women in general. I am learning what seems true for me as a unique and important individual, and choose to see each woman as a unique and important person as well. My increased understanding of women helps me to be more at ease in developing meaningful and intimate relationships with the women in my life."

4

UNDERSTANDING

WOMEN

COLETTE FLEURIDAS, PH.D.

This chapter guides us to a greater understanding of what it means to be a woman today and how to understand women as friends, lovers, colleagues, and employers. The goals include: recognizing and dispelling stereotypes about women which limit us; recognizing the societal, relational, and personal experiences in our lives which strengthen women's self-esteem, confidence, and well-being; and learning more about issues of importance to contemporary women.

What do young adults want to know about women?

Personal Reflections

Write a list of three or more questions you have about women; specifically describe what you would like to know about women. If you are a woman, you may wonder if other women share your beliefs, values, and experiences. If you are a man, you may wonder about women you know or about women in general.

I asked over 300 college students in the psychology of women courses which I teach to write a list of the questions they have about women. Questions asked most often included:

1. Of the common stereotypes about women, which ones are true?

2. What are some characteristics common to contemporary women?

3. How are men and women different and why? For example, why do women seem to have less self-confidence than men? Why are women perceived as inferior to men? Why are women more willing to share their feelings than men?

4. What do women value in their lives? What contributes to women's happiness and psychological wellness?

5. What do women value in their romantic relationships? (Often, male students want to know what women find attractive in men or

what women want in a romantic relationship.) Why are so many women unhappy if they are not in a romantic relationship?

6. What are the important political and social issues that concern women? What can we do to equalize the power and opportunities available to women and men?

Compare your questions with these: Students also asked numerous questions about the topics below. See the bibliography at the end for additional reading about them.

—women's appearance (body image and eating disorders)

—cultural, racial, and ethnic comparisons of women

—women's physical health

—combining multiple roles (career, spouse or partner, home-maker, and mother)

—women's sexuality

—women's friendships (with women and men, and competition between women)

—sexual and physical violence against women

—feminism and the women's movement.

What do you believe about women?

Personal Reflections

Write a paragraph or two about what you believe about women: What do you think is true about most women of a given age, culture, race, social class, and educational background?

Try completing the following sentences in your journal. Respond quickly and without much forethought:

1. Generally, women are more_____
2. Typically, in a romantic relationship, women prefer_____
3. Most women have a bad habit of_____
4. Today, educated women know that_____
5. Compared with men, most women are better at_____
6. Women would be better off if they_____
7. Above all else, women tend to value_____

8. If women had to choose between advancing in their careers or maintaining a healthy relationship with their romantic partner, they would probably_____

9. Most women who work do so because they_____

10. The changes that would most contribute to the advancement of the status and welfare of women in all societies are_____

You may want to repeat this exercise after replacing the word *women* with *men*. Also, complete each sentence in the first person; for example, "Generally, I am more _____ " Invite a friend to do the same, and compare answers.

➤
What are some common stereotypes about women?

Stereotypes are shared beliefs that certain qualities are assigned to groups of people based solely on their membership in that group. Research in the last three decades examining gender stereotypes in many countries and cultures have found certain adjectives still commonly associated with women or men.

Stereotypes about women:	Stereotypes about men:
affectionate	adventurous
appreciative	aggressive
childlike	ambitious
complaining	assertive
dependent	autocratic
dreamy	confident
emotional	courageous
excitable	cruel
fickle	daring
gentle	disorderly
meek	dominant
nagging	enterprising
nurturing	independent
prudish	logical
sensitive	rational
sentimental	strong

| sophisticated | tough |
| submissive | unemotional |

Circle the words which you believe have a positive connotation in our society. Are these traits attributed to women and men equally valued?

At the beginning of each semester, I ask my students to generate a list of adjectives that describe women in general; then we do the same for men. At first, the lists differ, but the longer they get, the more similarities appear. The class discussion which follows results in general agreement that BOTH women and men share most of the traits in both lists (women AND men are strong, sensitive, impulsive, rational, intelligent, and so forth), yet we also acknowledge that there are differences.

Stereotypes shape not only how we think about other people, but also what we tend to believe about ourselves and how we act from early childhood through our elder years. Most stereotypes are not based on reality for most of the people grouped together. Most are socially shaped beliefs and norms which have been perpetuated by prescribed gender roles, social systems, and the media. For example, for millennia women have been the primary caretakers of young children and the elderly (although archaeological evidence suggests that for tens of thousands of years, women and men in the hunter and gatherer tribes shared domestic tasks more equally).

Caretaking is a nurturing role, and requires gentleness, patience, sensitivity, and the ability to put the needs of others above one's own. It is understandable that women were seen as nurturers, and that girls were socialized to act in the same way. Furthermore, in societies where women were dominated by powerful and aggressive men, the women most apt to survive were submissive, dependent, and obedient. Once again, girls were trained to act submissively.

Many women are changing their roles and challenging restrictive gender-typed stereotypes. Most women in the United States work to support themselves and their families. Fewer women now depend on men for their support. Many women are the heads of households; some choose to be single and others choose to be "childfree."

Men also are changing their lifestyles, but apparently more slowly than women (see Chapter 3). There is more acceptance and encouragement in the industrialized nations for women to become employed full-time outside the home than for men to become full-time househusbands. Men are becoming more involved in parenting and household chores, perhaps due to the women's rights movements, the persistent requests of working mothers, and the gradual changes in social expectations.

Usually women continue to bear the responsibility of the home and children, even when they work full-time and have a male partner. Most women resent this imbalance (☞ see Baker, *Women*, and Ries and Stone, *American Women*). Many women with careers, myself included, do not want to be in charge of insuring that all the household responsibilities are done. That role often resembles that of a supervisor, making sure that everyone has done their chores. Rather, we prefer that our partners be self-motivated in doing their half of the work because *they* choose to be equally involved in these tasks. Regardless of gender, many households find it challenging to share the responsibility to insure that the important things are done.

The use of stereotypes often prevents us from realizing and appreciating the incredible diversity among people due to cultural backgrounds, ethnicity, education, age, vocation, sexual orientation, and role in relationship or family, not to mention the unique biogenetic characteristics of each of us. I agree with other psychologists who urge us to limit our use of the terms *feminine* and *masculine* to describe stereotypical female and male traits. These terms may perpetuate our stereotypes and dualistic thinking about people. Rather than label a person's behaviors or attitudes as feminine or masculine, it is more accurate to describe each individual specifically as gentle, intuitive, creative, strong, independent, or assertive.

What are some characteristics common to contemporary women?

Quality studies of random, representative samples of contemporary women have yet to be done; however, numerous surveys and nonrandom studies have investigated commonalties among women. Most studies have focused on differences between women and men. An overview of the field indicates that more women worldwide, but especially in industrialized nations, are obtaining an education. Contemporary women are pursuing a career in addition to or with preference over raising a family. Women today are freer to express themselves in what have been considered traditionally male behav-

UNDERSTANDING WOMEN   101

iors or traits. Fewer women remain passive and silent in abusive relationships. People are beginning to listen and realize that change is needed.

However, most societies continue to oppress and devalue women. This continues to limit women's views of themselves and their worth, and thus restricts their perceptions of what they are capable of doing and being. Social oppression explains why many women in the past had less self-confidence, less self-esteem, and more emotional problems like depression, than men. Women are socialized to experience and share emotional feelings more freely than men, which also explains why women report more sadness, depression, and anxiety than men.

Most patriarchal civilizations tend to empower men and value what are believed to be male traits and roles while deploring that which is associated with women: Competition and winning is more highly valued than cooperation and negotiation, autonomy more than interdependence, and reason more than intuition. We are not certain why most societies evolved in this manner, although several theories attempt to provide plausible reasons for the domination of men over women. Prehistoric evidence indicates that for millennia women were honored and worshipped as goddesses in more peaceful tribal units.

It is possible that with the rise of warring tribal groups, physical strength, military leadership, and domination became prized over nurturing, ritualistic relationship with the earth, and creative play. To increase the numbers and military strength of the clan, women and children needed to be protected. The division of labor and heroic role of the conquering warriors led to the leadership and domination of certain men over women, children, and over other men who did not share the status of the governing rulers. Consequently, those with less power and value became possessions of those who had more social power.

These values and practices were perpetuated by government policies and religious dogmas. For thousands of years in many civilizations, husbands owned their wives and children, and the men could do just about whatever they chose with them (☞ see books by Riane Eisler and Marija Gimbutas). This was true in the United States until the late nineteenth century: Husbands owned family property, had child custody, and were sanctioned to rule over and even to physically punish their wives.

None of the possible reasons for the oppression of women justify the continuation of this phenomenon. Feminists (men and women who advocate equal opportunity for all) claim that men as well as women benefit from valuing women; all societies are healthier when equally respecting and rewarding those characteristics which have traditionally been considered feminine, such as gentleness, cooperation, care giving, and parenting.

Probably some of the major problems in our societies would diminish if most of us believed in the value of care giving and in the equal value of all peoples, regardless of appearance, age, gender, or "productivity." For example, we need to change the rampant violence against women, children, the aged, and other oppressed people. The sexual and physical abuse of girls and women is epidemic in the United States. Conservatively, one-fourth of all women (and at least one-tenth of the men) have been sexually victimized at some time in their life; usually by a family member if a child, or by someone they know if an adult. The most common cause of injury to adult women is spousal abuse. Over half of all murders of women are committed by current or former partners whereas 6 percent of male murder victims are killed by their partners. Whatever contributes to this tremendous violation of human sanctity must be challenged and changed.

Why is a discussion of social values and the oppression and violence against women important in a section describing characteristics of contemporary women? Social norms and values shape beliefs and behaviors, all of which affect women's development. Women students stress the importance of open discussions about the prevalence of violence and sexual assault in our society. We need to ascertain how violence is perpetuated by the media, popular culture, some religious groups, and other traditional organizations, including law enforcement. I believe it can be reduced through preventive education for young people and children, quality parent education, public awareness, and boycotting companies which use depictions of violence or oppression to sell products.

We need to work for the passage of stronger laws against domestic violence, sexual assault, acquaintance rape, and for insuring the enforcement of such laws. Social action is necessary and helpful: Write letters to legislators, advertisers, newspaper editors, and speak out against social injustice, violence, and sexual harassment. Men, in addition to women, need to be involved in changing the traditional beliefs, language and behaviors which perpetuate the objectification and abuse of women and other oppressed peoples. (See bibliography for more on this topic.)

Violence against women, children, the aged, and those who are dependent on others for care or support, is probably a product of social values and norms which have not included the valuing of women or of nurturing. Ultimately, social values need to evolve. When women and children know they are valued and respected as well as men, they will value and respect themselves, and others will be less apt to abuse them. These are basic elements of a healthy society.

How are women and men different and why?

It seems that people have always compared women with men and often emphasized their differences. In the past two or three decades, feminists have shaped the psychological and sociological inquiry of gender differences. Feminist psychologists created guidelines for gender-fair research and methodology, and have greatly contributed to our understanding of this field of inquiry. There are many more questions and discrepancies in the research than solid answers about how and why women and men differ.

Personal Reflections

Answer the following questions in your journal, knowing that you can only speculate how your life might have been different if you were the other gender. Then ask a friend of the other gender to do the same. You may want to compare the answers of several friends.

If I were a _____ (the other gender),
1. My parents would have raised me to _____.
2. My teachers would have encouraged me to _____.
3. My mother would have _____.
4. My father would have _____.
5. After high school, I probably would have _____.
6. In college, I probably would have majored in _____.
7. I would pursue a career in _____. or I would _____.
8. I would choose a romantic partner who is _____.
9. My friendships would be _____.
10. My life would be different because _____.

When my students complete a similar questionnaire, very few believe that their lives would be basically the same if they were the other gender. Most say that each of their parents would have related to them differently; that their teachers, coaches, and counselors would have encouraged them to do different things with their lives; and that they would not have the same career or romantic aspirations that they do now. Some women respond that one major difference would be that they would not live in fear of being raped or physically abused. A few men share that they would like the option to conceive and give birth to a child; they also would like to be free to express a greater range of emotions.

Socialized gender roles affect us from birth and shape who and what we become. Researchers seem to agree that culture (social norms, beliefs, and behaviors) is a stronger influence than biology in creating and perpetuating gender differences in most areas. Gender role socialization is such a powerful and pervasive force that it is very difficult to uncover which psychological or personality gender differences are primarily biological, if any.

The three major biological causes for gender differences are genes, hormones, and brain organization. Genetic gender differences are limited to the genetic information on only one pair of chromosomes, out of a total of 23 pairs of chromosomes (the sex chromosomes are XX for females and XY for males). The Y sex chromosome is contributed by the father and dictates the development of the male gonads in the fetus, which then produce androgens (called male hormones because they are found in larger proportions in males). It seems that very little genetic information is carried on the Y chromosome. Therefore, recessive genes on the X sex chromosome are more apt to dictate the genetic make-up of males than of females who have two X sex chromosomes and a higher probability of a dominant gene on the other sex chromosome.

This is why recessive genetic traits which are sex-linked are more apt to appear in males than females, such as color blindness and hemophilia. To our knowledge, very few traits are genetically sex-linked. Although we know from identical twins studies that some personality traits (like shyness and extroversion) and cognitive abilities are influenced as much by genetics as by the social environment, these traits are not sex-linked or gender-specific.

The release of different hormones in male and female fetuses and after puberty does appear to cause gender differences, especially in animals, and specifically in sexual behaviors (in animals, sexual mounting behaviors), aggression, and physical strength. This seems to be due to the effects of the hormones on brain formation in the fetus and on physical development. For example, the release of different hormones during fetalhood affects the hypothalamus of females and males differently; it is part of the brain which regulates certain body functions, such as the monthly menstruation cycle from puberty through menopause in women.

Researchers are investigating the effects of different hormones on the development of the hemispheres of the brain but have yet to find anything conclusive about gender differences. Of course, there are biological differences between women and men, but these do not appear to account for most, if any, of the psychological differences between women and men. Across cultures, the major difference between the sexes is physical strength: Most men are stronger than most women, if matched for age and size—and there are exceptions even to this generality!

One biological difference between genders is the cyclic fluctuation of hormones in women. An average of about 50 percent of women claim to experience water retention, headaches, and/or irritability, and depression (among other symptoms) related to their menstrual cycle, commonly called premenstrual syndrome (PMS) or premenstrual tension (PMT). Research has yet to substantiate specifically what causes most of these symptoms. Good nutrition (a diet high in B vitamins, calcium, magnesium, low in sugar, salts, and caffeine), and regular exercise, appears to be effective in decreasing or eliminating many of the symptoms. Antiprostiglandin drugs, including aspirin and Motrin, have also been found to be helpful in reducing the severity of menstrual cramps, which usually occur at the onset of menstruation and may last two or three days. (☞ See the bibliography "Women's Physical Health").

Personal well-being and sociocultural expectations influence one's perceptions and experience of menstruation. Cultural variations in premenstrual mood swings have been found, even among Catholics and Protestants (with Catholics reporting more negative mood swings than Protestants). This does not mean that women imagine that they are feeling moody or irritable, but cultural attitudes and beliefs affect them. Research results on PMS are still tentative and contradictory: Some studies report that women do not experience cyclic and predictable fluctuations in their moods. A female reader commented, "It is insulting to blame emotional outbursts, depression, etc. on PMS."

Other studies document evidence of cyclic bouts of irritability, depression, and other feelings, such as increased sensitivity and tearfulness. A reader who kept track of her emotional states for a week before each expected period for six months found that, "I am quick to anger and cry four days before my period. Knowing that helped me considerably in the workplace." Still other studies have found that some women tend to experience an increase in well-being or a "premenstrual elation syndrome"! This variation may be due to the possibility that during the time just prior to menstruation, some women are more sensitive and aware of their emotions. This has yet to be documented consistently with research.

➤ Self-respect, a healthy lifestyle, and a good attitude toward our bodies, our sexuality, and our femaleness are important keys for women's health and psychological wellness.

We can also promote and support more research and medical training in areas of women's health such as breast and ovarian cancer and menopause; it is an area of medical research which has been sadly neglected.

There are a few personality traits which vary between men and women, however, research results are often contradictory. The most consistent gender difference is that men are usually more physically and verbally aggressive than women. Researchers speculate that this is partially due to the higher levels of the hormone testosterone in males, but is largely exacerbated by the cultural and social norms. In children, there is a tendency for boys to have higher activity levels than girls, perhaps for the same reasons.

Although the evidence is not as consistent, studies suggest (at least among white, middle class, and young or middle-aged Americans) that women may be more empathic than men, demonstrate less confidence (however, women may be more realistic) than men, and speak more intimately about personal feelings and thoughts with their friends than most men. All of these differences appear to be learned: We learn how we are to feel, think, and behave as either girls or boys by observing others (including TV, books, and other media), and through the training we receive from our parents, teachers, and friends. Afro-American girls, for example, do not suffer the same drop in self-esteem at puberty because their parents have taught them that the media images of femininity are wrong and unrealistic.

Take a stroll through a toy store for an instant lesson in how we socialize our children. Observe children of different ages and their parents, and see how the socialization is reinforced even with very young children. Ask the clerk what type of toy he or she would recommend for a three-year-old boy or for a three-year-old girl. Keep notes in your journal and reflect on changes we need to make to raise our children in a gender-neutral environment where both girls and boys are equally encouraged to play with whatever they want.

Reviews of research show that there are no consistent gender differences in general intelligence, learning, memory, reasoning, or creativity. The differences in verbal and math skills which had been documented a few decades ago (girls scored higher in verbal skills and boys in math skills) appear to be decreasing and minimal. The few modest cognitive differences that continue to appear after adolescence in studies of spatial perception, mental rotation tasks, and certain math tests are growing smaller, perhaps because more girls are being encouraged to take math classes than previously.

The focus of research has shifted from emphasizing differences to affirming the many similarities between the sexes, as well as the tremendous and rich diversity among people within each gender. Often, newspapers and popular magazines publish stories about a new research finding about how women and men differ. Unless you know how to evaluate the reliability and quality of the research, skepticism is warranted. Compare the results and methods of that study with those of others done on the same topic before drawing conclusions.

A common concept among feminists is that gender (as differen-tiated from biologically based differences) is a social construction. Thus, gender can be reconstructed through implemented changes in society. In most cultures, both genders are not equally encouraged to participate in the range of growth and educational experiences available. Another example is division of labor where only one gender is considered a viable parent or breadwinner or political leader. We are now in a position to challenge and reconstruct social forces which perpetuate these unhealthy differences.

Finally, actual and important differences between women and men need to be considered when forming social policies. One primary difference is that women are the child bearers and the ones who can breastfeed babies. It is personally and socially advantageous for men to be actively involved with the pregnancy and birth of their children, including bottle feeding their babies regularly, preferably with breast milk, and to recognize that mothers have special physical needs which must be acknowledged and honored. Women's careers should not in any way be threatened by these needs; employment policies and health care provisions should be designed to reflect the values of a society which honors the roles of women and cares for the well-being of infants and families.

Attending graduate school and building my professional career while having three children was an incredible but worthwhile challenge. Several factors contributed to my ability to manage: First, I believe in myself thanks to the positive influence of my mother. I share the responsibilities of family work equally with the childrens' father. We spend special time alone together almost every day, building a supportive and nurturing relationship. I work at maintaining an open, loving, and fun relationship with each of my children. Also important is that I try to live a healthy and balanced life. My professional success is also due to supportive social policies and educational scholarships, more of which are needed to assist parents to continue with their education and careers.

What do women value in their lives?

Personal Reflections

Before we consider what women in general value in their lives, consider what you value about your life. What beliefs do you cherish? What experiences, liberties, or things do you most value? Which beliefs, values, or qualities seem absolutely essential for your well-being? What do you think your friends or your romantic partner would say if you were to ask them these questions?

The values, beliefs, attributes, and experiences that both women and men cherish and appreciate are many: good health, safety and security, happiness, relative freedom, social support, adequate re-sources to meet hopes and expectations, meaningful relationships and work. One of the most important values, following safety, political freedom, and sustenance, is usually that of having a quality romantic relationship or of sharing intimately with close friends on a regular basis. Another important value for contemporary women, as well as men, is having meaningful, productive work. Some people place global issues such as world peace and harmony high on their list of what is most important in their lives; indigenous cultures are more apt to prioritize respect and care for the Earth.

When asked to write a list of what they value most in their lives, both female and male students respond that happiness, health, and family are the most highly valued aspects of their lives. Usually they attribute their happiness to healthy relationships (family, friends, and romantic) and to success (academic, career, and financial stability). Other important factors are also discussed, such as politi-cal and religious freedom, peace, environmental wellness, and physical safety. These values are shared equally by women and men.

Studies examining what factors seem to contribute to women's happiness or life satisfaction usually show that women who have both a family and a rewarding career (prestigious, demanding jobs) are most happy, even though they are more apt to experience the multiple stresses of the double duty of raising children, doing housework, and managing their careers. The emotional health of these women depends on the quality of their relationships with their mates, the demands and stresses of their work environment, and on the provision of quality child care for their children.

What do you think contributes to women's increased happiness when they try to be "supermoms" and "do it all"? Perhaps women with careers experience the increased value of their lives due to our social norms which place more worth on professions and contribu-tions made outside of the home (as you may have already sensed, I think this norm is unfortunate). Women who also earn money share more power within the home, because money conveys power in most families. These women are able to support themselves and their families, if needed, which is a comforting and empowering reality. As mothers, these women also may benefit from the personal fulfill-ment and enrichment of raising children. Women in meaningful and supportive intimate, relationships also receive all the benefits from these types of companionships.

Other contributing factors to working women's happiness include having social acquaintances, social support, and social status. If they are in a meaningful profession, they are less bored than women who work at home full-time as homemakers and mothers who are not involved in other volunteer activities. Therefore, given our social norms and personal values, it makes sense that, in general, women who "do it all," in terms of family and career, report more happiness and life satisfaction than other women.

Greater than our need for romance and success is our fundamental need throughout life to be loved and valued for who we are. This is essential for people to develop self-esteem and self-respect. People with low self-esteem are generally unhappy even if they are in a romantic relationship and have a successful career. If girls are not valued in a particular family or society, or if they are not honored as much as boys, they are less apt to experience personal self-worth. Success at school, at work, and in forming healthy relationships is related to one's self worth and experience of competence in each of these areas.

Carol Gilligan, a Harvard professor and researcher, is studying the development of self-confidence in young girls. She found that as they reach ten or eleven years old, their self-esteem drops significantly: Young girls change from feeling confident and capable to insecure and less assertive as teenagers. Other studies have not found this to be true for boys. More research is needed to document what contributes to this change, but evidence suggests that the emphasis on unrealistic beauty for girls and the increased attention that boys receive contribute to this unfortunate phenomenon. I asked my 15-year-old daughter what she thought contributed to this drop in girls' self esteem at that age, and her immediate response was the emphasis placed on girls' appearance. She does not believe that the popularity of boys depends on their appearance to the extent that it does for girls.

How can I build self-esteem?

A healthy society attempts to maintain nurturing social environments for both genders and for all types and ages of people. Generally, when people are devalued (especially as children) or given less personal and social power, they think and act differently than those who are honored. It is understandable that women would have less self-esteem than men in societies where men have been valued over women and where the social roles of women (mother and housewife, teacher, nurse, and librarian) have not been appreciated and esteemed as much as the roles traditionally held by men (breadwinner, manager, business and land owner, political and religious leader, military officers, news reporter and media star). You can also see why women scored lower than men in self-confidence in those areas where men are seen as experts. In addition to changing the inequities in our society, there are many things we can do to build our own self-esteem and confidence:

1. **Think highly of ourselves:** We need to value ourselves as women (or men) and as individuals. For some people, this means changing how we think about ourselves. We can learn to think positive thoughts that are realistic yet optimistic (see the affirmations at the beginning of each chapter in this book). For example, rather than telling ourselves that we cannot do something or that we are not smart enough, we can change our thoughts to: "I am capable and intelligent," "I am learning how to_____," or "I am a responsible person." Positive self-talk and visualizing success throughout the day can be a helpful tool for building self-esteem, if we embrace what we are saying and picturing.

2. **Be with people who value and respect women in general and who value us as individuals:** We need to develop friendships and romantic relationships with people who care for themselves appreciate us for who we are today. We can try to find a respectful and supportive work environment where people are treated fairly, equally, and with respect. We may benefit from joining or forming a support group; this is especially important if the home or work environment is not offering what we need. Also, participating in organizations which support the advancement of women can bolster one's understanding and appraisal of women, such as N.O.W. or N.W.P.C. (☞ addresses at the end of the chapter).

3. **Develop skills in areas where we want to excel and which we enjoy:** To build self-confidence in our scholastic abilities or in our field of work or in domestic tasks, we need to take the necessary steps to learn the tasks required to do the job well. It is helpful to find ways to learn these skills that are enjoyable or at least rewarding. Some important skills for all of us include communication skills, assertiveness training, and conflict resolution skills.

4. **Observe healthy role models:** See how others live their lives

with self-esteem and confidence, how they manage their doubts or mistakes as well as their accomplishments. Choose role models who exhibit the characteristics which we admire. Avoid making physical beauty the standard of a woman's worth or of our worth! The beauty of our bodies is in our health and in our minds. Beautiful people come in all shapes, sizes, and colors. Refuse to allow the popular press to dictate what is beautiful or attractive: The "ideal" portrayed by fashion magazines is an impossible and degrading ideal and not a helpful role model for any of us.

Remember that, given the basics, happiness depends on meaningful relationships and accomplishments, not on physical appearance. Let's build a society that honors inner beauty (honesty, joy of living, compassion, creativity, sensitivity,) and appreciates a much greater diversity of what we consider to be physical beauty.

5. **Be gentle with ourselves and have a sense of humor:** When we make mistakes or do not do as well as we would like, rather than blast ourselves with negative self-talk or cynical criticism, we should support ourselves. Positive self-talk with a smile or a sense of humor is helpful. Doing something that is self nurturing may also be what we need. Recognizing that we are learning from our mistakes and appreciating the lesson is also important: Many difficulties are opportunities for growth. Perfectionism is bondage; it is healthier to try to do our best with a sense of balance and lightness, given all we want to do and be.

6. **Take care of our whole selves:** Good nutrition, regular exercise, consistent sleep and relaxation, healthy fun and play, and developing an evolving sense of purpose or meaning in our lives are essential components of a healthy lifestyle (see Chapter 9). What we do to our bodies affects our minds and vice versa. If we want to feel good about ourselves, we need to take care of ourselves in a balanced and holistic way.

7. **Experience our interconnection with all that is:** We are all interconnected with one another globally and with this beautiful earth. Building self-esteem includes smelling the roses, creating ways to be in nature, and appreciating the beauty around us. Part of taking care of ourselves includes being active in doing something that promotes the well-being of others or the Earth: Volunteer work at a women's domestic violence or rape crisis center can be extremely enlightening, or helping to replant trees in a deforested area may be part of one's personal path to healing. Other less time-consuming

activities include recycling, donating money to social action groups, and writing letters about issues of importance to political leaders or to the editor of the local newspaper.

There are many other things that we can do to grow in appreciation of who we are (☞ see the books by Johnson, Steinem, and Wolf). Other options include: taking a class or workshop on building self-esteem, joining a counseling group, or doing some individual therapy with a psychotherapist. No one needs to live with low self-esteem. One of the joys of being a therapist is witnessing women, men, and children blossom into people who grow to love and care for themselves with newfound joy and confidence.

What do women want?

For a specific answer to that old question, we need to consider many variables: What women? At what time in their lives? In which social and ethnic group, class, and political-economic environment? We can say with reasonable certainty that, in general, most women want to be valued, respected equally with men, seen as unique but also as equals. Most women want to have equal opportunity and encouragement to succeed in all domains of social and professional life, with equal pay and benefits for comparable worth. Women want to be valued as caregivers, and live in societies where the roles of caregiver (parent, teacher, nurse, hospice employee, and so forth) are viewed as important and therefore highly rewarded.

Women want to be safe in their own communities and in the world at large: safe from abuse from their lovers, families, and friends (the primary perpetrators of abuse against women). Women want to be free from sexual harassment in their workplaces and in their communities. Women want children to be safe from abuse, hunger, and disease. Women want to live in societies where all people of all ages have the means to care for their basic needs and education.

I do not think that "what women want" is the mystery that has been posed in the past, nor does it differ significantly from what men want. Even when we consider what women want in their romantic relationships, there are many hopes and desires that are not at all mysterious.

➤
What do women value in their romantic relationships?

A cross-cultural study by Buss and his colleagues of over 9,000 mostly middle class people in their twenties, from 37 nations, reveals some interesting information about what people value in a potential romantic partner. Repeatedly, cultural differences outweigh gender differences, and usually women's and men's priorities are virtually the same. The most important characteristics of their ideal mate or marriage includes:

—mutual attraction and love,
—dependability,
—emotional stability and maturity
—a pleasing disposition.

Women and men in the United States put education and intelligence at the top of their wish lists. Women are slightly more similar to each other than to men in emphasizing the importance of their mate's earning capacity and ambition, whereas men favored physical attractiveness. Other similar studies, primarily in the United States, also suggest that women and men share similar values in regard to relationships: affection, intimacy, companionship, honesty, sincerity, and trust. Some gender and class differences are found; for example, middle class women are more apt to prioritize their independence and forming equal partnerships than are men or working class women.

Students in my classes place honesty and trust at the top of their lists and studies of students at other university campuses show similar results. College students also prioritize faithfulness, warmth, kindness, and a good personality, with few differences between genders in what they value in their potential mates.

Women report more happiness and overall psychological health when their closest relationships are healthy. Research shows that emotional health is highest for employed husbands and lowest for full-time female homemakers; employed wives score at the intermediate level. Recall that women with families who have prestigious and demanding jobs, and mates or spouses who share the household tasks equally, report more happiness than other women. Couples who believe they have happy marriages report the following:

1. high levels of education,

2. good communication and conflict resolution skills

3. best friends in their mates

4. both spouses are high in understanding, gentleness, affection, and self-esteem

5. if both spouses work, they share the household and child care tasks equally.

Many young women believe that they will not be happy or whole until they find their ideal mate or have a husband and a family. This view reflects a social norm that people should marry and have children, or at the very least, be in some sort of romantic relationship. Unfortunately, this idea perpetuates the discontent of single people; it may be particularly hurtful for women in their elder years, who are more apt to be single. A reader comments "I choose to remain single and have rarely seen it pointed out that I too can be happy." This is an example of a social value which needs to be modified. People can be happy and fulfilled in a variety of friendships and relationships, not only within a romantic partnership or in a family. This is an exciting time to be a woman with multiple options opening up.

The most important points to apply

♦ GENDER STEREOTYPES: We need to enhance our awareness about how gender stereotypes have shaped what we think about ourselves and our gender. We can take steps to compensate for limitations in our own lives (by learning new skills and changing the way we think about ourselves, and building self-confidence) and in reshaping our society (for example, through educating parents and teachers about how to promote gender equity).

♦ VALUING WOMEN: Although some societies, such as the Scandinavian countries, have made important changes in advancing the status and power of women, more changes are needed to help all of us value women (ourselves and the women with whom we are in relationship) and to appreciate and reward what have been women's traditional roles and characteristics. We need to redefine the "ideal" woman, not focusing on unattainable physical beauty, but on inner beauty, integrity, compassion, wisdom, creativity, humor, assertiveness, and other valued attributes.

♦ GENDER DIFFERENCES: Psychological differences between women and men are usually learned and are diminishing. Societal based gender inequities which impair our well-being need to be challenged and changed. Some biological differences are important and need to be recognized (physical strength, childbearing); others need to be studied in more depth (e.g., PMS) with the goal of enhancing all our lives.

♦ HEALTH AND HAPPINESS: Most people everywhere share similar life values. Basic needs and preferences are universal: health, food, water, shelter, clothing, freedom, safety, financial security, and quality education for all. Additionally, most contemporary women and men want meaningful and respectful relationships and work. Women who report the most happiness are women who "do it all."

♦ SOCIAL ISSUES: Critical social issues of importance to women include safety, security, equal opportunity, equitable pay, health care, respect, and freedom.

SUGGESTED READINGS

Mary Belenky, B. Clinchy, N. Goldberger, and J. Tarule. *Women's Ways of Knowing: The Development of Self, Voice, and Mind.* New York: Basic Books, 1986.

Susan Faludi. *Backlash: The Undeclared War Against American Women.* New York: Crown, 1991.

Karen Johnson. *Trusting Ourselves: The Complete Guide to Emotional Wellbeing for Women.* New York: The Atlantic Monthly Press, 1991.

Gloria Steinem. *Revolution from Within: A Book of Self-Esteem.* Boston: Little, Brown, 1992.

Rhonda Unger and Mary Crawford. *Women and Gender: A Feminist Psychology.* New York: McGraw-Hill, 1992.

WOMEN'S ORGANIZATIONS

National Organization for Women Caucus 1000 16th St., N.W. Washington, D.C. 20036

National Women's Political 1275 K St. N.W. Washington, D.C. 20005

You might also check on the American Association of University Women, Commission on the Status of Women, Business and Professional Women, or League of Women Voters chapters in your area.

ABOUT THE AUTHOR

COLETTE FLEURIDAS

Given the topic of this chapter, I share those things about me that I think are most appropriate. I am the oldest daughter of a woman who valued me as a unique individual and as a female. My mother taught me that women deserve an education and a career they enjoy, as well as a family. I am a mother of three incredible children (15, 12, and 7). My daughter genuinely appreciates herself as a young woman. I value her deeply, as I do her younger brothers. I am in a meaningful and egalitarian romantic relationship, and I treasure the other friendships which I have. I honor my body and maintain a healthy lifestyle by staying informed about health issues, and through self-discipline, flexibility, and doing things that I enjoy.

I explore the meaning and purpose of my life through various forms of work, play, social experiences, spiritual avenues, relationship with nature, and inner work (meditation, self-examination, therapy, and the like). Currently, I work (probably too hard and too much!) as an assistant professor of psychology, teaching courses primarily about counseling, family and relationship therapy, and the psychology of women. I am also a counselor part-time, seeing clients at the university's counseling center; in the past, among other things, I was a clinical director of a treatment center primarily for Native Americans.

SUPPLEMENTAL BIBLIOGRAPHY

Stereotypes:
Basow, S. *Gender and Stereotypes.* Monterey, CA: Brooks/Cole, 1992.

Lips, H. *Sex and Gender.* Mountain View, CA: Mayfield, 1993.

Contemporary Women:
Baker, M. *Women: American Women in Their Own Words.* New York: Simon & Schuster, 1990.

Olds, S. W. *The Working Parent's Survival Guide.* Rocklin, CA: Prima, 1989.

Matlin, M. W. *The Psychology of Women.* Fort Worth, TX: Harcourt Brace Jovanovich, 1993.

Paludi, M. *The Psychology of Women.* Dubuque, IA: Brown & Benchmark, 1992.

Ries, P. and Stone, A. J. (Eds.) *The American Women: 1992-1993 Status Report.* New York: Norton & Co, 1992.

Self-Esteem and Psychological Wellbeing:
Johnson, K. *Trusting Ourselves: The Complete Guide to Emotional Well being for Women.* New York: The Atlantic Monthly Press, 1991.

Rivers, C., Barnett, R., and Baruch, G. *Sugar and Spice: How Women Grow, Learn, and Thrive.* New York: Ballantine Books, 1992.

Travis, C. B. (Ed.) *EveryWoman's Emotional Well-Being.* Garden City, New York: Doubleday, 1986.

Sanford, L. T. and Donovan, M. E. *Women and Self-Esteem: Understanding and Improving the Way We Think and Feel about Ourselves.* New York: Penguin Books, 1984.

Gender Differences:
Fausto-Sterling, A. *Myths of Gender: Biological Theories about Women and Men.* New York: Basic Books, 1985.

Halpern, D. *Sex Differences in Cognitive Abilities.* Hillsdale, NJ: Erlbaum, 1992.

Hare-Mustin, R. T. and Marecek, J. (Eds.) *Making a Difference: Psychology and the Construction of Gender.* New Haven: Yale University Press, 1990.

Hyde, J. S., *The Other Half of Human Experience.* Lexington, MA: D.C. Heath, 1992.

Hyde, J. S., and Linn, M. C. (Eds.) *The Psychology of Gender: Advances Through Meta-Analysis.* Baltimore: John Hopkins Univ. Press, 1986.

Social Values, History and Change:
Diamond, I., and Orenstein, G. *Reweaving the World: The Emergence of Ecofeminism.* San Francisco: Sierra Club, 1990.

Eisler, R., and Loye, D. *The Partnership Way: New Tools for Living and Learning: Healing our Families, Our Communities, and Our World.* San Francisco: Harper, 1990.

Gimbutas, M. *The Language of the Goddess.* San Francisco: Harper, 1989.

Jackson, D. *How to Make the World a Better Place for Women.* New York: Hyperion, 1992.

Also see *MS* magazine.

Relationships:
Blumstein, P., and Schwartz, P. *American Couples.*
New York: William Morrow, 1993.

Brothers, B. J. (Ed.) *Equal Partnering.* Binghamton, NY: Haworth, 1992.

Buss, D. M., et al. "International Preferences in Selecting Mates: A Study of 37 Cultures," *Journal of Cross-Cultural Psychology,* 21, 5-47, 1990.

Dinkmeyer, D., and Carlson, J. *Taking Time for Love.* New York: Prentice Hall, 1989.

Kimball, G. *50/50 Marriage.* Chico, CA: Equality Press, 1993.

Norwood, R. *Women Who Love Too Much.* New York: Pocket Books, 1985.

Russianoff, P. *Why Do You Think Nothing Without a Man?*
New York: Bantam, 1981.

Women's Body Image and Appearance:
Sacker, I. M., and Zimmer, M. A. *Dying to be Thin.* New York: Warner Books, 1987.

Wolf, N. *The Beauty Myth: How Images of Beauty are Used Against Women.* New York: Doubleday, 1992.

Cultural, Racial, and Ethnic Comparisons of Women:
Bronstein, P. A., and Quina, K. *Teaching a Psychology of People: Resources, Gender and Sociocultural Awareness.* Washington, D.C.: American Psychological Association, 1988.

Collins, P. H. *Black Feminist Thought.* Boston: Unwin Hyman, 1990.

Duley, M. I., and Edwards, M. I. (Eds.) *The Cross-Cultural Study of Women.* New York: The Feminist Press, 1986.

Women's Physical Health:

Boston Women's Collective. *The New Our Bodies, Ourselves.* New York: Simon & Schuster, 1984.

The Federation of Feminist Women's Health Centers. *A New View of a Woman's Body.* West Hollywood, CA: Feminist Health Press, 1991.

Fine, M., and Asch, A. (Eds.) *Women with Disabilities.* Philadelphia: Temple University Press, 1988.

Lark, S. *The Premenstrual Syndrome Self-Help Book.* Berkeley, CA: Celestial Arts, 1989.

Lark, S. *Menopause Self-Help Book.* Berkeley, CA: Celestial Arts, 1989.

Women's Sexuality:

Anand, M. *The Art of Sexual Ecstasy: The Path of Sacred Sexuality for Western Lovers.* Los Angeles: Jeremy P. Tarcher, 1989.

Barbach, L. *For Yourself: The Fulfillment of Female Sexuality.* New York: Doubleday, 1975.

Hite, S. *The Hite Report: A Nationwide Study of Female Sexuality.* New York: Dell, 1976.

Hyde, J. S. *Understanding Sexuality.* New York: McGraw-Hill, 1990.

Voss, J., and Gale, J. *A Young Woman's Guide to Sex.* New York: Henry Holt, 1986.

Women's Friendships:

Bhaerman, S., and McMillan, D. *Friends and Lovers: How to Meet the People You Want to Meet.* Cincinnati, OH: Writer's Digest, 1986.

Eichenbaum, L., and Orbach, S. *Between Women: Love, Envy, and Competition in Women's Friendships.* New York: Penguin Books, 1987.

122

Sexual and Physical Violence Against Women:
Quina, K., and Carlson, N. *Rape, Incest, and Sexual Harassment: A Guide for Helping Survivors.* New York: Prarger, 1989.

Straus, M. B. *Abuse and Victimization Across the Lifespan.* Baltimore: John Hopkins University Press, 1988.

Sumrall, A. C., and Taylor, D. *Sexual Harassment: Women Speak Out.* Freedom, CA: The Crossing Press, 1992.

Walker, L. *The Battered Women's Syndrome.* New York: Springer, 1984

Feminism, the Women's Movement, and Women in History:
Anderson, B. S., and Zinsser, J. P. *Women's History.*
New York: Harper & Row, 1988.

Davis, F. *Moving the Mountain: The Women's Movement in America since 1960.* New York: Simon & Schuster, 1991.

Eisler, R. *The Chalice and the Blade: Our History, Our Future.* Cambridge, MA: Harper & Row, 1988.

Friedan, B. *The Feminine Mystique.* New York: Laurel Books(1962/1983).

Schaef, A. W. *Women's Reality.* San Francisco: Harper & Row, 1981.

✪Next... Despite many myths and stereotypes, it appears that innate differences between women and men are minimal. One of the delightful differences for heterosexuals is sexual anatomy and physical attraction to the other gender. Sexuality, including lesbians and gays, will be explored in the next chapter by a sex educator.

"I am alive to my senses. I am attractive and lovable, just the way I am. I am whole and complete with or without a partner. I am capable of passion and intimacy."

5

THE SECRETS

TO SUCCESSFUL

SEXUALITY

PAT HANSON, PH.D.

Chapter Goals

This chapter responds to questions most commonly asked by thousands of students in sexuality classes I have taught over the past 25 years. It will provide improved knowledge of fact versus myth concerning the physiology and psychology of sexual response. You will gain increased comfort with your own and others' values, attitudes, and practices. Throughout, the goal is improved skill in saying yes and no to sex assertively, within the confines of your own value system. Hopefully you will gain a greater understanding of major blocks and barriers to intimacy and healthy sexual relationships and discover how to dissolve them.

What is sexuality anyway?

Sexuality is a gift, and perhaps one of the most misunderstood and paradoxical forces known to us. Sexuality is much more than most of us think it is; sexuality is something we *are*, not merely something we do sometimes if we get lucky. It encompasses being alive to our senses and open to our eroticism, whether or not we have a partner. It involves how we express the gender role to which we were born, and it includes with whom we choose to play, to love, to work, and to live.

Being open to our sexuality can awaken us to sensations of pleasure, closeness, connection, and love; or it can be associated with discomfort, vulnerability, pain, and powerlessness. Only part of sexuality includes genital sex. Sexuality involves choices that today include the possibility of pregnancy, disease, and even death. Properly handled it can be a source of validating and expanding ourselves; but misused for power, control, or identity, it can become the source of endless traps and dead ends.

Fears faced with facts can disappear. Correct information can combat ignorance. Knowing that others share similar self-doubts can diminish unnecessary guilt and shame. Giving oneself permission to experiment and finding courage to take some well-thought-through personal risks can go a long way to improving intimate relationships.

As with any other aspect of our lives which is fraught with anxiety, we must first look to the sources of what we know and don't know, and choose to learn from accurate resources. No matter how conflicting our past sexual memories may have been, there are sources of support: books, groups, classes, counselors, and potential partners who can help us make our future choices in a manner that affirms our sexuality positively, and helps us to integrate this powerful force into the rest of our lives as a natural part of who we are.

The resources listed at the end of the chapter, and self-help groups available in most major cities, are highly recommended for fuller discussion of the keys to successful sexuality.

How can I ask for what I want sexually from my partner?

Many of us have been taught that we should know what our lover wants without having to ask. Many of us have been raised to feel that our partner's needs should come before our own. We have not been encouraged to ask for a kind of touch, a certain place or time for lovemaking, a favorite position or activity. Fairy tales, romance novels, Hollywood films, and television teach us that a good lover can magically read our minds, and will stroke us in exactly the right places and with the precise amount of tenderness or passion that we desire. Many of us fall into patterns of communication set early in childhood, either nonassertively ignoring our own wants and needs, or aggressively insisting our desires get met at the expense of others.

Both men and women need to give up the role of second-guesser, and give themselves permission to assertively state their desires in a manner that respects their own as well as someone else's boundaries. A model of *Compassionate Communication*, developed by Marshall Rosenberg, is useful in getting couples to be honest with one another, to realize the precise intent of each other's wishes, and to practice positive interaction. Practice the following exercise by writing in your journal.

═══════════ **Personal Reflections** ═══════════

When you (said or did) _____ . Be specific, brief. Name words describing the incident as specifically as you can.

*I felt*_____. (one or two emotions/see feeling words below) Avoid "I thought that" or "you felt."

Because I _____. Be *self*-revealing; admit vulnerability.

What I really want (or wanted) *is/was* ___ . Avoid blame. Put in the positive.

And I'm wondering if *you'd be willing to* ___ . Be specific and brief.

Feeling Words:

sad	guilty	happy	hopeful
hurt	angry	joyous	optimistic
disappointed	afraid	excited	encouraged
afraid	angry	enthused	inspired
concerned	upset	loving	peaceful
lost	rejected	peaceful	grateful
abandoned	perplexed	supported	empowered
lost	confused	welcomed	flattered
lonely	depressed	included	honored
betrayed	suspicious	relieved	turned on
hopeless	dejected	loved	appreciated
harassed	humiliated	receptive	aroused
put-down	stifled	relieved	
discounted	unimportant	validated	
attacked	violated		
misused	abused		
manipulated	exploited		
discouraged			

This model is sometimes called the **W.I.B.W.A.** model of communication. The initials of the first word of the five different sentences help the communicator to describe an incident or desire as specifically as possible, to reveal feelings rather than intellectualizing or blaming, to admit vulnerability, to state positively what one wants, and to specifically ask for cooperation in the future. Here is an example related to sexual communication:

When you pulled away from me the other night when I tried to move you to turn around so we could make love doggy position,
I felt rejected and disappointed,
Because I love to experience your vagina that way.
What I really wanted was to enter you more deeply and to stroke your G-spot with my penis,
And I was wondering if you would enjoy doing that next time.

An assertive response to this request might go something like this:
When you pulled out of me and turned me over the other night,
I felt abandoned and hurt,
Because you interrupted my sensations just as they were building up.
What I really wanted was for you to continue doing just what you were doing because I wanted to feel close to you and to be able to look at you.
And I'm wondering if next time before you change position, you would ask me how I'm feeling and if I'm ready to change.

The successful application of this communication model depends on lots of practice. Think about an improvement you would like in your sexual communication. Begin with easy matters and move to the more sensitive ones. Once the routine is established for stating feelings clearly and directly is established, it becomes easier to express one's attitudes and desires. The key to successful sexual communication is taking risks and revealing vulnerability. (Readers comment that this is easier said than done.) Having a partner you trust opens up many possibilities.

One of the topics to be discussed in sexual communication is sexually transmitted diseases. The U.S. Department of Health and Human Services reports that about 12 million people acquire an STD each year. Latex (rather than animal skin) condoms are a must; because they can come off or break, they should be coupled with use of a vaginal spermicide and not relied upon as safe. When in doubt, insist that you and a potential sexual partner take an AIDS blood test.

What exactly is an orgasm? And how can I be sure my partner has one?

Only in the last 25 years have scientists discovered exactly what constitutes an orgasm. Masters and Johnson's ground breaking videotaped high-tech research monitored the sexual response cycle of over 700 couples in the laboratory between l965 and 1970. They discovered that sexual response for both men and women consists of four stages: *excitement, plateau, orgasm,* and *resolution.* At each stage they charted pulse, blood pressure, galvanic skin response, and involuntary muscle contractions. In the early 1980s, sex therapist and writer Helen Kaplan Singer divided sexual response into three phases that most sexologists now commonly use to typify sexual functioning: the *desire,* the *excitement,* and the *orgasm* phases.

Because of the many factors that can influence desire (medical history, fatigue, mood, setting, family background, and the stage of the relationship), we know much more about the psychology and physiology of excitement and orgasm than we do about what goes on before the excitement phase begins. Physiologically, an orgasm is a release of muscular tension and vasocongestion, dispersing blood that flows to the genital area in the excitement phase, in a series of muscular contractions that are similar for men and women. The contractions occur in about 5 to 8 three-second spurts, in men accompanied by ejaculation of semen and, in a very small portion of women, female ejaculation from the urethra. To have truly success-ful sex, couples must learn to *minimize* the importance that has been placed on the big "O" in the over-sexualized nineties.

Shere Hite solicited sociological descriptions from over 7,000 men and women in the late l970s and early 1980s. They wrote about how it feels to have an orgasm, both with and without vaginal penetration, under all types of circumstances. These accounts go well beyond fictionalized love scenes in romance novels that people had depended on to describe how people actually experience this thing called an "orgasm." Hite's reports entail pages and pages of verbatim descriptions from men and women about their perceptions of intensity and levels of satisfaction from different kinds of sexual activity. Most of her respondents reported that satisfaction is more dependent on their mental state, than on the intensity of physical response.

Couples need to learn to know what they want from their

sensual and sexual experiences, and ask for them in nonverbal (such as gently moving a hand where you would like it to be) and verbal ways. Yes, it is wonderful to want to bring one's partner to this sensational release and yes, knowing the facts of basic sexual anatomy and functioning can give one the potential to put that knowledge to good use; but couples also need to realize that an orgasm is the ultimate physiological and psychological surrender to one's senses and is only partially involuntary.

The secret to success lies not in the hands or the tongue or the genitals of one's partner, but with one's Self! No matter how good a technician one's partner is, no matter how sexually experienced, or how sensitively and consistently he/she touches you (even if that clitoris, G-spot and/or glans gets stimulated very regularly), no matter what sweet-somethings your partner whispers in your ear, surrendering to the physical sensation of orgasm is a choice you allow yourself, and you have yourself to thank for it, not your lover.

Many couples get into power and control issues over whether or when they have orgasms. In a recent study of college students, 70 percent of the women, and 37 percent of the men reported faking orgasms. Certainly they are not doing this because it enhances their own pleasure. While it is natural to want one's partner to feel proficient, we must remember that our self-esteem is *NOT* inevitably linked to our sexual performance. The ability to surrender to an experience as psychologically and physically intense as an orgasm is extremely complex. Orgasm involves so many factors, both mental and physical, it is self-defeating to attach so much importance to it.

We are not our orgasms! We do not need to measure our own self-worth by a predetermined number of cries and moans on the Kaplan Singer or Masters and Johnson scale of performance. The key to successful sex lies not in galvanic skin response, but in the closeness, honesty, and connection between the couple. Maintaining passion in lasting relationships is an art that has to be nurtured and developed over time. Besides communicating effectively, couples may need to give themselves permission to experiment to keep their levels of response high.

It might be exciting to read or view erotica together, discussing what turns each of you on (or off) about specific films, stories, or images. Remember, good sex takes time. Save and savor several special hours every week for sex, making relaxing time together a priority. A reader asks, "Doesn't planning sex make it contrived?" No, planning a romantic date, dinner and dancing adds to the anticipation and this can be true of making love as well. Massaging with creams and oils, using Astroglide, tickling with feathers or furs, making love in different locations or in tandem with an erotic video, putting a mirror where you can see yourselves, sharing fantasies, and dressing up in costumes designed to entice are a few of the many things couples can do to stay playful with their partners.

How does a woman's sexual response system work? How can a woman be stimulated to orgasm?

A woman's sexual response is predicated as much on how psychologically turned on she feels as it is to varying degrees of direct and indirect stimulation of her breasts and internal and external genitals. A sound knowledge and appreciation of female sexual anatomy is the foundation for successful sexual interaction.

Most women's breasts react to stimulation, mental or physical, with nipple erection, but some do not. Nerve endings and hormones can be aroused by suckling breasts, bringing erotic pleasure and uterine and clitoral contractions. However, how and when to touch, kiss, rub, or fondle breasts is up to each individual woman, and may vary during her menstrual cycle. Close to half of all women experience some breast tenderness shortly before their menstrual periods. Some men have linked their capacity to bring a woman to orgasm with the presence or absence of visible nipple erection in women, but nipple erection is not an absolute indicator of the presence of orgasm.

Externally, women's genitals are as varied as their faces. They all have the same parts in a wide variety of styles and arrangements. *Vulva* is the term used to describe all the outer female genitals that you can see. The large *outer lips,* or *labia majora,* join at the top of the *mons pubis.* Smaller *inner lips,* called the *labia minora,* are located within the outer lips, and the *vestibule,* or almond-shaped *vaginal opening* lies within these inner lips. At the top of the vestibule is a tiny pinpoint of an opening: the *urethra,* the passageway for urine, and below it is the opening to the *vagina.*

The *clitoris,* the only organ whose sole function is to give pleasure, is located at the point where the inner lips join. There are more nerve endings in this tiny, pea-shaped organ than there are in the entire length and head of a penis. The clitoris has a shaft or body and a head or rounded area called a *glans*. It is normally covered with tissue of the inner lips, a hood to protect it. In its normal, nonaroused state, the clitoris is one-eighth to one-half of an inch in length; when stimulated by the touch of a finger, a tongue, a penis, or a vibrator, the clitoris becomes engorged with blood and doubles in diameter, withdrawing under its hood, because of its extreme sensitivity. The clitoris needs to be well-lubricated when it is touched, either with vaginal fluids, saliva, or a water soluble jelly. When orgasm is near, the clitoris retracts completely and can no longer be seen. It moves out again when stimulation is stopped.

Internally, a woman's genitals consist of: the *hymen* , a thin piece of tissue around the opening inside the inner lips, broken during childhood activity in many women; and the *vagina,* a muscular passageway that runs from the vulva to the *cervix,* a donut-shaped, rounded bottom of the *uterus* , the pear-shaped organ that holds a baby if and when pregnancy occurs. Inside the vaginal walls of a woman's internal sexual system are *Bartholins glands* which secrete a few drops of fluid when a woman is sexually aroused.

Most women also have a series of nerve endings on the front, upper, inner wall of their vagina called the *urethral sponge* or the *G-spot.* When stimulated, either by a finger or a penis in the right position, the nerve endings of this G-spot, which are actually connected to the clitoris, can produce an intense sensation sometimes feeling like a pressure to urinate, and can lead to orgasm. A few women release fluid from their urethra when they have an orgasm produced by stimulation of the G-spot. This is called female ejaculation.

In summary, there are three "magic spots": the breasts, the clitoris, and the G-spot that, when consistently stimulated, either separately or simultaneously, can produce an orgasm in a woman who is psychologically ready and willing to allow one. The secret lies in that last word, readiness. For many women that state of mind depends on many factors: the kind of day they've had, how they feel about their partner, where they are in their monthly hormonal cycle, and how able they are to surrender to a particular sexual moment. Many women choose to enhance their sexual arousal with fantasies, either by reading, viewing or sharing their erotic visual images with their partner, or by keeping them to themselves.

Just like all other body parts need exercise to stay fit, it is important for both men and women to keep their sexual muscula-ture in shape. Like any other organ, when allowed to get out of tone, sensations in the vagina can diminish. It is recommended that women regularly do exercises called "Kegels" (named after the physician who discovered them) by contracting their vaginal muscles. This can help with childbirth as well as to increase sexual sensitivity. If you can stop the flow of urine when you are first urinating by tightening your vaginal muscles, you can do a Kegel. Think of an elevator going up and down various floors, and attempt to contract the vagina from bottom to top and down again. Do this ten times at least twice a day. These strengthening exercises can be done routinely, when stopped in a car at a red light, while at work at your desk, as well as during sexual intercourse. Men are also capable of contracting muscles around the penis and scrotum, to prolong erection or stimulate their partners.

Masters and Johnson pointed out that being a spectator observing and judging one's sexual performance and response is a major barrier to sexual enjoyment. Focusing on what you find attractive about your partner, allowing yourself to listen to your surroundings, giving yourself permission to engage in fantasies and paying attention directly to the sensations that you are experiencing, are ways to step beyond the spectator role.

➢
What causes men to respond sexually? Does penis size make a difference? What is the difference between a circumcised and uncircumcised penis?

A man's sexual functioning, like a woman's, depends on what goes on between his ears: how he feels about what is happening and with whom, as well as his internal and external sexual system. Men, perhaps more than women, have been socialized to see sexual performance as inevitably linked to their self-esteem. Dispelling some of the major myths about male sexual anatomy and performance can relieve many men and their partners of much of the anxiety that can diminish sexual pleasure.

Men's external sexual system consists of the *penis*, a hairless muscular shaft, which has a head called the *glans* at its tip, in the very middle of which is the opening to the *urethra*, a passageway that runs the length of the penis and through which men both urinate and ejaculate semen. Some men have a fold of skin covering the glans of the penis called a *foreskin;* these men are *uncircumcised*. Other men who have the foreskin removed around the time of birth are *circumcised* (approximately 60-70 percent of those born in the United States, and only a small percentage of men from other cultures). Circumcised men have the *corona*, a ridge around the glans at tip of their penises, showing at all times. There is no difference between the ability or length of time it takes for circumcised and uncircumcised men to have orgasms.

One of the greatest myths of male sexuality is that "bigger is better," concerning penis size. When hanging flaccid in a limp and non-aroused state, the length of a penis varies greatly and differs among races. When erect, there is considerably less variation in penis size, the average penis being between 5-1/2 and 6-1/2 inches. Physiologically, penis size has nothing to do with either male or female orgasm and sexual functioning. The muscles of the vagina are a potential space, adaptable to whatever size penis is inserted.

Hanging behind the penis is a sac called the *scrotum*, which contains two egg-shaped organs, the *testicles*. Internally, a man's sexual and reproductive organs consist of these testicles, where sperm and male hormones are produced. Since they need to be just a few degrees lower than body temperature to develop healthy sperm, a man's body has a self-regulating temperature system whereby his scrotum hangs lower on hot days and pulls up closer to the body in colder environments, and just before ejaculation. Mature sperm are stored at the top of each testicle in a ridge of tissue called an *epididymis*, from which a tube called the *vas deferens* leads up from the scrotum, past a tiny *Cowper's gland* which releases a clear fluid immediately prior to a male orgasm that neutralizes the acidity in the urethra. When a man is ready to have an orgasm, sperm pass through the vas deferens, picking up about a tablespoon of white fluid containing fructose, some fats, and about 75 calories, from the *prostate gland*, which is located on the underside of a man's *bladder*. An *ejaculatory duct* involuntarily regulates the opening of the urethra so that a man can never urinate and ejaculate at the same time.

Our culture has placed a tremendous emphasis on the penis as the center of both male and female sexuality. One of the most serious stereotypes to overcome is the emphasis on penile-vaginal sex as the be-all and end-all. Research has shown that only a small minority of women achieve orgasm regularly with only penile-vaginal penetration. If couples allowed themselves to explore the unlimited ways sexual satisfaction can be brought about, they may

134

discover many different ways to achieve fulfillment that do not include penetration or center on the sexual peak of orgasm. Fulfillment depends on the needs and wants of each partner and may include something as simple as cuddling and just sleeping together, or may be reached by an agreement for an exchange of nongenital massage, mutual masturbation, or oral sex.

What couples need to do is to learn first their own, and then to appreciate their partner's responses, recognizing and acknowledging the similarities rather than the differences in their sexual anatomy and functioning.

Can masturbation become a habit that will interfere with partner sex?

Masturbation is purposeful touching of one's sexual organs to achieve pleasure, not necessarily orgasm, and it is practiced widely by both men and women. The Kinsey studies reported in 1948 and 1952 that 62 percent of women had masturbated to orgasm at some point in their lives and 33 percent masturbated regularly; 92 percent of men had masturbated. Almost all continued to do so regularly whether they were married and had regular intercourse or not. More recent studies show that between 65 to 70 percent of women of all ages masturbate on a somewhat consistent basis, including more than half of women over the age of 60. Men's rates remain consistent at about 85 to 95 percent.

Feelings about masturbation run deep in the fabric of our familial and religious upbringing. Many old texts on sexuality see touching oneself as a sin of "self-abuse." Commonly held myths about masturbation are that people can get hooked on it; that it leads to illness, blindness, insanity, or homosexuality, and that it is a sign a person is unable to form intimate relationships. These myths still exist today, in spite of the fact that they have been thoroughly disputed by sex researchers and therapists.

Couples need to realize that comparing masturbation to sexual intercourse is like comparing apples and oranges. For many men, masturbation is a lifelong practice that they associate with a combination of fantasy, tension relief, and viewing magazine pictures of practices they rarely if ever would do in real life. For many women it is a way of self-pleasuring and direct clitoral stimulation leading to orgasm more consistently than vaginal penetration alone. Many couples find mutual masturbation a turn-on. Some people, especially those who find themselves in long distance relationships, enjoy "talk sex," calling their partner or a 900 telephone number to listen to or exchange sexual stories while they masturbate.

Sexual enrichment manuals for couples published after ☛ Lonnie Barbach's landmark best-seller *For Yourself* in 1974 (Anchor Press) not only state that masturbation is healthy and normal but they encourage self-pleasuring as a way to know one's own timing, responses, and preferences before sharing them with a partner. Because a vibrator can stimulate one's genital nerve endings consistently, regularly and strongly, many people find using them a dependable way to assure themselves of an orgasm. Many partners enjoy pleasuring one another with vibrators.

We need to let go of conditioned concepts that enriching a human experience with a mechanical sexual aid detracts from, rather than enriches, the experience. While common sense tells us that there is a vast difference between a sexual experience culminated with a vibrator and one brought on by another human being, we must not let this fact interfere with our ability to choose from a variety of ways to experience sex at different points and times in our lives.

One of the best kept secrets of sexuality is to "know thyself" in every sense. Masturbating is normal, and so is not masturbating. With AIDS and an epidemic of sexually transmitted diseases encouraging couples not to exchange bodily fluids, an increase in both the acceptance and practice of masturbation is occurring.

I've never told anyone how I really feel when I look in the mirror. I don't think I measure up... does anyone else feel this way?

Our concept of how we appear to ourselves, our body image, is inextricably intertwined with our sexuality. One of the most burdensome myths imposed by our media-saturated culture is that there is only one "body beautiful." For women, that includes perfect facial features, clear skin, slim hips, a flat tummy, medium to large firm breasts, round buttocks, and shapely legs. For men, a square jaw, a full head of shiny, thick hair, muscular "pecs" and "abs," tight hips and "butt," and of course a large penis, are essential.

Concerning our genitals, especially for women, if we allow our-selves to look at them and think of them at all, it is often with disgust, disdain, and a sense of separation of who we are from what "we do down there." Because we also urinate and excrete from the part of our anatomy that has the potential to bring us limitless pleasure, many double messages remain from our childhoods. The words we use for our sexual anatomy and for the sex act reflect our cultural ambiguity about sexuality. There are few acceptable or even slang terms for the vulva, vagina, and clitoris; while many of the hundreds of hard, driving, words with strong images exist for the penis, although these limit any expression of tenderness or vulnerability.

Since it is important for us to know and accept our genitals, both in appearance and sensation, I ask my students to draw a picture of their sexual anatomy, both internal and external, listing the terms they use for each part of their anatomy, as well as writing several sentences that describe how they feel about the parts of their body between their thighs and their waists. (You might find it interesting to do this exercise in your journal.) Afterwards, when we share these pictures anonymously, the amount of negativity never ceases to amaze me. Perhaps the greatest lesson learned from doing this is the relief students feel, knowing they are not alone in their attitudes or their appearances.

For those brave enough to take improving their body image a step further, I suggest that you find a time when you are alone to stand naked in front of a mirror. Starting with your head, look at each part of your body, and state something positive about it. For example, "What I like about my hair is____," "One thing I like about my face is____," "What I like about my arms is____," and so on. In addition, make a list of things other people have told you that are wrong with your body, and then create a ritual of destroying this list.

━━━━━━━ **Personal Reflections** ━━━━━━━

Draw your body.

Make a list of things about your body that you dislike that *can* be changed, and things that *cannot* be changed, making a contract with yourself to make one change within a reasonable period of time. Draw your body, selecting different crayon colors for various parts. What does this exercise tell you about your body image?

Do this not because someone else wants you to, but because *you* want these changes to improve how you feel. Body image is an intimate part of our sexual identity. We need to be able to accept ourselves as fine the way we are.

I've heard that 10 percent of all people are gay, lesbian or bi-sexual. Am I not noticing something?

In almost all cultures, an often invisible minority of the population, close to 10 percent, loves, lives with, and has sex with members of the same sex. Yet homophobia, fear of homosexuality, or fear of being perceived as homosexual, is far more pervasive in our culture than is homosexuality itself. This is closely related to another condition called "heterosexism": the assumption that everyone is heterosexual, and if not, should be. The question asked above is a good example of heterosexism.

Homophobia limits each and every one of us, and is evidenced in ways ranging from how we express affection to members of the same sex, to giggling, laughing, or exhibiting fear, revulsion and disgust at the mention of gay, lesbian, or bisexual persons. It can be seen in overt and covert discrimination against gay people in social activities or jobs, and the most severe form of homophobia can take the form of violence, gay-bashing, and hate-crimes.

This section will briefly distinguish between gender identity, sexual behavior, sexual orientation, and sexual identity. It is directed to helping you sort fact from fiction about the many misconceptions regarding each of these concepts, in hopes that you will establish both publicly and privately your personal place on the continuum of sexual identity. Until you truly know where you stand along these lines, you will not be able to adopt fully intimate, rewarding relationships.

One of the most pervasive myths about homosexuality is that gender identity (the personal and private conviction each of us has about our femininity or masculinity and how we express it) is related to our sexual preference. Less than 10 percent of people who openly identify as gay or lesbian fit the stereotype of either an effeminate man or a butch woman. Unconsciously connecting how we dress, speak, and act along a scale of appropriately masculine or feminine characteristics that identifies people's purported sexual preference unnecessarily puts people into categories, and limits freedom of expression for all of us.

Sexual orientation refers to our attraction and preferences emotionally, socially, and sexually. As far back as the Kinsey studies in the early 1950s, studies have established that a large majority of men and women have had some preadolescent, adolescent, and even early adult sexual contacts with members of the same sex. Our sexual behaviors are just that: experiences we have had. Our sexual identity, the lifestyle we choose to internalize and accept as the truth of who we are, is what defines us. "Homosocial" might be a better word for men and women who find their primary emotional and sexual fulfillment with people of the same sex, as homosexual focuses too much on only one aspect of their lives.

Everything gay persons do emotionally, erotically, and sexually, straight persons also do. As far as intimate sexual relationships go, gay and lesbian men and women face the same possibilities, and have the same problems as do all of us. They have the same repertoire available to them in bed as heterosexuals: massage, kissing, fondling, breast play, manual and oral genital stimulation, and penetration (some lesbians but only a small minority use dildoes). They proceed through the stages of sexual response and orgasm as do all human beings. Masters and Johnson found that lesbian and gay couples spent more time on foreplay and were more verbally inquisitive of their partner's needs than were their married heterosexual counterparts in earlier studies.

We must learn to look for the similarities among people of all shapes, sizes, skin colors, and sexual orientation, rather than judge, separate, and categorize them. By countering homophobia when we see it, first in our own language and behaviors, we can work toward a world that is an equitable and loving place for everyone.

What effects do drinking and drugs have on sexuality?

It depends on the substance, the setting, and the person. The old adage "candy is dandy, but liquor is quicker" is partially true; alcohol definitely affects decision-making skills and has long been used socially to promote relaxation, overcome inhibitions, and lower levels of anxiety. When it comes to sex, the negative effects of alcohol far outweigh the positive ones. Alcohol has been mistakenly thought to positively affect each of Kaplan Singer's three stages of sexual response: desire, excitement, and orgasm; yet it usually creates more disinterest, dysfunction, and dissatisfaction than is popularly realized.

In small doses, alcohol can lower inhibition. But in moderate to high doses, alcohol decreases arousal, psychological appreciation, and may induce uninhibited, aggressive sexual behavior that can become offensive or violent. The Centers for Disease Control define both chronic and acute drinking as problematic. Chronic is defined as two or more drinks every day, and acute drinking as five or more drinks on one occasion on a weekly basis.

In moderate to high doses, alcohol decreases dexterity and contributes to a variety of sexual dysfunctions. While most sexual dysfunction stems from emotional causes, in women, perceptions of sexual arousal, as well as actual vasocongestion and lubrication, decrease with increasing levels of intoxication. In men, premature ejaculation, inhibited erection (inability to get it up), as well as ejaculatory incompetence (not being able to get it off once it is up), are all associated with increasing amounts of alcohol. Once an episode of secondary impotence associated with drinking happens, a self-fulfilling prophecy can occur.

Andrew Weil describes marijuana as an "active placebo," a chemical whose influence on behavior is actually the combined effects of a little relaxation and a lot of expectation. Because one's sense of time and space are distorted, the pleasure of sexual activity might *seem* prolonged. Long term use of marijuana, however, has been associated with lower levels of testosterone production and temporary impotence in men, and interrupted menstrual cycles in women.

Cocaine has supposed, aphrodisiac capabilities; taken in small amounts, it stimulates the central nervous system and produces a mild euphoria and a "rush" or "flash" on sniffing or injecting that has been compared by some to orgasm. It also appears to affect the brain by temporarily producing periods of confidence and allowing some individuals to do things they wouldn't do ordinarily. Yet, its powerfully addictive qualities, combined with the severe depression users feel when its effects wear off, start a cycle in many users that lowers their levels of sexual interest and ability.

Satisfaction, how we feel about what we do sexually before, during, and especially afterwards, is what counts. Can any experience that was embellished with substances be deemed completely successful? The secret to successful sexuality may lie in knowing ways to relax; to overcoming early, fearful, or negative associations with intimate relationships; learning how to ask to get one's needs met; and freely giving to meet another's needs, without dependence on special settings or substances to pave the way.

I have shameful, embarrassing feelings about sex that have been dumped on me since childhood. I don't know if I'll ever be able to fully enjoy and appreciate sex with someone I love. Where do I begin?

Most of us have some embarrassing or painful memories surrounding sexuality. Given the latest statistics on the incidence of adults molested as children—one in four women, and one in six to ten men—considerable healing is needed before we can fully participate in healthy intimate relationships. For those of us not hurt during childhood, the likelihood is quite high that we might find ourselves in love with someone who may have experienced some abuse in the past that could hamper his or her ability to trust and let go completely. It is important to accept someone's sexual past as just that, their past. What is important are the choices, feelings, and actions demonstrated between two people in the present moment.

Sexuality is inherently a positive gift, meant to express love and bring pleasure, joy, and closeness, even though many of us have learned that parts of it are shameful. We need to remember the difference between guilt, healthy shame, and toxic shame. According to ☛ John Bradshaw, in *Healing the Shame that Binds You* (Health Communications), guilt is an emotion resulting from acting contrary to our beliefs and values; it does *not* directly reflect on one's identity or diminish one's sense of self-worth. It is simply a painful feeling of regret or remorse for one's actions that comes from making a mis-take, from doing something you felt was wrong for you.

Shame, however, is more damaging. Healthy shame, the next step up from guilt, is a normal human emotion reminding us of our limitations and our vulnerability. Some shame can keep us grounded and help us to see the bigger picture in things, helping us remember that we don't know it all. It can allow us to see mistakes as opportunities for growth. Toxic shame is a state of being that takes over one's identity; it is a feeling that one *is* the mistake, not that one made an error. It can erode one's sense of self-esteem into feelings of worthlessness, helplessness, hopelessness, and depression. Paradoxically, shame can be the core motivator of both over- and underachievement, addictions and codependent behaviors, and dominant as well as submissive patterns.

Many people need help from sources outside themselves in order to heal patterns of toxic shame and get over guilt which may have them trapped in self-deprecating mental patterns that keep them from reaching their full potential to relate, to love, to create, and to think. It is a sign of strength to ask for help, and also the first indication that changes in attitudes from negative to positive can take place. A teacher, a clergyperson, or a counselor may be needed to sort out one's sense of self from past incidents, especially those that occurred in childhood for which we were not responsible. In almost every city there are free, confidential, twelve-step support groups for codependency, incest survivors, and for people for whom sex and romance have become addictions. These people may find themselves participating over and over again in sexual or relationship patterns that have negative consequences. The purpose of these anonymous groups is for people to support one another as they help themselves overcome behavior patterns that have become unmanageable.

It may be useful for you to remember that inside yourself is an "inner child," a free, spontaneous, beautiful spirit, who wants only to explore the world with his/her senses, to love and give to others, and who has unlimited potential. ☞ Many recent self-help books suggest many ways of learning to love and nourish this inner child: *You Can Heal Yourself* (Hay House) by Louise Hay; *Revolution from Within: A Book of Self-Esteem* (Little Brown) by Gloria Steinem; *Love is Letting Go of Fear* (Bantam) by Gerald Jampolsky; and Nancy Napier's *Recreating Yourself: Help for Adult Children of Dysfunctional Families* (W.W. Norton).

═══════════════ **Self-Reflections** ═══════════════

Try getting into a quiet place, use some deep abdominal breathing to promote relaxation, and imagine or visualize yourself as a child. Ask your inner child what your life is like, how you feel, and what you want or need. Then picture yourself responding to that child, re-parenting it in a loving, trustful manner that would allow all

142

of his/her needs for fun, for touch and affection, for curiosity and creativity to be fulfilled. You can end this visualization by imagining that this child is merged within you, and promising to take care of both of you from now on.

What about AIDS? Are heterosexuals really at risk for it? How is sex different in the 1990s as a result of it?

You gotta be crazy to have
Sex in the 90s, sex in the 90s
Sex in the 90s. "
　　　　　—Gloria Estefan

AIDS has forever changed the face of sexuality for all of us. This incurable, sexually transmitted disease is passed on by unprotected sex between HIV positive persons and their sexual partners who exchange bodily fluids, between intravenous drug users who share needles, and from mother to child during pregnancy. It is not transmitted by coughing, sneezing, toilet seats, dirty towels, or any type of casual contact. Because it takes an average of eight to ten years from infection with the virus until the immune system has broken down to such a point that one becomes sick with symptoms qualifying for full-blown AIDS, approximately a million people in this country who look perfectly healthy are walking around able to transmit HIV.

Fifty to 60 percent of the world-wide cases of AIDS have been transmitted heterosexually. The fastest growing group of new cases of AIDS in this country is among people 24 to 29 who got this disease as teenagers. One in five new cases of AIDS in the United States are females, who are seven times more likely than men to become infected with the AIDS virus from a single sexual encounter.

Other sexually transmitted diseases like herpes, venereal warts and chlamydia, are not fatal but can result in serious infections and infertility, and exist in epidemic proportions among sexually active people. Every year about 2.5 million U.S. teenagers are infected with a sexually transmitted disease. This represents one out of every six sexually active teens, and one-fifth of the nation's STD cases.

The secrets to success for singles in the 1990s are vastly different than before the AID-ees. Couples are being forced to communicate before they connect. While the popular song by Gloria Estefan "Sex in the '90s" says spontaneity is dead, so are a lot of men and women. Freed by the sexual revolution, gay liberation, and accessible birth control since the 1960s, they practiced spontaneity to the hilt.

Yet, there is hope. Taking a non-fear-based approach to the facts presented in this chapter can change one's perspective on the two-sided coin of sexuality, even in the 1990s. As the ancient Chinese definition of crisis is made up of two overlapping symbols: danger *plus* opportunity, sexuality in the decades to come has the power and the potential to be even *better* than in the past. We can reach new levels of relating and many of us can anticipate a heightened appreciation for the preciousness of each moment in the face of death. New levels of honesty and vulnerability can bring the sexes closer together. Eroticizing condom use can be fun, can increase couple communication, and has the positive side effect of lengthening the time it takes for a man to reach orgasm. To learn the art of self-loving, to be intimate, to enjoy a myriad of low risk ways of exploring one another's bodies without exchanging bodily fluids, can heighten sexuality.

══════════════ **Personal Reflections** ══════════════

1. Did any of your reactions to this chapter surprise you?

2. Did you learn anything new from reading this chapter? Where have you learned most of what you know about sexuality? Is this the optimal way to learn about sex? If you had children, how would you explain human sexuality to them?

3. Have you taken time to draw your body and write down how you feel about its various parts? Where did you learn to feel positive or negative about different body parts?

4. Are most of the people you know taking healthy precautions against sexually transmitted diseases? Are you? Why or why not?

5. How would you like your sexuality to develop over the next decade? What do you most like about your sexuality?

The most important points for me to apply —tips for truly successful sexuality:

◆ *Know your SELF first.*

The'"M" word is normal, healthy, and OK; many sex therapists recommend masturbation as an exercise in self-knowledge and self-loving.

♦ *Discover what you REALLY want, and practice asking for it.*
If it's nurturing, ask to be cuddled.
If it's relief of tension, masturbate or exercise.
If it's connection, intimacy, and passion, ask your partner for sex.

♦ *Each time you have sex, act as if it were the first time.*
Preserve a sense of fascination, exploration, creativity, and innovation, as if you were alien creatures exploring one another, trying to get the other to know you better.

♦ *Remember that great sex takes time!*
Sexual response is learned; in spite of what the media depict, our reactiveness depends on the amount of time we spend each time, our previous experience, as well as the duration and depth of the relationship.

♦ *Remember that your partner's orgasm is NOT your responsibility!*
Really paying attention to our partner's needs, while attempting to get your own needs met, is the most elusive and erotic act of all. We allow *ourselves* the involuntary muscular contractions of orgasm.

♦ *There's validity in exercising the muscles* you need for any extremely important area of your life; sexuality is no exception. The mind, the heart, and the genitals need attention to keep fit and fully functioning.

♦ *Change core negative beliefs into affirmations by nurturing your inner child.*
Let go of stereotypes like "men use love to get sex" and "women use sex to get love." Change them into affirmations such as "I already have what it takes to attract a partner who is sensitive, sensual and meets my needs."

♦ *Communicate compassionately.*
Use self-revealing verbal and nonverbal tools to create intimacy between you and your partner.

♦ *Always look for opportunity in every problem or crisis.*

SUGGESTED READINGS

Lonnie Barbach. *For Yourself: On the Fulfillment of Female Sexuality.* New York: Anchor Press, 1974. *For Each Other: Sharing Sexual Intimacy.* New York: Anchor Press, l984. *Going the Distance: Secrets to Lifelong Love.* New York: Doubleday, 1991.

Patrick Carnes. *Don't Call it Love: Sexual Addiction in the Nineties.* New York: Bantam, 1991.

Laura Davis. *The Courage to Heal. The Courage to Heal Workbook.* New York: Harper & Row, l990. *Allies in Healing: Partners of the Sexually Abused.* New York: Harper & Row, l992.

Betty Dodson. *Sex for One: The Joy of Self-Loving.* New York: Crown. 1992.

Jack Hart. *Gay Sex. Manual for Men Who Love Men.* Boston, MA: Alyson Publications,1991.

Charlotte Davis Kasl. *Women, Sex, and Addiction: A Search for Love and Power.* New York: Harper & Row, l990.

JoAnn Loulan. *Lesbian Sex, Lesbian Passion: Loving Ourselves and Each Other.* San Francisco: Spinsters: Aunt Lute, l987.

Bernie Zilbergeld. *Male Sexuality.* New York: Bantam, 1992.

* Each of these and many more are available through a catalog of books, films, and sexual enrichment aids from:
The Sexuality Library, 1210 Valencia Street, San Francisco, California 94110. (415) 550-7399.

ABOUT THE AUTHOR

PAT HANSON

I have been a health and sexuality educator for over 25 years. Currently I teach health courses at California State University, Chico and am president of Health Matters, a consultation and media production firm. I have taught and trained professionals to integrate a positive approach to sexuality into their respective fields, as well as conducted workshops around the country on issues related to healthy relationships, sex education, countering homophobia, sexually transmitted diseases, death and dying, the relationship between sexuality, spirituality, and all addictions, and reducing "AFR-AIDS" (people's fears of AIDS).

I have produced several slide/music programs: "Quilt of Sorrow/Quilt of Hope: I Want to Know What Love Is," about the New York Memorial AIDS Quilt; and "Memory, the Faces of AIDS," as well as two television series aired by PBS affiliates. As a freelance writer, I have published articles in popular and professional journals. My wish for young people is that they accept the gift of sexuality with awe, reverence, *and* a sense of humor! Cherish this gift.

❂Next... Good sex is certainly part of the glue that bonds a couple, but not enough to ensure a viable relationship in the long run. Intimacy skills are described in the next chapter by the author of several books on marriage and parenting.

"I am capable of creating a loving, equal relationship that improves with age like a quality red wine."

6

HOW TO SUCCEED IN LOVE

GAYLE KIMBALL, PH.D.

Chapter Goals

This chapter discusses how to succeed in selecting a mate and nurturing an intimate relationship. Most of us want a vital and egalitarian relationship, but the fact that more than half of the recent marriages end in divorce is alarming. Our culture trains us for divorce by teaching us that love is about excitement and being an adult means hiding most of our feelings. Yet, intimacy is based on disclosure, and love is about comfort, trust, deep caring, respect, humor, expansiveness, having compatible goals, interests and values, and enjoying each other on a daily basis. Love is not just thrills and chills. Day-to-day domesticity is not usually exciting, although it can stimulate profound growth, and be deeply affectionate and satisfying.

Most of us want a relationship between equals who share the work of running a household, but employed wives do 70 percent of the family work. Despite lip service, egalitarian households where family work is shared 50/50 are rare. Because of these contrasts between our expectations and the reality of daily living, a good marriage must be attended to rather than put on cruise control. This chapter outlines the relationship skills you need to cultivate your potential to love and be loved.

How do I meet single people?

You rarely meet a new friend at home, so make a rule to go out at least once a week, with no pressure to meet someone special. It is enough to make the effort without any attachment to results, so that any effort is a success. Participate in groups that correspond with your interests, e.g., clubs that cycle or hike together, political campaigns, or service groups. Find out about activities for singles sponsored by organizations ranging from churches and synagogues to the Sierra Club: Check the newspaper for meetings. Take adult education courses and lessons—dancing, acting, financial management, a foreign language. Attend conferences and workshops. Try answering or putting in a single's ad in the newspaper, meeting in a public place. Ask your friends and colleagues if they know of single people with interests similar to yours. Take walks in your neighborhood, because a common way to meet someone is living or working in the same area. Go to parties. The policy is to engage in at least one activity a week.

A reader asks how to initiate a conversation with someone you do not know. Make a comment about something you both are observing or ask for information such as the time or background about the place. You could comment on something you admire about her clothes or appearance. Try wearing an unusual hat to establish contact. You could be frank and say something like, "I have a hunch you're a really interesting person. Would you be willing to share five minutes with me to see if my intuition is correct?" Nothing ventured, nothing gained.

Remind yourself every day about your positive traits and what is likeable about you, so that you create a positive aura that attracts other people to you. Post positive affirmations on your mirror: "I deserve the best." Then when you are with other people, focus on learning about them rather than thinking about the impression you are making. Do not accept your first judgements as accurate; they can be the opposite of what is possible for the two of you together. Take time to get to know someone you find interesting, even if he is not initially attractive to you. This may be a good sign that he is not triggering an habitual, irrational infatuation response on your part.

A common mistake is to think that the search for the beloved is the crucial task, rather than deepening one's ability to love, as explained in the ☞ classic *Art of Loving* by Eric Fromm (Harper & Row). The most important preparation for meeting Mr. or Ms. Right is learning about your unconscious, the part of the psyche that is like the mass of the unseen iceberg under the water. A relationship is the joining of two conscious personalities plus many more unconscious subpersonalities, such as your inner child, parent, adult, and shadow. ☞ See Connie Zweig and Jeremiah Abrams' *Meeting the Shadow* (Tarcher) for an explanation of the part of our psyche we usually repress and fear the most. The more you understand your sub-personalities, the less likely they will sabotage a healthy relationship and the more you can include them in developing a richly layered couple interaction. Useful tools in this lifelong exploration of the self are dream analysis and the active imagination, as ☞ explained in Robert Johnson's *Inner Worlds* (Harper Collins).

How do I select an egalitarian mate?

For women, according to interviews I've done with hundreds of couples, the best biographical indicators that a man will be an egalitarian spouse are from two ends of a continuum: Either his parents provided an equitable model of sharing responsibilities and his mother did not wait on family members hand and foot, or his mother was so subordinate that he vowed he would never treat his wife like a servant. Good predictors for a role-sharer are that he likes and respects his mother, he and his sisters and brothers did the same kinds of jobs around the house, he has spent some time living alone and cooking and cleaning for himself, he has liberal attitudes about gender roles, and he believes that equality is good for men and women. The most important trait to look for is that he has an independent sense of his own masculinity that does not depend on the opinions of others. He is not threatened if neighbors see him washing clothes or doing other traditional female tasks.

My female students appreciate men raised by mothers who did not cater to them and thus helped them understand the necessity of sharing housework. (I keep this in mind as I raise my son.) Women should remember that, especially if you become a mother, he will probably treat you the way he treats his mother who is the molder of his feelings about women. On some emotional level, he will expect the same services from you as his mother provided, even if intellectually he knows this is unfair for dual earners.

For men, the best indicators that a woman will hold up her end of an equal relationship are similar, with emphasis on the self-confidence it takes to expect equality. Study her interaction with her father carefully as this shaped her attitude toward men. Does she expect to be taken care of, financially and emotionally, or does she expect to role-share? Studies show that the most satisfied women have both a career and a family because career-minded women have their eggs in more than one basket. Women with more than one role have fewer symptoms of emotional and physical distress and more self-esteem than women who are full-time homemakers. (Of course there are many exceptions to any general pattern, as when women work in menial jobs and homemakers are leaders in community service.) It is a good idea to look for a woman who expects to be a breadwinning partner rather that one who expects that the Prince will take care of her happily ever after. Remember that it takes time and probing to get at these unconscious expectations. ☛ *50/50 Marriage* (Equality Press) has more information about how to select an egalitarian partner and create marital equality.

How do I know if this is Ms./Mr. Right?

The single most important rule for deciding on commitment to a partner is to ask yourself, Is this my **best friend**? Best friends find it easy and enjoyable to talk together and make time for frequent discussions. The secret is like peeling an onion, uncovering layer after layer of interesting qualities about the other, year after year. The synergy of the couple's interaction makes the whole greater than the sum of its two parts. When the two of you are together, you should feel larger and expanded rather than constricted. If you are best friends, if your interest in and respect for each other keeps growing, and you have a good sexual chemistry, you are building a solid foundation for a lively, long-term partnership.

The breakup of the marriage of Princess Diana and Prince Charles is an example of the dangers of not marrying a best friend with common interests and of confusing infatuation and sexual attraction with love. They did not take enough time to get to know each other well before they married. Since it takes time to differentiate between love and infatuation, it is crucial to give yourself this time as divorce prevention. There is no hurry in making one of the most important decisions of your life; if you feel pressured into making a decision to marry, he or she is probably not the right person. Love is based on trust and respect which simply take time to develop.

Other pressures propelling some people into making a poor decision to marry are their family wants them to, they are afraid they will not find someone else, they feel they are at the age where they should settle down, they do not want to hurt their partner's feelings by saying no to marriage, or they have engaged in sexual intercourse. Timing can be like quicksand: Just because the timing is right now does not guarantee the necessary ingredients for a solid marriage. Think about other reasons why your acquaintances have married, and do not repeat those mistakes. To avoid divorce, do the preparation work outlined in this chapter before deciding to get married.

When two people come together it is not just two flat surfaces rubbing together, smoothing out incompatible bumps, and fitting together compatible bumps and indentations; it is more like two multifaceted cubes interacting. The complex interaction between two sets of emotions, preferences, bodies, conscious and unconscious minds, spirits, and different personal histories means that it will **take time** to understand the complex interfaces and the games being played. You cannot make a rational decision about being soul mates in the first stages of infatuation because too many unconscious forces are activated. The process of awareness is like constructing a jigsaw puzzle because it takes a while to put enough pieces together to see the picture.

Sometimes we are strongly attracted to someone we do not even like, because of sexual chemistry or the magnetism of two complementary, unconscious patterns that hook each other. Sometimes we get hooked on the excitement of anxiety, of not knowing what is going to happen next in the romance, and mistake that intensity for love. A British study looked at attachment of puppies to their master. They watched three groups of puppies; the first was consistently well-treated, the second was consistently poorly treated, and the third group was alternately poorly and well-treated. The last group was the most attached to their masters. We need to avoid the kind of intense excitement generated by uncertainty—Will he/she phone?—or at least recognize that it does not equal love. (Many readers recognize themselves in this puppy story.)

What happens in infatuation is that the other person serves as a movie screen for our unconscious projections. The excitement comes from the projective charge of the psyche's attempt to become recognized and integrated, not from the beloved. That is, the power comes from the stirring of our unconscious energies, not from the other person who just acts as a spark that ignites existing inflammatory material. That is why the half life of infatuation averages three months. When the bubble of projection is burst by an incursion of reality, we ask, "How could I ever have wasted so much energy on that jerk/bimbo?" The symptoms of infatuation are insomnia, butterflies in your stomach, loss of appetite, anxiety, weak knees. This sickness is not a sound basis for a partnership, but it is a very useful tool for understanding our unconscious attitudes about men or women.

Carl Jung believed that the anima and animus, our unconscious image of the other gender, often determines our romantic love choices. We fall in love with unexpressed and unconscious parts of our psyche as we project them on someone else. The most popular symbol of men's archetypal anima (Jung's term for the female part of the male psyche) is Marilyn Monroe. She expresses the childlike sensuality and vulnerability prohibited in the cult of masculinity. The female animus (the male part of the female psyche) falls in love with men—Clark Gable to Robert Redford to Mel Gibson—who are in charge, strong winners, and have other qualities prohibited in the feminine role.

Ask yourself if you fall in love with individuals who manifest an underdeveloped part of you. ☞ See Robert Johnson's *She* (Harper Perennial), *He* (Harper & Row), and *We* (Harper Collins) for an interesting discussion of anima and animus and romantic love. Enjoy the excitement of infatuation, but do not marry in this stage. The goal is to become aware of and incorporate our repressed selves rather than fall in love with someone who temporarily expresses them for us.

Offering a male perspective, therapist Steve Flowers reports, "Usually it's our unconscious that does the choosing. We usually don't even see our own patterns, let alone others'." We have an uncanny knack for picking what is familiar to us, even though it may not be obvious at first. A common example is being drawn to alcoholics because a parent was an alcoholic. **Think carefully about the patterns in your previous relationships**, what to avoid and what to repeat; a neutral observer such as a therapist is useful.

─────────────── **Personal Reflections** ───────────────

1. Make a list in your journal of people you've been attracted to, even media stars.

2. Are there common themes/patterns in your relationships? If so, what do you want to continue and what themes do you want to change?

3. What qualities and talents do you want to develop in yourself? Thinking of your life as a novel, what are your themes?

4. Make a diagram of your family as far back as you can research to plot the relationship themes. How would your family describe a good woman? A good man? How would you describe a man and a woman worthy of your respect and emulation? What family relationship patterns would you like to repeat and what patterns would you like to change? How are your romantic partners like or unlike your parents?

5. Describe your ideal life partner, if this is a goal for you. Then number the characteristics in order of importance to you. What gifts do you bring to an intimate partnership? What changes would you like to make in order to be capable of the fullest possible connection with your mate? What change would you like to make in the next month?

If there are themes that do not work well for you, such as being drawn to a victim who wants a rescuer, or to a self-absorbed person who will not challenge your fear of closeness, or to a parent-figure who wants to dominate you like a child, consciously avoid your pattern. This is easier said than done, but awareness is a tool for improvement. Sometimes it takes months or years to see that an old pattern is at work. ☛ Maggie Scarf's *Intimate Partners* (Random House) provides a guide to becoming aware of your emotional patterns.

Counselors report that often what originally attracts a couple to each other gradually repels them as they mature. A common example is a young woman who marries a dependable daddy-type who makes her feel secure while her partner wants a dependent girl who makes him feel important and expresses feelings for him vicariously. Then she arrives at age 30, as ☛ described in Gail Sheehy's *Passages* (Bantam), and dumps "daddy" for someone who treats her like an adult. (Women are more likely to initiate divorce, probably because they have higher expectations for marriage.) What would you say is the main draw between you and your present and past loves? How do you project the attraction between you and your present partner will develop over the next decade?

The patterns that Steve Flowers sees in his counseling work with couples include: "the age-old dance between the seeker and the sought, the emotional pursuer and the emotional distancer, the active and the passive, the pusher and the pushee, the optimist and the pessimist, the realist and the idealist." What part do you usually take in this couple's dance? Steve recommends reading ☛ a fun, illustrated book called *The Two Step,* which shows how to change the dance of the seeker and the sought by Eileen McCann, (Grove Weidenfeld) and Harville Hendrix' *Getting the Love You Want: The Guide for Couples* (Harper Perennial). Steve explains that opposites attracting are caused by the desire to compensate for a soul injury in childhood.

In his marriage, Steve is the sail that propels their boat forward and his wife Mary is the deep keel that keeps them balanced and grounded. Their aim is for him to learn balancing functions and for Mary to learn propelling functions so that they will gradually move beyond depending on each other to a purer need-free love. Steve's goal is to "participate consciously with the Creator; to move in harmony with the Creator, and join with the flame which unites us." He is deeply appreciative of Mary's delight in his masculinity and his contributions to their household and vice versa.

Analyze together with your partner the ways in which you **comple-ment and balance each other**, watching that you do not allow one person to do the emotional expression for the couple and the other to do the rational planning. You will probably get resentful—and should if you are healthy—about having part of your personality ignored.

It's important to **spend time with the parents and siblings** of a potential partner because we, like baby ducks, imprint on our parents, as ducklings follow what they first see as they hatch out of the egg. It's a safe bet that we behave like our parents or in reaction to them. Most of us had close contact with only one adult male and one adult female as we grew up (or maybe just our mother, unless we were close to our extended family or had stepparents), so it is not surprising that our parents shape our attitudes about relationships.

A marriage is really the union of two people plus their family patterns and beliefs; one could say that four entities are joining together. How would you describe the ghosts or baggage you bring to an intimate relationship? What ghosts accompany your partner? How do you feel about these two sets of ghosts that influence your interaction as a couple? They can be positive as well as negative. You must identify these ghosts in order to be able to rationally apply the relationship skills outlined in this chapter.

Readers report trying to apply communication skills outlined in this chapter and meeting with resistance, blame, anger, denial, lack of interest and other blocks from their partners. In this type of situation, the mother or father ghosts must be communicated with first. If you have a hunch about which ghost is blocking progress, try pretending to set it in a chair and interview it. Respectfully ask it what it wants and listen without making judgments as your partner tries to speak for the ghost; Is it afraid of being controlled? What steps can be taken to accommo-date this fear? If you don't make progress in dispelling the anger or fear that is preventing you from rational communication, seek a therapist's assistance. Men are taught not to seek help (even when asking for directions in the car), but it makes sense to consult an expert. Every human is imperfect and can use some fine tuning. Going to a therapist does not mean that you are mentally ill; it means that you care enough about yourself and the relationship to want to increase your under-standing and learn new skills.

We can connect with another person emotionally, intellectually, physically, spiritually, as playmates, parents, and team members with common goals. Ask yourself and your partner how well you connect in these areas and **identify other connections** that are important to you. Decide if there are some areas where you can do without a close connection to your partner and some areas of connection that you value too highly to give up. For example, is emotional closeness important to you, but is intellectual stimulation something you can get from others? Identify underdeveloped potentials to cultivate together, since a major joy in a relationship is growth and discovery, while stagnation is boring. A relationship goes forward or it goes backward. Avoid complacency; live as if death were always over your shoulder reminding you to take action.

Going on a trip where the two of you are together nonstop, making decisions about what to do and where to go, can be a useful indicator of how well you operate as a team. You might want to do this before deciding whether or not to live together. Also, **discuss the questions at the end of this chapter** with your partner in order to check out your assumptions. ☛ A list of 235 other questions are provided in *The Book of Questions: Love & Sex*, by Gregory Stock (Workman). Unspoken expectations, usually based on the way we grew up, can cause strains for a couple. Steve Flowers points out, "Becoming your own parent can greatly contribute to not exerting unrealistic expectations on your spouse." ☛ He recommends *How to Be an Adult* by David Richo (Paulist Press) as a good book about growing up.

In this process of analysis, some couples have compared their expectations for marriage and decided to break up when they realized how different their goals were, say, for child rearing. They have learned exactly what they do want in a mate. It takes substantial work and time to nurture a relationship, to practice effective conflict resolution, to risk voicing uncomfortable feelings, to trust and be tolerant: Are you and your partner willing to make this effort? Do you want to grow old together, to be across the dinner table from each other for the next 50 years or more? Is your potential mate likely to be an onion with many layers to peel as you continue to explore each other? Are you?

Studies indicate predictors of divorce; think about minimizing these factors. Spouses are more likely to divorce if they have stressful living conditions caused by marrying in their teens, not earning enough to maintain their desired lifestyle, the husband's unemployment, not completing college, or addictions. A U.S. Census Bureau study tracking 24,000 people over four years, released in 1993, found that the divorce rate is highest when the father is unemployed (14 percent over the four years), and about 8 percent when both parents are employed full-time, compared to 5 percent when the mother works part-time. This study indicates that the man is still expected to be the main breadwinner and that this role is still important for marital success.

Couples are more likely to divorce if they do not have children, if their parents were divorced, if they were previously married, if both are greatly work-focused and do not have nurturing personalities (take Sandra Bem's Sex Role Inventory), and if the woman has a higher degree and earnings than the man. In regard to the last factor, this depends on the husband's attitudes about gender roles; if traditional, he suffers stress if he is not the main breadwinner; if egalitarian, he is happy to have a fulfilled wife and enhanced family earnings.

Think about birth order; sometimes two first-borns, for example, may clash if both want to be the leader or two last-borns may both expect to be babied. In *The Birth Order Book* (Fleming H. Revell), Kevin Lehman summarizes birth order differences, suggesting that it is a better balance to marry someone whose birth order is different than yours. See which characteristics apply to you and your partner, with the caution that scholarly review of the studies of birth order do not find any consistent correlations. Just for fun, do you tend to be

    a. a perfectionist, reliable, well-organized, critical;

    b. a mediator, avoid conflict, have many friends, a maverick,

    c. manipulative, charming, blame others, a good salesperson?

These traits supposedly describe first, middle, and last-borns.

Children of divorced couples observe causes of divorce first-hand. My students and I surveyed 82 young people for an advice book for children of divorce (in progress). In response to a question about why their parents divorced, the most frequent answer was that they did not get along, they argued, and were too different. For some, this was because their parents married too young and grew apart. For others, the incompatibility was caused by one of the partners being an alcoholic or drug user and one sexually abusing his daughter. Some parents were snowed under by financial problems and did not communicate well. Their incompatibility sometimes led one of the spouses to have an affair.

The conclusion we can draw from these eyewitness explanations is that you need to have **common interests and values** (Charles and

Diana did not). You need **compatibility as roommates**, team members, and possibly as parents, who will support each other's goals over the long haul. Opposites may attract, but often they cannot live together harmoniously. This does not mean you have to be peas from the same pod. Many couples tell me that they have similar values but opposite personality traits which balance each other; often they say something like "she's hyper" and "he's easygoing." Differences which complement and instruct can add spice and promote balance and growth. And growth is one of our main purposes for being on the planet.

Another lesson to learn from the children of divorce is that any two people who live together get on each other's nerves and irritate each other, as you have probably experienced with roommates. Several respondents say that their parents simply did not try hard enough to work through their differences. The magical way to overcome this friction is to plan good times together, making love, going out and having fun, accomplishing projects together—whatever nurtures mutual happiness, exhilaration, and joy. Fun must be planned regularly as it is the glue that holds the relationship close and creates tolerance for each other's imperfections. (These principles hold true for your relationships with your children as well; it's important to have fun with them, create family rituals, and hold enjoyable family meetings to work through current issues and validate each other—not just tell them what they're doing wrong.)

Most importantly, identify the relationship patterns and expectations each of you brings to your partnership and consciously decide what kind of partnership you want to evolve. **Checking out your assumptions** as you become aware of them prevents many misunderstandings, disappointments, and hurt feelings. Think about when you feel hurt: Is it because your expectations are disappointed? Do not expect your partner to be a mind reader. Tell him or her what you want so she or he has the opportunity to comply or to explain why compliance is not possible. Carrying around unresolved resentments is harmful to your immune system as well as the couple bond. (☞ See books by Louise Hay [Hay House] correlating diseases with specific emotional disorders.) Select a partner who is willing to do this kind of exploration of the deeper self now; do not make the mistake of thinking your mate will change once you're married.

How can i be successfully single?

If a relationship does end, it can be painful, especially if the other person initiated the breakup. How can we deal with this pain and longing? Realize that webs of connection grow between two people who are intimate and that even if the webs are not healthy or become outgrown, it takes time to undo them. Part of the pain can stem from feeling rejected, withdrawal from an addictive relationship, or fear of being alone. Scientists relate that romance stimulates natural amphetamines in the brain which produce feelings of euphoria in the first two or three years of a relationship. These subside and are replaced by endorphins, with similar chemistry to morphine, causing feelings of peace and calm. During sexual activity, the brain secretes oxytocin, which stimulates feelings of attachment and satisfaction. (☞ See *Time*, February 15, 1993.) Withdrawing from stimulation of these chemicals in the brain can be difficult, just as it is for someone addicted to artificial amphetamines or morphine. Try to replace the stimulus with exercise or some other natural inducer of euphoria.

Do not try to repress or ignore your grief; the only way to heal a wound is to open it up and clean it out. Find a supportive friend or therapist and tell him or her everything you remember and feel about the relationship. Repeating memories is usually necessary to release emotions to allow healing to begin. All your friend needs to do is listen attentively and not stop the flow with advice or telling her or his own stories. Having a good listener and setting aside focused time to grieve "fans the flames to burn off the dross," says Steve Flowers.

Emotions have to surface, be acknowledged, and worked through in order to be released so we can move on. Repressing painful feelings guarantees being burdened by them, even if we refuse to allow them consciousness. Steve observes in his counseling practice that helplessness, rage, and shame, as well as grief, often surface after a breakup. This is an opportunity to acknowledge and sort out these feelings and trace their origins. A breakup often reactivates previous unresolved experiences of rejection or failure, giving both a double punch and a double opportunity to progress. Pain is often our best teacher and deepens our capacity for joy, as ☞ Kahlil Gibran explains in *The Prophet* (Knopf).

Let yourself mourn with a closing ritual to finalize the end of the relationship, like a funeral. Consider a ceremonial burning of old

letters and momentos and make a list of all the reasons the relationship should end and what you learned from it. Did you repeat any
old patterns? Take advantage of all the surge of feelings surfacing
through this open window to go to a counselor and discover more
about your psyche. Do this before the curtain gets stuck down again
on the influx of feelings as you return to a daily routine.

Keep track of your dreams to learn how your unconscious mind
is processing the breakup. Writing them down in your journal allows
you to discover your personal dream symbols and align yourself
consciously with your unconscious evolution. The unconscious is
not just a passive storehouse of memories; it actively processes them,
as your dreams illustrate. Carl Jung explained that the goal of life is
to become whole by bridging the conscious and unconscious minds.
If you're interested in exploration of the psyche, ☞Jung's books—
like *Memories, Dreams, and Reflections* (Vintage), are fascinating.

Here is an example of how the dream process works. I was in a
relationship where I needed to become assertive and end it. I had a
series of dreams about being asked to teach math—one of the most
fearful disasters I can imagine. In dream after dream, I tried to figure
out how to cope, asking my good students to help, etc. In the last dream,
I said to the school administrators, "I'll teach anything in social sciences,
but I won't teach math." They readily agreed. My unconscious was
practicing saying no and soon I was able to end the relationship.

════════════════════ **Personal Reflections** ════════════════════

As you go to sleep tonight, instruct your unconscious mind that
you would like to remember your dreams and have the various levels
of your mind work together for growth and understanding. Have
your journal and pen by your bed. When you wake up, immediately
make your mind a blank screen and wait for images to come up, like
film developing in processing chemicals or a TV turning on. As you
write down your memories, often a second and third dream will be
remembered. After a month or so, reread your dreams to look for
your personal imagery and to identify what your unconscious mind
is processing. We commonly dream about our anxieties and our
physical desires, as well as working through our daily experiences,
but some dreams are more instructive of important growth. What
themes do you remember from previous dreams? What are the
relationship themes in your dreams?

Avoid seeing your "ex" for awhile until you are more disconnected from each other, as a relationship can be an addiction that contact activates. Think about how long it took to heal after past breakups and how you feel about those people now. Imagine the kind of partner who will appreciate you and the kinds of interaction you would like to have, building on what you learned from your previous relationship. Start a new activity, like joining a new group or taking a class, so that you do not let depression and inertia bog you down. Do not rebound into a new relationship without taking time to get centered and digest what you need to learn.

Establish a daily routine of constructive activity, such as exercise, meditation, taking a walk, doing community service, talking with friends, and achieving small goals. Make lists of your admirable and likeable qualities and post them. Do nice things for yourself, like arranging flowers in your room, getting a massage, or taking a trip to a place with programs for singles, like Club Med.

Living alone is an opportunity to learn about yourself, your own rhythms and tastes. It is an opportunity to learn to fly with your own wings, Steve says. Being single is a good time to be self-indulgent, to enjoy the luxury of wearing comfortable old clothes, sleeping when you want, and not caring what you look like or having to be gracious. It is a time to figure out what is really important to you and spend a lot of time doing it well, without needing to accommodate someone else. It is a good time to get to know various kinds of people and experiment with different activities you are curious about. This is an opportunity to help others, such as doing volunteer work as a Big Brother or Big Sister, or getting involved in local politics.

Appreciate this time to do what you want to do, because the statistics indicate that you will live with a partner sooner or later; well over 90 percent of Americans marry. Your time to be completely independent and self-directed may not last long so use this time well. You cannot have a healthy relationship until you are balanced by yourself. Being needy is a formula for a disastrous relationship. Appreciate your freedom and use it thoughtfully for self-exploration and for community service. In the process of giving you may meet interesting people.

➤
How can I make my marriage successful?

When you do get together with Ms. or Mr. Right, I know you strongly want to avoid adding to the divorce statistics. This section summarizes what I have learned from interviewing hundreds of married and divorced persons for *50/50 Marriage* (Equality Press) and *50/50 Parenting* (Lexington Press), from reading hundreds of studies of marital satisfaction, and from my own experiences. This intensive research revealed the critical factors for a successful marriage. When my students and I surveyed hundreds of people of various ages, about what makes them happy, at the top of the list were friends, family, mates—the people we love, not making money. (Other factors were achieving a goal and engaging in enjoyable leisure activities such as sports or being in nature.) Yet many of us get seduced into pouring our best energy into work. We need to focus on our relationships as much as or more than we do on career success.

The first step is having **realistic expectations** about what family life is like today. A New Hampshire family law attorney observes in his divorce clients that, "Most of the time, people don't put in the work. They let things go too far and their expectations are so crazy." A husband in Pittsburgh defines working at the relationship as talking things over and compromising.

I asked hundreds of California State University college students at Fullerton (near Los Angeles) and each semester at Chico (north of Sacramento, where I teach) to describe a typical day in their lives fifteen years from now. Their essays are amazingly similar year after year. Students usually expect an intact marriage, with two or three children—most often a boy is the first-born, reflecting our sexist biases. Most are dual-earner couples, but men and women still have different attitudes about their roles. Men often view the wife's job as for her personal satisfaction rather than as an economic necessity, because his job is primary. She is primarily responsible for family life, taking long maternity leaves, then working part-time to care for their children, while his career keeps moving up the ladder of success.

Men are portrayed in the essays as very helpful, but the sense is that he is *helping her* rather than doing his fair share of the work. Many men do want to spend more time with their children than their fathers spent with them. When the mother works full-time, the children are frequently cared for by baby-sitters in the home or by grandparents. Parents arrive home at 5:00 P.M. or earlier, spend time with their children, take time to exercise, then have two or three hours to talk together and make "mad, passionate love" after the children are tucked into bed.

The differences between women and men are interesting. In a 1993 comparison at CSU,Chico of 46 female and 43 male students, the main differences were that women were much more likely to predict job flexibility, being home to pick up children after school, for example (22 women versus 5 men). A hopeful sign is that men were twice as likely to mention specific family work tasks, such as driving their children to school or helping them with homework. Only one of the men said his wife did not work, while all the other women were employed. Television beat out mention of sex (15 men and 9 women included TV, compared to 8 women and 7 men who mentioned making love.)

Looking at 200 CSU,Fullerton students' essays written several years ago, with a few more women writing than men, 89 percent of the women mention being married, as compared to 63 percent of the men. Seven percent of the men mention dating, but none of the women do. Most telling is that 29 percent of the men make no mention of marriage or family, compared to only 11 percent of the women. Women twice as often mention spending time with their spouses than men. Of the students who describe family responsibilities, such as getting children off to school in the morning, almost 75 percent are women. The most frequent family work mentioned by women was fixing dinner: 35 of them do it themselves and 20 share preparation with their spouses. Only ten men mention cooking dinner and three more say their wives do it. Thirty men mention owning luxurious toys such as Porches, Lamborghinis, and boats, and salaries in the six figures, compared to only 13 women. Men are more likely to mention owning their own businesses, exercise, travel, attractive spouses, and sex; while women are more likely to mention successful husbands, flexible work hours, and part-time jobs to accommodate family needs. These essays reveal that traditional roles are still pervasive, with women focusing more on family and men on their breadwinning role.

What is unrealistic about the almost uniform future described by hundreds of college students? The divorce rate in recent marriages is around 50 percent, so many readers will be single parents then remarry and form stepfamilies. Few jobs allow much flexibility and suburban dwellers may add several hours to their workday by commuting. Families are so mobile that many do not receive support from extended families and in-home baby-sitters are expensive and often quit to take better-paying jobs. Over 7 million children are latchkey kids and many other children are cared for in a patchwork-style child care arrangement. Polls reveal that Americans are not satisfied with the trilemma of lack of affordable quality care. Sick children are a frequent complaint of employed parents who dread "the call" asking that they pick up their sick child, which can lead to "the debate" about which parent should miss work.

Couples often find that their marriage is put on the back burner in the face of more pressing demands from work and children. They are so tired after the children are in bed that they collapse on the couch with a newspaper and fall asleep, rather than make love. ☞ Arlie Hochschild's *The Second Shift* (Viking) provides a description of the rather joyless life in dual-earner families. Fatigue puts a damper on ardor. As long as a man earns more, unequal division of family work follows, sometimes with unspoken resentment on the part of the wife.

Part of expecting to have it all is the expectation of professional careers for both spouses. Many young women are not prepared for the glass ceiling which accelerates men's career progress past women's after the first five years on the job. A kind of schizophrenic outlook prevails among my college students. On the one hand, students are well aware of the high divorce rate and worried about how to escape it. On the other hand, they expect to have the kinds of families they see on television where houses are always clean (with the exception of Rosanne's) and problems are solved quickly. U.S. students watch so much television—more time than is spent in the classroom by the time they graduate from high school—that it creates a second view of reality.

The media image of the superwoman creates dangerous expectations for young women who think they should exercise to sculpt a hard body, wear elegant suits and carry a brief case, come home and whip up a gourmet meal, and be a nurturing mother and sexy wife. An ad copy asks a suited career woman holding her daughter's hand, "Is your face paying the price of success?" The ad reminds women that their most important avenue to success is being attractive to men.

Men too are loaded with impossible expectations by media portrayals of loving, involved fathers shampooing their toddlers' hair, while at the same time being expected to devote the long hours and the competitive drive necessary to succeed at work. For example, a 1993 magazine ad for Silhouette romance novels states about a hero, "He drives a car fast, a bargain hard, and women to distraction." Even ads showing fathers in nurturing roles with their children call them heroes establishing a dynasty for eternity, to compile current ad phrases. Television and films, along with our education system, certainly do not prepare young adults for their future roles as employed parents.

Today a man cannot expect that his employed wife will have the time and energy to cheerfully do most of the family work. A woman cannot expect the Prince to carry her off and support her happily ever after, because he will not earn enough to make house payments and pay for the children's education on his own. Besides, the marriage is as likely to end in divorce as it is to survive; if it remains intact, the average age of widowhood is around 56. Clearly, young women need to plan on a lifetime in the work force.

Most parents cannot afford to take long parental leave because mortgage costs consume almost half (44 percent) of one person's income. The average real income for families headed by parents under age 30 has dropped over 25 percent since 1973; as a consequence, both spouses must work. Few jobs allow for flexibility, so most workers are compelled to work full-time from 8:00 to 5:00, plus commute. The average employee works over 50 hours a week, leaving family with just the leftover time and energy.

A realistic view is that both partners will need to be employed and share parenting rather than one supporting the other in the traditional "Father Knows Best" division of roles. June and Ward Cleaver types of families now constitute less than 10 percent of families; June has gone to work and maybe she and Ward have divorced and formed stepfamilies. The divorce rate is higher in second marriages with children, so it is possible that one of them will divorce a second time. What are the implications of these trends for you? Being forewarned is forearmed. If you think about the strains on contemporary families you can build buffers of understanding and support systems to protect your family from dissolution.

In addition to realistic expectations, it is well worth emphasizing that being **best friends** is the important key to success. The hallmark of friendship is that the pair likes to talk with each other and spends a lot of time communicating. Talking to one's spouse is the main tool for successfully maintaining a marriage. Couples talk about their goals, experiences, thoughts, and feelings—which requires turning off the television. A husband contentedly married for eighteen years reports, "Not being afraid to talk about things carries a vitality in itself. That's what a relationship is about and what keeps it meaningful. Communication is at the heart of it." Honest disclosure of feelings prevents manipulative behavior and generates trust, an important ingredient of any friendship.

A study of 161 happily married couples reported that the spouses became more interesting to each other over time. The authors (☛ Jeanette and Robert Lauer, '*Till Death Do Us Part* (Harrington Park Press) define the four keys to a successful marriage as **friendship**, **commitment**, **agreement on fundamentals**, and **humor**. Friendship is enhanced by enjoyment, taking time to have fun together and to enjoy each other's sense of humor. Pair bonding is based on the **shared memory of good times**, not on arguments over bills, kids, and messes. This is a major problem area for dual-earner parents whose energy and time goes mainly to work and children.

Another ingredient of marital satisfaction is **intimacy** (into-me-see), based on disclosure of one's feelings. Personal growth requires learning about the "untapped inner world: turbulent emotions, unexplored terrors, accumulated hurts, unclear meanings." It follows that, "The fastest way to grow is through accepting the experiences we normally resist, such as our hurt and pain," ☛ as John and Kris Amodeo point out in *Being Intimate* (Viking Penguin). They have since divorced, indicating that experts too face major changes in their relationships. Disclosure is not easy, since we risk rejection and judgment, and our own unconscious patterns often strongly resist change. It's as if subpersonalities cling to their own survival: Please keep in mind that you may have to do battle with your own unconscious in order to be capable of intimacy. But disclosure must be risked in order to continue peeling the onion skin; that is, learning about one's self and each other to keep the marriage dynamic. Disclosure thrives on trust which frees up all kinds of emotional and sexual expression.

Steve Flowers agrees with author Norm Jampolsky that we have to become students and teachers to one another. Steve says, "We have to learn about surrender, compromise, and fair play. All of us are pathetically impoverished when it comes to background and role models. Developing an egalitarian relationship is an incredibly challenging goal. It takes considerable maturity, courage, and self-examination, not to mention compassion, love, and committed investment."

Intimacy requires studying each other like an ambassador studies a new culture, including our original families and the different ways girls and boys are raised. For example, Deborah Tannen observes that in their conversations, girls share secrets with each other, while boys exchange practical information and struggle for dominance. This leads to different expectations for adult relationships, as when women relate the details of conversations during their day and men summarize theirs in a sentence or two. One husband observes that marriage is like diplomacy between two foreign countries. Sociologist Barrie Thorne writes, "Men and women live in two alien cultures oddly intertwined." Another sociologist, Jessie Bernard, thinks that men and women live in two different worlds, as she describes in ☛ *The Female World* (The Free Press). In the feminine world, little ladies do not get angry, say anything unpleasant, not be nice, initiate sex or talk about sex. Withholding is a barrier to intimacy, including repressing anger or sexual needs. Women may need encouragement to break the good girl rules.

In the masculine world, little boys do not act like sissies who reveal feelings other than anger or the joy of winning. Steve Flowers reports,

> For boys, the real danger of being vulnerable is that this will be used against you by other boys. You learn in kindergarten that being vulnerable is equated with getting picked on or beaten up. Shutting down means that men cannot develop the kind of internal warning systems or the radar women are encouraged to develop, where they zoom in on feelings. If men expressed them, their deep feelings would probably include shame, grief, loneliness, confusion, and guilt. The grief stems from the lack of freedom to be who you really are. Overworking keeps men from facing the emptiness, grief, shame, and anger that result from their role.
>
> As a consequence, midlife men shaken up by a recent divorce are likely to say, "I don't know who I am," and they really do not know.

Mothers often lean on their sons to make up for disappointments with their husbands, Steve observes, so boys learn that they must become the responsible ones. This causes men's fear of loss of control. Steve describes an image of a man gripping the steering wheel of a car in a storm, driving white-knuckled, afraid of letting go, for who else would guide the car? He reports that many men feel unappreciated for their struggles, feeling like they're climbing uphill with sweat pouring off their bodies, dragging heavy weights like house payments, bills, and protecting their children.

The male climber may feel trapped in a meaningless job, struggling to pay his family's debts, afraid to soften or give up the edge he feels he needs to keep struggling. He feels responsible and guilty for not doing even more and isolated and lonely because he cannot allow himself to disclose his fears and confusions. His fear of loss of control is compounded by dependency on women for validation of his worth as a man.

Women can encourage men to share the burden of being the responsible person in charge and not expect men to always be strong and decisive. A reader comments this was true for him because his ex-wife did not listen when he tried to explain the pressure he felt. Another reader in her early twenties says, "I never realized that men are under a lot of pressure." Just look at magazine ads featuring men and see how many of them look tight, tough, and unsmiling, like the Marlboro man. This tension is not good for health, which thrives on relaxation and fluidity, and it is not conducive to intimacy, which thrives on vulnerability.

Men are often suspicious that if they give an inch, women will want a mile, because they appear insatiable in their desire for talking about feelings. A safety valve for men is to set clear limits, as in talking about feelings for a half hour, or clearly spelling out in writing who will do what in the home. Some married men seem confused about their roles because they are doing more around the house than their fathers did, but it never seems to be enough for their wives. Steve advises that when men disclose their feelings, women should not "meddle, interfere, interpret, or comfort, and should never use what is revealed as a weapon."

Men may think of women as unexplainably moody, governed by PMS, unpredictable, and manipulative. If sometimes true, some of these traits follow from women's subordinate position; women who are direct and assertive may be judged abrasive, unfeminine, pushy, sexually unsatisfied, and difficult. Some women do feel more emotional before their monthly period, but studies do not correlate female performance on tests with their monthly cycle. If in doubt, a simple solution is to ask what is going on. There are explanations for the seemingly irrational ways we interact as men and women. A look at differences in our gendered language styles reveals a lot, as described in ☛ Deborah Tannen's *You Just Don't Understand* (William Morrow).

Men need to understand that women may funnel various emotions, including anger, through tears; women need to understand that men may funnel all kinds of emotions through anger. In my workshops with Randy Crutcher on "Bridging Men's and Women's Worlds," young men explained that they do in fact have deep feelings and sensitivities but are expected to hide them. They reported that women are often content to be just friends with nice guys but are attracted to jerks who seem invulnerable. Men get mixed messages—be tough/be sensitive, be liberated/pay my way, open the door for me/don't open the door for me, be successful on the job/have time for me.

Very true! report most men who read this paragraph and some women acknowledge that they indeed are attracted to the tough guys rather than the nice guys. One of them explains, "I liked the excitement of not knowing what he would do next. I have grown out of that and am currently very happy in a relationship with a nice guy. So, encourage the men out there that there is hope!"

Women may condemn men as being insensitive without thinking about the cultural definition of masculinity—the tough Rambo, the Terminator, and various hunks versus the dreaded wimp. Many best sellers tell women that men are jerks and that foolish women love too much, picking immature Peter Pans. This "male-bashing" does not account for the restrictive ways in which parents bring up their boys and the expectations women have of men to be Prince Charming. Making an effort to understand the pressures on the other gender builds empathy and a sense of being supported by one's partner. This is one of the most important gifts we can provide our mate.

An effective partnership requires learning **communication skills** that most of us were not taught by parents or teachers, although they are essential to solve the inevitable conflicts and misunderstandings that occur between two imperfect humans. Most of us were taught that becoming an adult means stifling our feelings to maintain an aura of calm control. We're taught that it is not polite to mention petty irritations or show anger. However, couples report that it is essential not to "gunnysack" resentments and irritations, but deal with them soon after they arise to prevent future blowups and feeling distant from each other. Trying to protect one's partner by not telling her or him the truth is treating that adult like a child. One of the best feelings is mutually facing a difficult situation, where both people may be angry or threatened, and successfully working through it together. This is how trust is built, knowing I can count on you to work with me even though your buttons are being pushed.

Specific skills are involved in effective communication, including conflict resolution, active listening, and using "I feel" statements rather than blaming "You always" statements. Blaming statements may be accurate but they evoke defensive counterattacks rather than cooperative moves toward a solution. Active listening involves encouraging your partner to discharge his or her feelings without interrupting the process with tales of your similar experiences or giving advice.

Giving total attention is a wonderful gift that allows the speaker to release emotions which clear the way for problem solving. It does not work to try and brainstorm a rational solution until the anger, fear, guilt—whatever emotions are surging—are discharged. Giving complete attention is a basis for feeling loyally supported, the foundation for friendship. (☞ Re-evaluation Counseling is a peer counseling system which teaches how to effectively release old feelings and shape new emotional patterns. RC groups are found in many cities. Headquarters are P.O. Box 2081, Seattle, WA 98111.)

Steps to Successful Conflict Resolution:

1. **Identify the problem** area (e.g. , I'd like more frequent sexual intimacy with you.)

2. **Identify your feelings** evoked by the problem without blaming your partner: I feel____ because____. You might say, "I feel less connected, less desired, less loving, and less tolerant when we do not find time to make love." A blaming statement, "You never make love with me anymore," evokes defensiveness, as in, "Well, you never____." Then your partner does active listening to restate what he or she heard you say: You feel____ because____," without adding judgments or excuses; "You're not feeling as close to me as you'd like and you'd like to make love more often."

Blame, sarcasm, placating, retreating into rationality to avoid expression of feelings, and bringing up past grievances are all forbidden in fair conflict resolution. Sticking to one issue means "that reminds me of when____" is unfair fighting. If you feel swamped, it is fair to take a break or walk around the block with a commitment to resume negotiations. The check-in process avoids the common mistake of making unspoken assumptions about what your partner is feeling and thinking. The keys are to avoid blaming because it causes a defensive reaction and to stick to how you feel because it generates an empathetic willingness to find a solution. "I feel you're a slob" is merely a disguised "you" message; just say how you feel, as in "I feel frustrated trying to cook in a messy kitchen."

3. **Ask for a specific solution**. This is the main component of conflict resolution because it provides a positive, workable suggestion rather than a defeating condemnation: "I'd like to save every Saturday as date night so we can renew our courtship mode, and I'd like to hire a housecleaner for 6 hours a week so we're not so tired." (☞ Harriet Lerner's *The Dance of Anger* (Harper & Row) and *The Dance of Intimacy* discuss how to clearly identify what you really want.)

4. **Negotiate a compromise** solution agreeable to both parties, to be reevaluated at a specified date. ("OK, we'll save every other Saturday night to go out and we'll hire a housecleaner 3 hours a week. We'll formally sit down and talk about our progress in two weeks.") ☞See Roger Fisher and Scott Brown's *Getting Together* (Houghton Mifflin) and their earlier book, *Getting to Yes*, to learn how to negotiate a win/win solution.

Throughout the process, partners can do what counselors are paid a lot to ask: How are you feeling about what I just said? Fill in the blanks can be used: As I sit here listening to you, I feel____. If my sadness/anger could talk it would say ____. End the process with appreciation for how each partner conducted his/her part of the dialogue, a reminder of what originally attracted you to each other, and other validations. Praise should become a daily routine, as regular as brushing your teeth, including the love notes and little surprises that often cease after courtship. Make a game out of seeing how much you can delight your partner. Pick out books about communication and intimacy to read together and discuss or give each other book reports about different books, reading key portions aloud to your partner. Learn from watching how a therapist does active listening and probing.

Readers ask, "What do you do if your partner is not willing to go through this kind of analysis?" You can model doing it yourself, not asking him or her to reciprocate until feeling less threatened and more comfortable. You can praise and reward the progress your partner makes even if it is slow. Women can remember that they may seem unbounded in their desire for closeness, so a clear limit can be established: "We will talk about our feelings for an hour a week and no more, then renegotiate in a month." Or you can decide there are other aspects of the relationship that make it worthwhile to continue, despite lack of communication. Finally, you can take a stand and say, "I won't stay in a relationship without a mutual commitment to growth. Perhaps we could use the help of a neutral third person like a counselor. But if you are not willing to join me in learning intimacy skills, despite all your good qualities, I see no choice but to look for someone who will."

Since every close relationship produces conflict of some kind, there must be a method for fair resolution of differences. One person usually giving in to the other or keeping disagreements under the rug is unfair, blocks intimacy, and breeds resentment. Of course, we all make two steps forward and one step backward; perfection is impossible. What counts is the intent to face issues as they surface. It depends on what you value, so this might be a good time to identify your bottom line in your journal.

A component of conflict is the often unspoken and unconscious struggle over power and control. Take a piece of paper, each holding two corners, and try to get it away from each other. Or, have a tug-of-war with a sock. Have a pillow fight. Get just one little piece of a treat that you both love to eat. Just one of you gets a back rub. Who gets the goodies? Do these before reading further. See what these simple exercises reveal about your power issues. Is one person more likely to give in than the other? Is one person more aggressive or insistent that his/her wishes be satisfied? Is one more suspicious and less trustful? How do you try to get what you want? How does your partner try to get her or his needs satisfied? What do you do if you disagree? What did each of your sets of parents do?

Do not duck power and control issues during courtship, thinking that you will assert your real needs and likes in the marriage. This is dishonest and asking for trouble. Face power issues now, as every human relationship has some jockeying for power. These struggles can be humorous if you acknowledge them, because they often come from our inner child, who might be satisfied by a lively pillow fight but frustrated by a logical debate.

Good marriages are characterized by a **commitment** to not withdraw, quit, or blame when difficulties, arise and to be tolerant of the partner's foibles. In return, we can ask for forgiveness of our faults. Couples report that marriage has ebbs and flows like waves and seasons and spouses should not catastrophize about the low/dry period as a cause for a divorce. With patience, work, attention, and a leap of faith, another good wave appears, just as spring follows winter.

Part of commitment is to be aware that work can be seductive and addictive: Do I work to live or live to work? (☞ Anne Wilson Schaef describes how our workplaces function according to an addictive/unhealthy system in *When Society Becomes the Addict* (Harper) and *The Addictive Organization* (Harper) coauthored with Diane Fassel. One wife comments, "Your marriage will be only what you put into it. If you work at it, it will grow; if not, it will die," just as plants wilt if they are not tended or a car stops running if it is not maintained. However, fairy tales and romance novels end with, "And they lived happily ever after." We are not given much education about how to succeed in marriage in a culture whose goddess is money and power.

We are expected to concentrate on the couple bond during courtship, then after the honeymoon he focuses on breadwinning and she focuses on family. Your love certainly deserves more time and energy than you spend earning and maintaining possessions. Specifically state and write out your priorities as individuals and as a couple and decide how to be true to them. Do not let work sap your best energies.

Commitment is especially required when babies arrive on the scene. Numerous studies show marital satisfaction as a U-shaped curve, dropping with the arrival of the baby and rising when the last child leaves the nest. Becoming servants to the demands of little ones is not romantic. Having a baby should be delayed until the partners have time to bank fun times together, with spontaneous sex, travel, sleep, dates, and other enjoyable activities that are likely to diminish after a baby arrives. In stepfamilies with children on the scene from the beginning, the couple *must* take time to create romance, reminding themselves that the solidity of their bonding is crucial for family solidarity and that the divorce rate is higher in second marriages. A reader in a second marriage reports that she has not had one day alone with her husband during their seven years of marriage. I advised her to correct this formula for divorce quickly.

Commitment is also needed when the inevitable conflicts between any two roommates arise. Issues that most often cause marital conflict are different attitudes about child rearing, money, in-laws, and sexuality. Newer conflicts to add to the list are equitable division of household work, competition over career success, and how to use scarce leisure time. Dual-earner couples surveyed for *Empowering Parents* report that their main causes of disagreement are frustrations over lack of free time, disagreements about finances and child rearing, and dissatisfaction over division of household labor. These tension areas should be discussed before marriage and before deciding to become parents.

As well as utilizing effective conflict resolution, these potential conflicts must be offset by scheduling frequent times for fun and time to talk together as a couple. Two goals are a weekly date night and taking turns listening to each other talk.

What can I do to enhance intimacy in the face of so many demands on our time?

♦ The most powerful step is to take regular time to actually **listen** to each other, giving our total attention without offering advice, judgment, or interjecting our own experiences. Learning not to give advice while listening may be especially difficult for men who have been trained to be the problem solver like Batman. This exchange should be scheduled at least once a week for a half hour or more of uninterrupted time for each person.

♦ Discuss your **dreams** with each other before you get up in the morning, remembering that their language is symbolic and visual rather than literal. Record your dreams in a journal. Patterns will emerge as you read over your dream journal and the message of the dreams will become clearer as you learn your personal symbols. Dreams are the most direct window into the unconscious and therefore are treasures of insight, often better than years of expensive psychoanalysis. Sharing your dreams is one of the most valuable tools for intimacy.

♦ Do guided **visualization**/day dreams/mediation with each other, such as one partner talking the other through a journey in a forest where they arrive at a magical house with a treasure box. What's the treasure? Or, what animal do you discover waiting for you as your guide? What does it say to you? Or, you walk down a spiral staircase (or escalator), find a door with ancient symbols on it, enter the room, and sit at a table. You invite the different parts of your personality to join you at the table. Your partner can interview the different characters, ask what they'd like, and how they can work together. When I did this I got a little girl who wants to play more (she doesn't like all this book writing), a fairy princess with spiritual advice, a gnarly old tree that just wants to achieve goals, and a snail. ☞Do exercises together to explore your **inner child**, as described in Lucia Capacchione's *Recovery of Your Inner Child* (Simon & Schuster).

♦ Simply **hold your partner** in your arms for fifteen minutes, giving her or him permission to relax completely.

♦ Say at least one thing you like about your partner daily, establishing a habit of offering **validations**. Write down a list of qualities and attributes you like about your partner and post them.

♦ Take the Myers-Briggs **personality inventory** published in Keirsey and Bates' *Please Understand Me* (Prometheus Nemesis Books). It is a useful tool for realizing that we have different approaches that can be irritating when not understood, as when one partner sees the other as "flaky" and is seen by the other as rigid. Reading the book reveals, for example, that one person requires open options and the other requires structure, and that neither style is better than the other.

♦ Make a **list** of how you feel most nurtured and affirmed by your partner and what you think is nurturing for him or her. Follow through with at least one activity from your list each week.

♦ **Trace yourself** on a large piece of paper, and color in where you feel love, hate, pain, or pleasure.

♦ Gather five objects and privately assemble them to create a **sculptured** environment, like therapists have clients arrange small objects on a sand tray. Don't watch each other. Interview your partner about how she or he feels about the "world" created, the relationship of the objects to each other, and so on. Swap objects and see how you assemble them differently.

♦ Identify different **subpersonalities** in your psyche, such as the child in you, or the rebel, the actor, the jock, or the clown, and let that personality speak. Ask your child-self to write to you and to your partner, by using your nondominant hand. Popular media figures can be used to describe subpersonalities. One person can be the interviewer, finding out about one of these subpersonalities. You can make up a fictional character to be interviewed by your partner, who pretends to be a national news reporter, perhaps using accents. Improvise fictional characters and dialogue, picking up this game from time to time when you feel playful.

How can we keep romance alive?

Intimacy is nurtured by satisfying sex, frequent touching, and verbal expressions of love and appreciation. (See Chapter 5.) An interesting explanation of the importance of touch is that as infants, we associated it with love and caring. Primates bond by touching, grooming, and cuddling. Because real men are supposed to know what their lovers like without asking and ladies are not supposed to talk about sex, most of us need to overcome some inhibitions about sharing our sexual likes and dislikes and our fantasies. You might get ideas from ☛ Nancy Friday's *Forbidden Flowers* (Pocket Books) and Lonnie Barbach's *Pleasures* (Harper & Row) about women's sexual fantasies. Also, *Deep Down*, edited by Laura Chester (Faber and Faber) and *The Ladies' Home Erotica* (Ten Speed Press) are collections of erotic writing by women. Various magazines are devoted to men's sexual fantasies, as you know.

I interviewed a couple married for 50 years who still have an active sex life because they maintain foreplay throughout the day. They touch, pat, hug, and kiss as they pass each other in their daily routines. She says that she feels like she's 40 in bed with her husband, although occasionally she gets a cramp that reminds her she's 75. Fidelity is tied to the trust which is the groundwork for intimacy, although studies report that one quarter to one-half of spouses have an affair. If a partner starts getting restless, this is a signal to take a romantic trip, to plan a surprise date, to think up sexy skits, to take the time to listen to and appreciate each other and go to a counselor to do some renewal work on the partnership.

Romance Enhancers

Create a one-day holiday: Spend the day in bed, with the children away, the phone answering machine on, candles and Christmas tree lights over your windows, incense, music, and tasty finger food to delight all your senses. Read Anais Nin's erotic diaries aloud and do some of the communication exercises listed below. Or spend the night in a nearby hotel with a hot tub, jacuzzi, a pool, and dancing. Be a tourist in your own area. Explore an activity you would not ordinarily do, such as going to a concert, automobile races, a fair, or an unusual ethnic restaurant, taking transportation you don't usually use.

Do what you enjoyed as a child: Buy a toy such as bubble-making solution, go to an amusement park or zoo, play games such as tag, hide-and-go-seek, or 20 questions; play a ball game together. Read aloud to each other, make up round robin stories where you take turns as narrator, have a picnic, and give each other oil massages. Simultaneous feet rubs can be exchanged while you talk. Take a bubble bath together, wash your partner's hair, and feed each other.

Create romance with imagination. Go on a double date, the women and men arriving separately at a public place where you pretend that you have never met before and want to get to know each other. Pretend that one of you is a seductive stranger who comes knocking at your door. Go out for dinner and dancing in your most elegant clothes (shop at thrift shops or rent formal attire). Read erotic books together. Wear sexy clothes to bed. Create rituals to celebrate special occasions, such as the day you first met. One couple uses each full moon as their special time together, planning a fun activity such as a train ride or just going out to dinner by themselves.

Create fantasy scenarios to act out in the bedroom: Spouses interviewed in Seattle found this greatly enhanced their sexuality, after becoming parents diminished it. One of their fantasies is that they are at an orgy, and they report to each other what they see going on around them. Another scene is to pretend that he is an American exchange student, a virgin, living with a Swedish family with a teenaged daughter. One evening she comes to his room and ...

How can I have a 50/50 marriage?

Equity issues are a major new area of concern for spouses. Today about two-thirds of married couples are both employed, but wives do 70 to 80 percent of the family work. A survey of 15,000 wives revealed that those in poor marriages rarely had husbands who shared equally in the family work—only 8 percent, compared to the 63 percent sharing among the wives who said they had excellent marriages.

Couples usually think of their marriages as fair because inequality feels natural and he usually earns more. Even men who say they share family work equally do little more than traditional men, according to a ☛ large survey described in *The American Couple*, by Philip Blumstein and Pepper Schwartz (William Morrow). However, national surveys still show that husbands with employed wives only do around 10 percent more family work than husbands with homemaker wives, who do around 20 percent. The test of fairness is that each partner has an equal amount of leisure time.

A reader responds, "I thought my marriage was egalitarian because I helped out around the house. I never even thought about all the schedule making and mental notes my wife does. I'd come home and ask, 'What's for dinner?' Even though she is working full-time, I failed to recognize the inequality of such actions." This is a typical pattern, repeating what is familiar to us from our childhoods, which I would like you to look for in your family.

Other evidence of the husband's privileged status is that couples are much more likely to move to another city for his career than hers and marital satisfaction diminishes when the wife earns more than the husband, unless the husband has feminist beliefs. Stanford historian Carl Degler concludes, "Women's work in the main is still shaped around the family, while the family is still shaped around the work of men." This will continue as long as men earn more than women; even today the typical wife earns less than half what her husband earns. Techniques for equal division of family work are explained in the next chapter for dual-earner couples.

The most important points to apply

♦ Take an active role in looking for a partner; define what you would like and think about where you might meet such a person.

♦ Marry your best friend only after you check out your expectations and assumptions with each other and analyze your emotional and unconscious patterns.

♦ Do not take the marriage for granted or put it on the back burner. Structure in regular time for fun, for talking about your feelings, and for cuddling and sex.

♦ Consciously create "tingle" by leaving your house, going on weekend trips, exploring new places and adventures. Remind yourself that pair bonding is based on the shared memory of good times.

♦ Expect that a long-term relationship is like an ocean wave that ebbs and flows. There will be low periods but make a commitment to work through them, trusting that the wave will peak again.

♦ Consciously determine your values and priorities and then stick to them. Learn to say no, to delegate, to hire work done, or to trade services with other families. If your top commitment is to family, this may require giving up high earnings. What would you want written about you in your obituary; that you earned a lot of money and accumulated many possessions, or that you experienced love and grew in depth of character?

♦ Intimacy and role sharing both require learning how to negotiate, solving conflicts, actively listening, and using of "I feel" messages rather than blaming "You always" messages.

♦ The aim of all this work is growth which is exhilarating and much more interesting than numbing oneself with television, alcohol, cigarettes, other drugs, incessant work, and other ways to avoid facing our self-defeating habits.

♦ The society is unhealthy; it is workaholic, sexist, and racist. Speak up about the need for realistic changes and advocate solutions (see *Empowering Parents*).

SUGGESTED READINGS

Harville Hendrix. *Getting the Love You Want*. New York: Harper Perennial, 1990.

Robert Johnson. *Inner Worlds*. San Francisco: Harper, 1986.

Gayle Kimball. *50/50 Marriage*. (Equality Press, 42 Ranchita Way, Suite 4, Chico, Ca. 95928). *50/50 Parenting*. New York: Lexington, 1988, or from Equality Press.

Maggie Scaarf. *Intimate Partners*. New York: Ballentine, 1988.

180

ABOUT THE AUTHOR

G A Y L E   K I M B A L L, P H. D.

I'm the author of *50/50 Marriage, 50/50 Parenting, Empowering Parents,* and editor of *Women's Culture: The Women's Renaissance of the 70s.* I am a professor and the mother of thirteen-year-old Jed. I have produced videotapes on gender and family, including "Dual-Earner Families," "Parenting," and "Men's Changing Roles." I like to jog, dance, ski, backpack, travel, and would like to play more. I wish I had known the information in this chapter when I was 20, and look forward to hearing from you about how you build on these skills, and welcome your questions and comments. Write to me at CSUC, Chico, CA, 95929-420.

Questions to Discuss Before You Make a Lifetime Commitment to Marry

1. What do you like and dislike about your own parents' marriage?
   a. What ways are you similar to or unlike your parent of the other gender?
   b. What ways are you similar to or unlike your same sex parent?
2. Make a list of people to whom you have been very attracted; include some of the characteristics you like and dislike about each person.
3. What ways are you or your partner similar or different in:
   a. family background
   b. interests
   c. values

    d. religious beliefs

    e. sense of humor

    f. energy level

    g. attitude toward work

    h. biorhythms: sleep patterns, energy level, time spent alone, etc.

    i. desire for sexual frequency

    j. degree of emotional closeness desired

    k. intellectual interests

    l. political beliefs

    m. definition of fun

    o. other_____

4. List five qualities you like about:

    a. your partner

    b. yourself

5. What would you do if you were on a business trip in another city and met an extraordinarily attractive person who wanted to have a one-time sexual fling with you?

    a. How would you expect your partner to react in a similar situation?

    b. Would you discuss the event with your partner?

6. How would you like your partner to react to someone else's flirtatious behavior towards you?

    a. Do you plan to retain friends of the other gender and/ or go out with friends of the same gender?

7. What division of responsibility would you like in each of the areas listed below—use percentages:

    a. housework (including cooking, cleaning, and shopping).

    b. child care

    c. child discipline

    d. initiating affection

    e. initiating sex

    f. initiating conversations

    g. earning income

    h. financial planning

    i. care of the yard and car, and home repairs

    j. planning use of leisure time, social activities, and tasks such as sending greeting cards and buying gifts

    k. other_____

8. What percent of time and energy do you expect that you and your spouse will give to:
   a. career
   b. family
   c. personal interests
9. Do you want to have a baby?
   a. Why?
   b. When?
   c. How many?
   d. How will the child be cared for in its early years?
   e. Who will make child care arrangements?
10. If you both have an important meeting the same day your child comes down with the flu, who will stay home?
11. What do you think are the best methods for teaching children good behavior and setting limits?
12. Who will pay bills, budget money, determine how much to save and how to invest your earnings?
   a. Are you similar or different in how you think money should be spent and how much should be saved?
13. Whose career will be most important or will they be equally important?
   a. What would you do if each of you gets a desired job promotion to a different city?
   b. Will you expect your spouse to be involved in your work-related social activities?
   c. Who will take time off from work for children's activities?
14. How much time do you think is appropriate to spend with your own parents and your in-laws?
   a. With whom will you spend major holidays?
15. How neat and orderly a person are you?
   a. What roommate issues, like toothpaste being squeezed improperly or kitchen cleanliness, have caused you the most irritation?
   b. How have you resolved these conflicts with previous roommates?
16. What are tolerable amounts for you of consumption of alcohol, cigarettes, drugs, and junk food for yourself and for your partner?
17. Do you consider yourself an extrovert or an introvert?

    a. How much time do you like to spend by yourself and how much time do you like to spend with friends?

18. What causes conflict between you and your partner?
    a. How do you resolve your disagreements:
        1. One person usually gives in.
        2. One person usually initiates discussion.
        3. One person usually manipulates indirectly.
        4. Compromise.
        5. Other_____

19. How do you like to be appreciated, shown affection, and other expressions of love?
    a. How do you like to provide these expressions of love to your partner?
    b. Do you feel free to explain your feelings and needs to your partner? Why or why not?

20. Take the Temperament Quiz in *Please Understand Me* by David Keirsey and Marilyn Bates and compare your characteristics.

21. Is your partner one of your best friends?
    a. Do you spend a lot of time talking with each other?

22. What are your goals for your marriage?
    a. How would you define a successful marriage?
    b. What internal and external factors do you think will help or hinder you in growing toward these goals?
    c. In what ways have you grown in your relationship so far?

23. What other facets of a relationship are important to you that have not been mentioned on this list?
    Enjoy!

✪Next... The major strain facing marriages today is juggling work and family and finding the time to nurture the couple relationship. Survival techniques for dual earners are described in the next chapter, written by the author of three books on contemporary family issues.

"Trying to be superparent is unrealistic: I do the best I can with 24-hour days. I act on my priority of family as #1."

7

HOW TO SUCCEED IN A DUAL-EARNER FAMILY

GAYLE KIMBALL, PH.D.

Chapter Goals

This chapter defines the major issues faced by dual-career couples, how to cope and how to share family work. It provides time-savers to free up leisure time.

Why are families so stressed today?

A social revolution has occurred as evidenced by the fact that the majority of mothers of infants are employed. Yet the U.S. lags behind other industrial nations in its family support system. Most other industrial nations provide a national family policy, paid parental leave and extended periods of unpaid leave. In countries like France most three- and four-year-olds are in high quality preschools that are part of the educational system and therefore low cost to parents, and national health insurance is an old tradition.

The reasons the U.S. is so low on the family-friendly chart are that its national character rests on a fierce belief in rugged individualism and a suspicion of social solutions as anti-American, saddled with the still-strong nineteenth century belief that the family and child rearing are a feminine sphere. Since females are treated as inferiors, whatever is classified as feminine is devalued and considered soft and not worthy of much funding. Star Wars programs got more money than child care programs, for example, although our future as a nation depends on the quality of care and education our children are given.

Examples of the subordination of women are that women earn less than men even in the same professions; when women enter a formerly male profession, the pay drops; and the Year of the Woman in politics (1992) produced only six women in the Senate and 48 in the House of Representatives—although women are a majority of the population. Many women use subordinate speech and body language, as in not using declarative statements, adding tag questions, ("Don't you think so?"), allowing themselves to be interrupted and touched, and listening while men average two-thirds of the talking in mixed sex gatherings. The equation is family equals feminine equals soft. The outcome is shown by the national budget; in 1992 defense received almost a quarter of the spending compared to around 6 percent spent on children, although one in five children live below the poverty line.

What needs to happen to make the U.S. family friendly?

The elderly provide a model of effective lobbying. AARP (American Association of Retired Persons) is probably the single most powerful influence on Congress because members are highly organized, engage in letter writing campaigns, and vote. Parents Action is a fairly new national organization, still small and impoverished, struggling to organize parents in much the same way that the elderly are organized. You might want to join and receive the newsletter. (☞ Their address is B & O Building, 2 North Charles St., Baltimore, MD 21201.) We need to lobby for change in legislation, at the workplace, in schools, and in religious groups so they take active steps to practice what they preach about the importance of strengthening families. Models of family resource programs are provided in my *Empowering Parents*. This chapter suggests individual solutions for employed parents, and reminds us that these are band-aids. As long as we live in an inflexible society designed for "Father Knows Best" families, employed parents will experience unnecessary strain, fatigue, guilt, and self-blame.

What are the major issues I will face in a dual-earner family?

Here are typical couple issues to discuss with your partner, based on quotations from couples previously interviewed for *50/50 Marriage* and re-interviewed a decade later. What kind of advice would you give these couples? How would you handle these situations if they came up for you? And they probably will...

Workaholism: *(a female human resources consultant)*
He gets jealous of my obsession with work. He feels that I sacrifice attention to him for attention to work. He also feels that I sacrifice attention to him when I'm paying attention to my daughter.

Balancing two careers: *(a male psychologist)*
I don't think everyone can survive a dual career marriage. It takes an incredible amount of energy and achieve-

ment orientation. Even with all of that, you're going to pay a certain price for trying to have it all. You don't see each other as often as you would like. There's all the coordinating. In our marriage, there has always been a certain degree of tension because we've always been very independent. What holds us together is the support that we have for one another.

(a female in public relations)
When we got married we decided that one career would be the focal point because trying to have kids and two careers would be pretty much impossible. I've had this job almost 20 years; lots of promotions have come along, and I've turned every one of them down because they involved relocating or more hours. He's been jealous of what's been offered. I'd be surprised if they offered me anything else. I'm 42 and probably on the descending ramp now.

Her husband says, "I guess I'm still the man of the house, my job still has the edge."

Housework: *(a female health administrator)*
I said to my husband, "Either you do more or we've got to get someone else to do it. I can't cover this level of housework." He said, "Your level of housework is neurotic. Why should I deal with your neurosis?" I would get pissed off like crazy. He said, "Call someone." So, I lined up a cleaning woman who came in once a week.

(A manager whose husband used to do at least half of the family work: It changed when he went to work with five other professionals.)
They all had stay-at-home wives. When he mentioned some of the things that he did around the house, they were appalled. They talked about the things that their wives did for them. I think that had a tremendous influence. And as he got older, he just got lazier.

He says about her, She likes to stay busy at something. She will spend more time in the kitchen than necessary, just like I might spend more time in the yard than necessary just because it's an interest.

Parenting: *(a male attorney)*

Sarah's involvement with the children really cut out everything else in the world. She was always mad at me for not putting enough into the kids and I was mad at her for putting too much in. We spent a long time talking and accommodating. I did more, even though I thought it was unnecessary and she started doing less, even though she thought it was not right. We had some real bad blowouts. As the children got older, we grew back together.

Sex and Parenthood: *(a mother on leave)*

All of a sudden, I felt pawed over and grabbed at and sucked at all the time. The notion of someone else coming in with a physical need was enough to make me ill. He got tired of my hormones and my hysteria and this demanding baby. He was really not getting his at any level. When we talked about it, it got better.

(a female technician with 8- and 11-year-old sons)

It's still really great. It's never the same way twice. We both get a lot of joy out of it. We always come to each other wanting it, and wanting to enjoy each other, and having a good time with it. We both have a sense of humor about sex. It helps to take a weekend off and get away without the kids... We're both very pro-monogamy. We look, but that doesn't mean anything. It helps to realize that you can be sexually attracted to someone you're not married to and you don't have to act on it.

(a male factory superintendent, married 22 years)

The tingle is gone. The more familiar you get with one another and aging has a little to do with it. The stress, no time, it all eats at it a little bit. The man always wants sex more than the woman. We still love each other.

(a female social worker)

We had gone astray from each other, from being over-loaded and losing focus. He has a style of taking on too many projects. What brought it to a head was that I started to fall in love with somebody at work. I never did have an affair because I stopped it. We went to a counselor. Our goal is to scale down so that we have a slower pace in our lives and time to do things together. I felt that I had brought that up before, but he didn't hear it.

Effects of Dual-Earner Parents on their Children:
(a 14-year-old girl with dual career parents)
The kids that I know who have dual working parents seem a lot more independent and go out on their own and do stuff. I'm more of a take-charge and move-on kind of person.

Leisure Activities: *(a female health administrator)*
I married a guy who doesn't like to do anything I like to do! He likes sports, puzzles, word games, and television. I hate all of those. I like theater, museums, and reading. There is no way I'm going to go to a baseball game.
(a female salesperson)
Being an employed parent means giving up time for yourself, time alone, the time where you sit back, listen to the news, and read the newspaper. It was shocking to me after we spent a week in Hawaii for our tenth anniversary to realize that it had been seven years since we'd had more than a weekend away together. It was like wearing a beeper for years and we suddenly got to take it off. I never relaxed that deeply at home.

Power: *(male attorney)*
When people share a life, there's always a jockeying for control. When things go along really well, and you have a really good relationship without a lot of bumps in the road, maybe the big thing you fight over is doing the dishes. When it gets down to something that low, it means things are going pretty well.

In-Laws and Elder Care: *(male therapist whose family wanted him to move back to New York after his graduation, whereas his wife wanted to get away from their families)*
I felt angry because of the pressure I felt from Deborah. We really had different values. I guess I feel I capitulated to her. You can win the battle and lose the war. It drove a major wedge between us. We remain in a power struggle but stay in an alienated marriage because with both of us there is an underlying insecurity. Neither of us has a very high sense of self-worth. We got married too young, because she got

pregnant, and with three kids, we did not make the couple relationship primary.

(a male computer programmer)

My father is quadriplegic and my mother is alcoholic. We had to move them up near here, plus I'm managing fourteen people at work. So that really is quite stressful.

Money: *(female manager)*

We've never had "his" and "her" money. We always turn it all into the same pot and do joint decision making on financial expenditures. I've never made a big deal out of the fact that I have always made more money than my husband.

=================== **Personal Reflections** ===================

If you have a partner, you might both write your responses to these real-life experiences in your journals, then compare your viewpoints. Take each of the topics, respond to the quotes and state your position on workaholism, balancing two careers, division of family work, and so on.

Also discuss the following questions, two of the most problematic for dual-career couples. What if one of you gets an exciting promotion requiring a move across the country? (Some couples agree to alternate this kind of move; would you?) What would you do if each of you has an important day scheduled at work and you get the phone call telling you that your child is sick and needs to be picked up right away?

How can we cope with the strains of role juggling?

The main strain experienced by employed parents is feeling pressured to do our best as spouse, parent, and employee without adequate time and social support systems. Unrealistic media standards for the appearance of our homes and our bodies add to the strain. Draw a circle in your journal, dividing it into wedges according to how you spend your time. Then draw another circle, dividing the wedges into your most important values. Does your time allotment match your values? If not, brainstorm ideas about how to bring the two in line.

The following suggestions about how to cope were made by employed parents interviewed for *Empowering Parents*; their responses are grouped by gender.

Prioritize

Mothers have these suggestions: "I've decided what my priorities are and what has to be done versus what is optional." "Set realistic goals and eliminate the 'shoulds.' " "By setting small goals, making lists, and crossing items off, it gives me a feeling of accomplishment." "At work do not think about what has to be done at home and forget about work at home." " Reward yourself with a fun activity after getting work finished." "A mess is less important than one's sanity," says a Minneapolis woman.

Men suggest : keep work in perspective, make family as important as work, make schedules, do not overcommit your time, take issues one at a time, do the most important things first, and ask, "Is it really worth my time to be upset about this?" "Simplify life by living in a less expensive house and driving an older car so you can cut back on your work hours," an especially important point to consider.

Maintain Health

These parents recognize the value of exercise, eating low fat unprocessed food, and getting enough sleep. A father plays golf to "forget the day's events," and a mother jogs home from work in order to "feel vital and alive to be able to deal with my son."

Relax and Have Fun

Men mention making time for hobbies, playing a musical instrument, listening to music, getting a massage, playing games with family members, inexpensive trips, and playing pool in the basement. Women plan family activities and dates with their spouses, read, listen to relaxation tapes, do hobbies such as photography, take hot baths, and schedule lunches with friends. An Illinois mother says, "I treat myself well, get manicures, take naps on weekends, and plan to exercise more." Another mother tries to do something nice for herself every day.

Take Time For Yourself

Women suggest, "I insist on at least a few hours of time to myself each week, if only to go to the library to read or write letters." "Women need to get over feeling guilty about selfishness; women think it's not right if they don't give, give, give." "I treat myself to a sunset instead of keeping my hands in dishwater," says a British Columbia mother.

Share Family Work

Men advocate that each parent take turns with primary responsibility for their children and arranging child care trades with other parents. Women suggest assertively delegating housework and then praising children and husbands rather than being critical about their work. Lower your standards of home beauty and do not try to keep up with the Joneses so there is more time to play.

Cut Back On Work

A banker, a mother of two young children says, I changed my priorities; I left my high pressure position and overtime for a lower paying 40-hour-a-week job. I am not challenged at work and sometimes I long for the work status I had before, but I'm happier. I almost didn't have any children for fear that they would damage my career. Thank God my husband talked me into it. They are so much more rewarding than my career ever was.

Communicate

A husband says, "I let off steam by telling my wife the stuff that happened that day that really bugged me." Women advocate learning better skills by reading articles and books on marriage and parenting, or attending classes. They suggest setting aside specific time to spend with family members and turning off the television. Telephone calls should be screened with an answering machine. Some women vent their frustrations by screaming into a pillow or in the shower, something that men did not mention to doing.

Change Expectations

Women have to struggle to give up the traditional image of wife and mother learned from their own mothers and from the media. The perfectionist image is unrealistic and hazardous to women's health. Women realize that, "I'm not Ms. Corporate Business Person of the Year" and "Supermom doesn't exist or, if she does, she has a housekeeper." Like an addiction, they struggle with "getting over the Supermom Syndrome, trying to carry everyone else's load." *Newsweek* magazine recognizes that the Superwoman myth is "fading fast, doomed by anger, guilt, and exhaustion." The daughter of an employed mother predicts that future generations of women will not be burdened with the same load of guilt because she finds it easier than her friends to be a working mother and does not feel guilty.

A woman says, "My house is not always spotless, nor is my son. My hair, makeup, and clothes are not always in style or perfect. I don't always have my act together and sometimes I feel that I fail as a Supermom." She copes by telling herself, "I am me. I love my family, my job, and myself." When another mother catches herself visualizing some media image of perfection, she says, "I usually just laugh. No one made me God." Women suggest accepting the reality of less than perfect houses, career progress, romance, and children active in every sport, music lessons, and so on.

Develop a Positive Attitude

Humor helps some parents, and others are strengthened by their spiritual beliefs, prayer, or meditation. The women I surveyed are much more likely than the men to emphasize changing their attitudes, being thankful, and counting their blessings. They make comments like, "Even though our daily life is not as I envisioned it to be in my childhood dreams, it's something I cherish and I try to make the best of what we have." "I try to remember to have fun with whatever it is that I am doing, to not expect perfection." "I try to be satisfied with less than a spotless house and perfect teaching." "I get up thinking today will be a good day and I will survive." "I cope with the guilt by acknowledging that I literally would lose my mind if I became a stay-at-home mother." Studies reveal, however, that changing one's attitude is not as effective a coping technique as taking action, such as actually sharing family work equally.

Join a Working Parents' Group

Some women join working mothers' groups to learn that other mothers are going through the same difficulties in trying to give up being Supermom. One mother wishes she could be pen pals with other working mothers to learn how they are feeling because it "feels good to write down your frustrations." Men talk with friends, fellow workers, and some are in men's or fathers' groups that they find very supportive.

If we are both employed, how can we achieve equality in the division of family work?

When both spouses work, the typical pattern is that the wife does 70 to 80 percent of the family work, even when they profess a belief in equality and say their division of labor is fair. This is not much different than the 80/20 division typical in single-earner families. We continue what is familiar and seems natural—the woman being responsible for bread baking and the man responsible for bread winning. If you want to achieve equality, good intentions are not enough, especially when a baby arrives. Structure is required, as described in the following suggestions made by employed parents.

Ten Steps to Role Sharing

1. Institute equal division of work, responsibility, and leisure **from the beginning**; otherwise the partner who does less will feel like the rug is being pulled out when change is expected—usually with the arrival of a baby. Give parents you know a break and care for their toddler for a weekend to see how child care changes your life; then divide up family work equally in preparation for the demands of parenthood. You may think, "My child would not behave like that," but this is not realistic.

2. **Women must give up control** of the home, including imposing their standards and tastes. Men's main complaint is, "She doesn't like how I do the job, so why should I do it?" Women need to give as much praise as criticism. Men need to develop competency at home by taking on full responsibility for half the tasks. Women's main complaint is that men say they will help when asked, which assumes that the woman is the administrator and the responsible one. Being in charge is an energy-draining burden for women who are always thinking ahead, checking their lists, doing errands, planning, telephoning, and organizing. Discard the idea that the man is *helping* the woman around the house they share, as this implies he is doing her a favor by washing the dishes and toilets he uses.

A reader fears that if the woman gives up control, "the whole house will go to pot." Single fathers manage their households just fine; there is no gene for vacuuming or cleaning counters. Male interviewees for *50/50 Marriage* responded to logic and fairness. Some responded to the woman going on strike, not giving in to the waiting game, and refusing to rescue them by doing the man's agreed upon tasks. The couple should agree upon consequences for doing or not doing their share of the tasks. If a person cannot tolerate housework or cooking, then they might want to hire someone to do it for them. If something is very important to you, like a clean kitchen floor, then take that as your permanent job.

What matters is that each person has an equal amount of leisure time and that one person is not stuck with all the undesirable jobs like cleaning toilets. These kinds of jobs should be alternated. It is important to discuss the underlying power and control issues, the gender beliefs, the unfinished business with our own parents (for example, a man who feels his mother is controlling may resist doing his share of family work because he feels controlled in the process), and unspoken resentments which may get in the way of a rational division of family work.

3. **Use charts to allocate tasks,** which can be divided with points (i.e., three points for watering plants, ten points for cooking dinner) or rotated weekly. Make a list of all the jobs involved in maintaining your home, then post it on the refrigerator for a week to add jobs as they occur to you. Include social and administrative tasks (such as planning get-togethers, doing correspondence, errands, and making lists of things to be done). Include traditional male jobs such as repairs, financial planning, and yard and car work. Charts can remove the chore of being the taskmaster from the woman, who fears being a "nag" or "bitch," and therefore does the work herself. This fear is a major reason for inequality in the home.

Keep a time diary for a typical week. If one person has more leisure time, reassign chores so that leisure is equitable. The person with less time at his/her disposal is playing a subordinate role. Factual evidence of unfair division of labor is essential, since most people tend to think they work harder than other family members.

4. **Attach consequences** to doing tasks. A job that is important to everyone, such as cooking dinner, may be given regularly to a person who resists doing housework. The weight of disapproval from hungry people will be heavier than from people who dislike dirty floors. A common tactic to get out of a job is to delay, do it poorly, or say, "You do it better." Do not rescue the delayer or feel flattered by praise. (This is an old strategy to keep women in their place. In the nineteenth century women were put on a pedestal as a way to keep them from competing at work or in politics; women were told they were so angelically pure that smoke-filled rooms would devastate their delicate childlike natures.) If logic and charts fail, the person doing more work may have to go on strike and not give in to a waiting game where one person knows the other will jump in due to less tolerance for an uncompleted task.

5. Because child care is the most powerful influence pushing

couples back to traditional roles, **parenting must be shared from the baby's first day**. Recognition should be given to the fact that caring for a young child is more demanding than most paid work and that it is amazingly impossible to accomplish much with a baby in the household. Spending **time alone with a child** is imperative to developing a sense of expertise and confidence. Tasks should be structured, such as alternately putting children to bed or chauffeuring them. If this kind of plan is not made, parents will likely revert to the familiar and "natural" unequal division of labor practiced by friends and family.

6. **Learn a broad range of skills.** Take a class in cooking or auto repair. Women need to develop competency in dealing with repairs, cars, finances, and other areas regarded as masculine—although these tasks do not consume much time on a daily basis. Men need to develop parenting knowledge by reading, talking with other fathers, and spending time caring for their children. Pleading lack of skill is an unacceptable ploy to get out of family work, most of which is easy to learn. Studies show that women tend to do the more menial jobs, like changing diapers, while men do more fun tasks, like playing with children.

7. **Establish family as priority over work**. This means saying no to overtime work, and perhaps to job transfers and promotions. Role sharers value family above work, which is not easy to carry out in a workaholic culture. Recognize that giving lip service to valuing children and families is hypocritical in a country where millions of children are without adult care in the afternoons, and millions more youth are dropouts and functionally illiterate. Every parent will tell you that children grow up quickly; plan to slow down your career path when your children are preschoolers.

8. **Lobby** with employers, schools, hospitals and government on all levels to provide the kinds of support needed by contemporary families, such as flexible work hours, quality preschools, after-school care, parent education classes, and family-support legislation.

9. **Join together with other role-sharers** to provide emotional support and time-saving services for each other, such as pot-luck dinners, work bees, and child care exchanges.

10. Gain perspective and **learn useful techniques** by reading, attending workshops, starting a support group, going to a therapist, etc. since we have few models of egalitarian relationships.

How can I save time doing family work?

Cooking

Prepare casseroles, a turkey, lunch sandwiches, etc., on the weekend. Freeze dinner portions and microwave them during the work week. Use a crock pot to start a main dish in the morning. Change standards to preparing a big family meal just on Sundays, with other meals consisting of soup and salad or quick meals such as tostadas, fried tofu, Chinese stir fry, and vegetables and rice. A *Glamour* magazine survey shows that few Americans are sitting down to traditional meals; less than 15 percent of meals are cooked in conventional ovens, and about one-fourth of our meals consist of frozen dinners and fast food purchases. ☛ Quick gourmet recipes provided by Joan Jackson are listed at the end of this chapter.

Laundry

Provide each family member with three clothes baskets in their closets—for darks, whites, and delicates. Each person should have her or his own basket for clean clothes and put them away. Even very young children can do these chores. Children should get their clothes for the next day picked out in the evening and be responsible for identifying their clothes that need to be mended.

Housecleaning

A messy house seems overwhelming, so tackle it bit by bit: Clean one room Monday, do the laundry on Tuesday, and so on. Establish a firm rule that when through with an object it is put away before moving on to another activity, or else it is confiscated to be redeemed with a chore. Pay a teenager in the neighborhood for household help. Use Ziploc bags to keep puzzles and other small items belonging to children in one place. Evaluate whether cleaning needs to be done the way you think it should; for example, do children's sheets need to be washed every week? Close the door on children's rooms. Lower your standards. A mother explains, "I do my cleaning faster and less completely to steal enough time to do what I really want to do."

Distinguish between what must be done and what should be done

My homemaker mother, for example, made beautiful Halloween costumes for me. I assumed that I should make my son's costumes if I was a good mother and spent many hours at the sewing machine. It took me years to realize that he preferred an inexpensive, purchased costume. My mother also made birthday cakes from scratch and presented them as a surprise. My son helps make his cake from a mix but is just as excited on his birthday as I was. Expectations from our childhoods need to be examined and perhaps discarded.

Do Two Things at Once

For instance, try folding clothes with children, or talking on the telephone while cleaning out a drawer (See Chapter 1 for time management techniques).

What should we know about combining a baby and two careers?

I asked parents to offer suggestions for young couples, based on hindsight. "Having a baby is a whole other ball game," a father says. Parents tell couples who are thinking about having a baby to realize that their **life will change greatly.** Spontaneity will vanish: "It's much harder than you think" and "It won't be what you expect." They suggest talking to experienced parents and babysitting for a young child for a week. Reading books on parenting is useful, but even with that research, "Nothing can prepare you mentally and physically for the changes in your life brought on by a baby," explains the father of three children.

New parents must be willing to give up their free time. They should think seriously about why they want a baby. If it is because other people expect them to or because they hope it will save a shaky marriage, they should not have a baby. Nor should they have children if their top priority is work. "You will have to give more of yourself than you have ever given before," parents say, especially because being a parent, spouse, and worker can be full-time jobs. Be prepared to **put your career development on hold** during the child's early years.

Parents advise thorough **discussion of expectations** of each other before making the decision to get pregnant. This discussion should include specific issues such as who will change diapers late at night, how parents' work hours will change, and who will take the baby to appointments and to child care. Some suggest that it is useful to involve a neutral third person, such as a counselor, in these discussions of goals and expectations. A carpenter with a 5-year-old suggests, however,

"Don't be attached to your expectations. Strive to make your dreams real but if it all blows up, and it probably will, do your grieving, but don't stop dreaming. I like to think of it as God's way of perfecting us, purifying our spirits. Change is the only constant."

In terms of the marriage, parents feel strongly that couples should **delay parenthood** until they know each other well and have had time to have fun together. Some women advise not having a baby until both parents are committed to spending equal amounts of time caring for the baby. "Wait at least a few years or you are asking for disaster," states one father. The first year of infancy is so difficult a transition, if only because of the sleep deprivation, that the couple needs a reservoir of happy times together. "Parenthood is not the Donna Reed show," a mother explains.

Both mothers and fathers suggest waiting until education is completed, and careers and a financial base are established. Ideally a house is purchased before the birth, as children are expensive. Many suggest saving enough money so that one or both parents can work part-time during the infancy period or one parent can stay at home with the baby full-time for at least six months. "You will not want to leave the baby," mothers predict. The mother of a 17-month-old toddler relates, "It absolutely wrenches your heart to leave your baby. Today was the first day when my baby didn't cry when I left her." A reader reminds us that young children often do cry at separation from their parents—but not for long. A divorced mother advises women to "keep working because of the high divorce rate and kids don't need you 24 hours a day."

Once a baby is added to the family, parents advocate building in time to **talk and have fun** with each other. "Happy parents make happy children," most say. "Share hobbies, sports, cooking, and other activities," recommends a father. The key to a successful marriage is "talking about everything," including child-rearing policies. "Beware of shoving problems aside and letting them become monsters," warns a father.

In California, Laurel relates, "It's hard to believe but one of the biggest arguments after that first year of unrecognized communication breakdown after Whitney was born was literally about taking out the garbage!" A father suggests going to a counselor several times a year as maintenance, just as one periodically tunes up a car.

Child care should be researched during the pregnancy because affordable infant care with the proper low staff-to-child ratio is hard to find. Visit at unexpected hours to observe the child care setting. Find out about cooperative parent babysitting organizations, where no money changes hands. Research what employers offer in the way of health benefits, child care, and parental leave; be prepared to argue with your employer, advises one mother. Try to obtain flexible work hours or a part-time job. Another mother suggests lobbying with government officials for changes like paid parental leave.

In terms of **priorities**, parents advocate looking at children as "gifts and challenges, not burdens." They are struck by how quickly children grow up and how important it is to spend time with them while they are little, before they turn to their friends as the most interesting people in their lives and then leave home. Women suggest hiring household help, such as a student. Parents tell us not to put children second to work. Children should come first, because they are dependent on their parents. We give children material things rather than ourselves, the mother of teenagers believes. She sees "gourmet" children indulged rather than spending time with their parents. We should distinguish wants created by the media from actual needs. Although parenting is difficult, "it is worth it," parents conclude, when "a smile from your child warms your heart, and makes you forget about your hard day at the office."

If you are not a parent, write in your journal how you think having a baby would change your life and what changes you would need to make to enhance this new love relationship. You cannot expect your life to be the same with just the baby added like frosting to a cake. The cake, too, will change.

How can fathers be encouraged to parent equally?

Studies confirm that children gain social, academic, and emotional skills such as empathy, when they have involved fathers. Children need contact with their fathers as much as they need their mothers. Babies light up when dad enters the room, because they know they will have more lively play than with comforting mom. Write in your journal how you feel about the fathering you received and what you would like your children to experience with their father. The young men I survey are usually very intent on being hands-on dads who get children ready in the morning, drive them to their activities, and help them with their homework. It looks like the twenty-something generation strongly values involved parenting by both men and women. Here are specific steps fathers can take:

1. Regularly **get up with your new baby** at night and burp her and change her diapers. You will bond with your child by spending this time with her. If your child calls for both parents when he wakes up at night or gets hurt, you will know you are doing 50/50 parenting.

2. Spend regular **time alone** with your child.

3. Remind your wife that she must give up the gratification of being the child-rearing expert; **she should not impose her standards** when you are "on" with the child.

4. **Become an expert** on child rearing; read books and magazines about parenting skills and take classes for fathers. Do not turn to your mate as the expert; she probably hasn't had a lot of experience with babies either.

5. Develop **men's support groups** with acquaintances who have children of similar ages to discuss issues of concern, compare experiences, get new ideas, and compare men's and women's styles of parenting.

6. Take time to talk with the child, such as by **alternating** the bedtime **routines** with your spouse or by driving the child to activities. Reduce television viewing.

7. Plan weekly times for **fun activities** with the child.

8. **Look critically at the amount of time taken up by work** and decide if this matches your values and priorities. If not, take a stand and cut back.

9. **Talk with your own father** about his hindsight on parenting.

10. **Press for social supports for involved fathers**, such as flexible work hours and slowed down promotion timetables.

An example of a workplace with wonderful support programs is the Los Angeles Department of Water and Power. Some of the benefits for male employees include: access to beepers when a baby's delivery date is near; birth and lactation classes to help them coach their mates during and after childbirth; four months' unpaid paternity leave; a fathers' section in the family resource library and in the quarterly newsletter "Parents at Work"; various parenting workshops; a monthly fathers' group, and a special celebration of Father's Day such as a lobby display where viewers try to match photographs of fathers with their children.

"Staff pound into us that DWP Dads are making a difference," George Fogelson reports. Fathers tell me that the knowledge gained in workplace parenting programs led them to be more involved dads than they might have been with less information to apply at home. As the child-rearing expert, they couldn't sit back and read the paper.

The most important points to apply.

♦ Clearly define your values and periodically check to see if you are holding true to them in your daily life.

♦ Good intentions are not enough. Structure in involvement with children, such as alternating the bedtime ritual.

♦ Time is your most precious resource. Save it for your family by hiring, delegating, and sharing work; lowering perfectionist standards; and slowing down career progress when your children are young. Mark fun activities on your calendar so that regular time is saved for family bonding.

♦ Lobby for family support programs at work, in schools, in community groups, and in legislation.

SUGGESTED READINGS

Rebecca Sager Ashery and Michele Margolin Basen. *Guide for Parents with Careers: Ideas on How to Cope.* Washington, D.C.: Acropolis Books, 1988.

Beverly Treuille Benz and Susan Schiffer Stautberg. *Managing It All: Time-Saving Ideas for Career, Family, Relationships & Self.* New York: MasterMedia Limited, 1988.

T. Berry Brazelton. *Working and Caring.* Reading, MA: Addison-Wesley, 1987.

John Fernandez. *The Politics and Reality of Family Care in Corporate America.* New York: Lexington Books, 1990.

204

Lucia Albino Gilbert. *Two Careers/One Family.* Newbury Park, CA: Sage, 1993.

Gayle Kimball. *50/50 Marriage* and *50/50 Parenting* Chico, CA: Equality Press (see last page of this book.)

ABOUTTHE AUTHOR

G A Y L E   K I M B A L L, P H. D.

I'm the author of *50/50 Marriage, 50/50 Parenting, Empowering Parents,* and editor of *Women's Culture: The Women's Renaissance of the 70s.* I am a professor and the mother of 13-year-old Jed. I have produced videotapes on gender and family, including "Dual-Earner Families," "Parenting," and "Men's Changing Roles." I like to jog, dance, ski, backpack, travel, and would like to play more. I wish I had known the information in this chapter when I was 20, and look forward to hearing from you about how you build on these skills, and welcome your questions and comments. Write to me at CSUC, Chico, CA, 95929-420.

The Basics for Cooking Quick Gourmet Meals

Joan Jackson is a newspaper food columnist, instructor, and gourmet chef.

A quick meal does not necessarily mean a meal filled with prepared, store-bought foods. These foods contain a higher amount of sugars, salts, and fats than their homemade equivalent, and we must pay the high price of preparation and packaging. It is very satisfying to know that the pantry and freezer are each stocked with home-prepared foods just waiting for final assembly or heating.

Cooking Tips

1. Maintain a pantry of little jars of **condiments** to aid in the assembly of a variety of quick, savory dishes. For example, have basil pesto, cilantro pesto, chutney, olives, salsas, mustards (spicy brown, sweet hot, and Dijon style), Hoisin sauce (a tangy Asian sauce found in most supermarkets) and soy sauce, and an assortment of vinegars, including balsamic, rice vinegar, and both red and white wine vinegars. Also, bottled capers and marinated artichoke hearts will keep for months, and will add the kick needed in many a meal.

2. When cooking **rice**, prepare at least twice as much as needed, then freeze the remainder in meal-sized portions in freezer bags, labeled and dated. Try to keep an inventory of several types of rice including Basmati, Wehani (available in most health food stores), or another robust brown rice, and pearl grain white. Rice will reheat in a microwave, in the oven, or on the stovetop. Try reheating some rice in a casserole dish in the oven with ingredients such as cooked bits of poultry, artichoke hearts, and canned whole tomatoes. Try frozen rice thawed and tossed with Italian salad dressing and crunchy vegetables as a salad.

3. A **well-stocked pantry** should contain bottles of extra virgin olive oil, plain vegetable oil, pure olive oil, peanut oil, sesame oil, and a flavored olive oil—which can be made by infusing the oil with herbs, garlic cloves, or sun dried tomatoes. Invest in an assortment of herbs including oregano, basil, bay leaves, dill, tarragon, mint, and cilantro (coriander). You may be able to grow some of these in your own herb garden. Also, have small stocks of the following spices: cinnamon, cloves, nutmeg, cumin, garlic powder, several different curry blends, and both fresh and dried ginger.

4. Keep packages of **pasta** of different shapes on hand for quick hot or cold dishes; keep fusilli for salads, linguini or penne for hot meals, and small shapes like elbow macaroni or orzo to add to a soup to make it into a full meal. When preparing pasta, prepare extra portions and freeze or refrigerate the leftovers. Leftover spaghetti, unseasoned, can be added to beaten eggs and vegetables to make a quick frittata. Cooked pastas are quick to reheat in a microwave, covered, or on the stovetop in a covered pot with the addition of a few tablespoonfuls of water to keep the bottom from sticking. Leftover pastas can expand on otherwise plain meals.

5. Soak **beans** in water to cover and store in the refrigerator several hours or all day, then drain off the soaking water, rinse, add enough water to cover the beans again, and bring the beans to a boil. Boil hard for 5 minutes, then reduce the heat to low and cover. Cook for a few hours, without salt or seasonings, until tender. This can take as little as 40 minutes for some beans such as small limas, or up to 3 hours for large red kidney beans. Always cook extra beans and leave some unseasoned. When tender, drain and rinse some of the beans for a bean salad, and season the remainder to taste. Bean salads can be quickly assembled from cooked beans, or in a pinch from canned beans, with a few simple additions.

6. Save the **cooking water** from simmered meats and poultry and fresh vegetables, with the exception of broccoli, cauliflower, sprouts and cabbage, which may be too strong tasting. Freeze in ice cube trays, then label and store. These cubes of flavored ice will assist in building the flavors in a dish, whether in gravy, as part of the liquid in cooking rice or pasta, or to create an assortment of quick soups. Add to these any of the stored cooked beans, pasta or rice, add a few chopped vegetables, and season with herbs, salsa, pesto, or chutney to taste and the basic soup is made.

7. With **leftover vegetables**, pour enough Italian salad dressing over them to just wet all the pieces, and store in a tightly sealed jar in the refrigerator. The vegetables can be eaten as a side dish or appetizer for another meal and will be delicious from marinating in the dressing. Or, add the leftover vegetables to soups, casseroles, and stews in the last few minutes of cooking, just long enough to heat them through.

8. **Leftover meats**:
* Use them chopped finely and mixed with mayonnaise or dressing as a sandwich filling.
* Combine them with salsa and cheese and use to fill tortillas. Heat and serve hot or cold.
* Mix the meats with egg and bread crumbs, capers and chopped celery, and form into patties. Coat with crumbs and fry in a non-saturated oil. Serve hot with raw fruits and marinated leftover vegetables.
* Stir them into a pasta sauce and serve hot, over pasta.

With any of the above ideas, it is possible to create a delicious and healthy meal in a few minutes. These ideas imply an input time of several hours a month in the organization and preparation of some of these labor-saving ideas. Timing is also important: When cilantro is cheap in the markets, make lots of pesto, then freeze it flat in zip top bags. By freezing flat, it is possible to break off chunks to add to sauces and soups, or for seasoning meats. When basil is inexpensive, either prepare pesto or put it unseasoned in the blender and then freeze the purée to be seasoned into pesto at a later time. Pesto is comprised of pine nuts, olive oil, either basil or cilantro, and parmesan cheese.

Examples of Quick Gourmet Recipes

Fried Rice—combine the following ingredients:

1-1/2 c. leftover cooked rice	2 Tbsp. celery, finely chopped
2 Tbsp. peanut or vegetable oil	1 Tbsp. soy sauce, or to taste
1/4 c. fresh or frozen peas	1 egg
1/4 c. green onions, chopped	
1/4 c. toasted peanuts, slivered almonds, or cashews	

Basil or Cilantro Pesto

4 c. fresh basil or cilantro leaves	1/2 c. olive oil
1 or 2 peeled garlic cloves	1/4 c. pine nuts
1/2 c. freshly grated parmesan cheese	

Put the leaves of the basil or cilantro in a blender or food processor. Reserve the stems for flavoring soups. Add the oil and garlic to the leaves and process until the pesto begins to look like mashed leaves. Add the pine nuts and parmesan and blend until the pesto looks fairly smooth. Store the pesto in zip top bags, pressed as thin as possible and flat, so it will be easy to break off a chunk for flavoring different dishes. Pesto will keep in the freezer for several months. Use to flavor pizza, soups, pasta, fish, and poultry.

Pasta Al Pesto

1 pkg. linguini, fettucini, or spaghetti

1 Tbsp. olive oil	2 Tbsp. salt
1 Tbsp. butter	4 Tbsp. basil pesto (see above)

Cook pasta according to package directions, using the salt and olive oil in the water to season the pasta. When cooked to taste, drain and toss with the butter until the pasta glistens. Add the pesto and toss to blend. Serve with grated parmesan cheese. This can be stored in the refrigerator for up to 4 days and reheated.

Chicken Breasts in Pesto
1 or 2 boneless, skinless chicken breasts per person
1 Tbsp. basil or cilantro pesto per person
1 Tbsp. olive oil per person (not per chicken piece)
Heat the olive oil in a sauté pan over medium heat. Add the chicken breast pieces and sauté a few minutes until one side of the chicken develops some golden bits. Turn and sauté the other side a few minutes until the chicken is just pink and firm. Add the pesto to the pan and stir the chicken pieces well into the pesto and butter mixture. Cover and cook a few minutes longer until the chicken is done to taste. Remove from pan, add a few tablespoons of water, turn up the heat and stir the bits of chicken and pesto into a sauce. Serve the sauce over the chicken pieces.

Bean Salad
2 c. cooked beans, several varieties of different colors—black beans, white beans, garbanzos, kidney beans, etc., drained
1 c. fresh green or yellow wax beans, steamed until tender-crisp
1/4 c. finely diced celery   1/4 c. finely diced carrot
1/3 c. thinly sliced red onions   1/2 c. Italian salad dressing
Combine the beans in a serving bowl. Add the diced raw vegetables and steamed fresh beans and toss to combine. Add the salad dressing and mix well. Best if left to marinate for several hours or overnight. You may replace bottled dressing with: 4 Tbsp. olive oil, 2 Tbsp. red wine vinegar, 1 tsp. sugar, 1 Tbsp. parmesan cheese, 1/4 tsp. dried oregano, 1/8 tsp. pepper, 1/4 tsp. toasted sesame oil. Shake well and pour over the beans.

Black Beans, Yogurt, Rice, and Salsa
2 c. cooked, white long grain rice
                    2 c. cooked black beans
1 c. nonfat yogurt, drained   2 Tbsp. fresh cilantro, chopped
1 c. fresh tomato salsa, purchased in refrigerated case in market
From your ready freezer stock of cooked rice and cooked beans, select the varieties listed in the recipe and reheat in the microwave or on the stovetop. Drain the whey from thick plain

yogurt and keep it chilled. The contrast between the cold yogurt, the hot temperature of the beans and rice, and the spicy heat of the salsa is what makes this work. Put the salsa in the center of individual serving plates and arrange the beans, rice, and yogurt in a triangle around it, overlapping the edges slightly. Be generous with the salsa. Sprinkle the cilantro over all. Serve with wedges of lime, olive oil, and freshly ground pepper for individual embellishment.

Chinese Cabbage Salad
3 green onions, chopped, white part and some of the green
1 pkg. "ramen" noodles   1/3 c. butter
1/3 c. slivered almonds   1/2 c. vegetable oil
1/2 small head of green cabbage, shredded

Dressing: 1/3 c. sugar   1/2 c. vegetable oil
1/3 c. rice vinegar   1 tsp. toasted sesame oil
1 Tbsp. soy sauce

Break the ramen noodles into small clumps and reserve the flavoring package for another use. Sauté the ramen noodles and almond slivers in the butter until a toasty brown. Reserve until just before serving. This can be done several hours in advance. Make the dressing by mixing together all the ingredients in a screw top jar. Shake well to dissolve the sugar. This can be prepared ahead too, then stored in the refrigerator for several days. Just before serving, top the crunchy cabbage and onion pieces with the noodles and nuts, pour the desired amount of dressing over and toss. Serve immediately. This can be prefabricated by keeping a supply of shredded cabbage in a zip top bag, some chopped green onions in another bag, the toasted nuts and noodles in another, and the dressing ready to add to a delicious and different salad.

Greek Pilaf
3/4 c. orzo or broken lengths of spaghetti (1 inch maximum)
3/4 c. long grain white rice, raw
2 Tbsp. olive oil
1/2 c. finely chopped green onion
3 c. vegetable or chicken stock, heated to boiling
1/2 pound seafood from the following: scallops, oysters, mussels, or cubed firm-flesh fish such as salmon or halibut.
Heat the oil in a large frying pan with a lid. Add the orzo and

chopped green onion and stir, then cook until the pasta is golden brown and the onions are wilted. Add the rice, stir and add another tablespoon or two of olive oil if needed, then cook over medium heat until the rice gets a bright white appearance, and no longer looks translucent. Add the boiling stock and stir. Cover, reduce the heat to low, and cook for 15 minutes. Add the seafood, stir to incorporate into the rice, then cover and cook 5 minutes longer. Fluff with a fork and serve. It may be cooked without seafood and used as a side dish.

Grilled Gruyère and Kalamata Sandwich
per person—2 slices French style bread
thin slices Gruyère cheese   4 pitted Kalamata olives
olive oil   mayonnaise
scant 1/8 tsp. minced garlic
3 slices of sun dried tomatoes, rehydrated in boiling water 1/2 hour

Heat a frying pan (ideally cast iron) on medium heat for 5 minutes. Lightly brush both pieces of bread with olive oil, one side only. Combine the garlic with a few tablespoonfuls of mayonnaise, spread over the un-oiled side of each piece of bread. Place cheese slices on one piece of bread, top with tomato pieces and slivers of olives. Top with the remaining piece of bread. Put the sandwich into the heated frying pan and grill on both sides until the bread is golden and the cheese is melted. Serve hot with a salad

This brief culinary journey will start you on your way to cooking delicious and nutritious meals for yourself and your friends. When you want to splurge on desserts and want to make them yourself, watch for my future book of desserts. In the meantime, enjoy what you cook!

✪Next... Studies reveal that the most taxing role is parenting. Many parents report that it is their most rewarding role. Contemporary parenting issues are the topic of the next chapter, written by a professor of child development who has a therapy practice and is the mother of two young adults.

"Babies arrive without directions or guarantees. Raising them undoubtedly presents the greatest challenge we will ever face. However, we can thrive in our parenting roles and derive tremendous pleasure from the process, benefiting both our children and the world."

8

HOW TO BE A SUCCESSFUL PARENT

BARBARA POLLAND, PH.D.

212

Most of us are not given education about how to be an effective parent. This chapter provides information about common concerns, including coping with a new baby, selecting good child care, discipline, non-sexist child rearing, and fun family activities.

My partner and I are thinking about getting married and we both want to have children someday. We know we should talk about our ideas on raising children now, to minimize conflicts later. What are some of the topics we should discuss?

Begin by discussing material that is readily available; each of you has memories of your own childhood and what you liked and didn't like about how you were raised. Share those reflections with each other. You can learn a lot about each other through this process. Once you have a child you'll see how we automatically begin repeating what our parents did with us. You can help each other to change unwanted behavior and to implement the behaviors you liked about your own parents.

Create a list of what each of you considers really important in child rearing, then prioritize the list on your own and compare notes. One of the goals might be wanting children to have positive self-esteem. If that's a goal you both agree on, then talk about how you will work on it. Nagging, criticizing, and constantly saying no is not how children learn to feel good about themselves. Read and discuss books with each other, such as ☛ Briggs' *Your Child's Self-Esteem* and Polland's *Guideposts*.

If you both value creativity you might begin a notebook of creative child-rearing ideas. You'll be amazed at how quickly the pages will fill up if you keep your eyes and ears open. Television, newspapers, magazines, books, workshops, observing parents and children, and visiting schools are a few ways to gather ideas.

=========== **Personal Reflections** ===========

1. Make a list of what you most liked and disliked about the way you were raised by your parents.

2. How would you be different if you had been raised as the other gender? How would you feel if you were a parent to all girls or all boys?

3. What kind of child were you? What parts of your child-self have you retained as an adult?

4. Do you really want to have a child(ren)? Why or why not?

5. Define your child-rearing values; that is, what is really important to you about bringing up a child?

6. How do you plan to balance careers and parenting with your partner?

When is the right time to have children?

This is a matter of individual choice. The important issue is planning together so that pregnancy isn't an unwanted surprise. Having a wanted, planned-for child is a magnificent experience. Children deserve this kind of beginning. The ages of the partners, the woman's biological time clock, school and career aspirations, and the family's financial picture all make a difference. Some people love being young parents, while some people feel that a successful career will give them a better feeling of self-worth and they'll feel more capable as parents.

How will having a baby change my life?

One of the first things that usually hits in the first months of having a child is the overwhelming responsibility. A baby requires around-the-clock parenting. There's no how-to guide for your baby. You can have all the child care knowledge and ideas in the world, but your baby is her own unique self. Your life will change DRAMATICALLY! Having a baby is the most challenging new beginning for anyone, anywhere, and raising a child is a lifetime commitment.

Focus on getting acquainted with your baby and discovering how to meet your little one's needs. A new baby provides precious moments and you will want to be rested and ready to really enjoy him. Put a sign up in a few different places that states, "Our house is clean enough to be healthy and dirty enough to be happy." Nap when your baby rests: The phone and the cleaning can wait until later. It is important to think about how you can keep your priorities straight. You can limit visitors to one room that you keep very clean and give up on the rest of your place or meet them away from home so no one has to worry about how their house looks. Go for a walk together or to a park: Fresh air is wonderful for babies and good adult conversation is great for the parents.

Because the first months with your new baby can be sleep-deprived, read about the first year of life during your pregnancy rather than just focusing on the birth which is over in a day.

We disagree about how long a mother should stay at home with a baby. Is it silly to discuss this before we are even married?

When you identify issues that could create serious problems later on, it is never silly to try and resolve them. Discussing these sensitive topics can help you to know each other in meaningful ways. The truth is any decisions you make before having children cannot be carved in stone. Some of the most devout career men and women find themselves wanting to stay at home after a baby arrives. They don't want to miss any part of their child's life and people who thought they wanted to be at home full-time might change their mind, as discussed in ☞ Kathleen Gerson's *Hard Choices* (University of California Press). Some parents find ways to minimize work hours in order to maximize family time. However, many parents today do not have a choice about working because of the high costs of housing and other expenses. Over half the mothers of infants are employed.

If both of you need to work, there are a number of child care alternatives like baby-sitters, neighbors, home care providers, and child care center settings. Talk with other couples who have successfully dealt with this issue. During your pregnancy, find out what is available in your neighborhood. See if there is a child care resource referral agency near you which provides information about how to choose good child care. Some employers provide this referral service to their employees (e.g., IBM and AT&T). Discuss what you can afford and how you feel about taking a baby to another setting or keeping the baby at home with a baby-sitter. Having a plan ahead of time can help smooth the way.

How can I select good child care?

Parents who already have children in child care are a terrific resource. Ask them what they like about their program and what they would like to change. Find out if they are learning about parenting from the staff. Spend time in the setting. Talk to other parents in the community who selected other programs and ask them why. Encourage them to tell you anything negative they have heard about the care you are considering. It is worth every minute of time it takes to carefully research where to send your child.

How to Select Child Care

♦ **Family needs**: half-day or full-day, travel distance, cost (tuition and additional, incidental fees)

♦ **Your child's needs**: An introvert may not flourish in a large center and an older child may be bored in a small home care without a curriculum.

♦ **Philosophy** goals and objectives

♦ **References**: Are providers really doing what they profess? What do other parents and professionals say and what is their community reputation?

♦ **Safety**: enough adult supervision, equipment in good condition, rules the children understand, emergency plans, first aid kit

♦ **Health**: cleanliness of the staff and the facility, teachers wash hands frequently. Sick children are immediately isolated and sent home.

♦ **Ratio** of teachers to students: enough to meet the needs of each child

♦ **Qualifications** of staff: degrees, licenses, certificates, credentials, years of experience, and training in child development

♦ **Teacher turnover**: Stability is crucial. Much of the high turnover is caused by low wages for child care providers.

♦ **Personality** of staff members: self-confident or anxious, friendly or withdrawn, enthusiastic or passive

♦ **Student population**: ages, backgrounds. Your child can learn from interaction with both older and younger children. Do the children seem to cooperate with each other?

♦ **Social and emotional environment**: cooperative interactions, happy children, enthusiastic adults. Staff is appropriately affectionate with the children and the staff values the positive self-esteem of children. Ask staff what they do to help children feel capable.

♦ **Discipline**: What is their approach? Spanking is never acceptable. What are the rules and do children participate in formulating them?

♦ **Intellectual environment**: exciting, challenging materials; a curriculum that is child-centered rather than teacher-focused, plenty of time for unstructured learning. What is a typical daily schedule? Is this rigid or can children continue with a project if they wish?

♦ **Stress level**: Do the children and teachers seem relaxed or pressured? Is there academic pressure (for example, pressure to learn numbers and letters) which is inappropriate for young children?

♦ **Nutrition**: What kinds of snacks are available? What food rules does the school have? Sugary, salty, and fatty processed foods should not be regularly available.

♦ Indoor and outdoor school **environment**: Is there enough space, quality, and quantity of play equipment?

♦ **Creativity**: Is there music, movement, art, science? Can children dictate stories for staff to write and children to illustrate? Check for walls/bulletin boards and evidence of children's creativity or inappropriate teacher cutouts. Does all the art work look the same or is it the unique work of each child?

♦ **Field trips**: how often and where? (Do not sign a blanket field trip permission slip that covers all future trips.)

♦ **Assessment**: what kind of records do teachers keep on the growth and development of each child? Do they have a developmental program plan?

♦ **Parent involvement**: What is the policy on how parents and children should separate at the beginning of the day? Are drop-in visits allowed? Can you have lunch with your child? Are there brown bag parent meetings or evening gatherings to learn more about the program and about child rearing? Is there a home/school partnership or do they want the parents out of the way? Are parents invited and encouraged to share their expertise with all of the children?

What can we do to help our young children enter a child care setting?

There are many steps parents can take to help their little ones feel comfortable in a child care setting.

♦ Visit the program together for a short time. Go through as much of the daily routine as your time permits. You might want to visit once in the morning and a second time in the afternoon. This will give both of you familiarity with the entire day. Take some photographs of the child care providers and the setting to look at with your child at home.

♦ Take some photographs from home so that your child can look at them during the time away from you.

♦ Make a tape recording of music that you and your child love. Include songs that you like to sing to your little one for the child care provider to play for your child.

♦ Use a sandwich-size, Ziploc bag to store a handkerchief doused with a favorite cologne or after-shave lotion from dad or a perfume from mom. Use a scent that the child has connected to one or to each of the parents to be kept in the child's cubby, available at any time, to use all the senses.

How will being in child care affect my child?

If you can afford to be at home with an infant and you want to be, it's preferable for at least six months to get to know each other and enjoy the experience of falling in love with your baby. If you do need child care, take the time to look for the best possible situation to enrich your child's life. Many people believe they are more effective parents because they have career and financial satisfaction; they feel more effective with their children because they are not full-time parents and appreciate the hours they share.

A multitude of studies show that quality child care is good for children. The current debate centers around the possibility of less close bonding between parents and babies in all-day child care, but the differences in bonding are not great. Poor quality child care can be detrimental to children. Early childhood settings need to have a low staff-to-child ratio to ensure safety and stimulation and contact for every child.

Some parents who don't work outside the home do not share quality time with their children. Across the board, looking both at parents who work and who don't work, we would probably find that very few parents spend much quality time with their children. So many chores have to be done that daily life often is functional survival. We are not in the moment because we're so busy looking backward and thinking forward. Children can tell if we are really focused on them or preoccupied with other matters. We want them to be well aware of how important they are to us.

The busiest parents can take at least fifteen minutes every day to be 100 percent present with their child. Everything else must be blocked out. Don't take phone calls or answer the doorbell and do turn off the television. Find an activity you know your child will like and do it together or sit and cuddle reading a book or rubbing backs. Take advantage of these brief periods of focused, joyful time with your child. Babyhood and childhood rush by and you can't get them back.

When a baby is fussy, experiment to find the kind of music he seems to like. Put on music and dance with the baby or walk with her. Some babies are comforted when they are rocked, while some go to sleep in a car or in a wind-up swing. Getting to know your baby's likes and dislikes will help during rough spots.

Also, plan moments in your hectic schedule to take care of youself. Think about what makes you joyful and happy. Have a list of things that could be really pleasing to you that don't take much time like a bubble bath by candlelight, reading a chapter in a good book, or a phone conversation with a friend. You need recharging activities that bring you pleasure while you are meeting the demands of parenthood.

I get nervous when I think about having to go to work when my child is ill. What do other parents do?

Plan ahead for this. Some parents use sick days and vacation time from their work to stay home with an ill child. Some spouses split the day staying home from work, one staying home in the morning and one in the afternoon, or they alternate missing a day at work. A list of alternatives will help you in an emergency, including relatives, friends, college students, neighbors, baby-sitters, and child care centers for the mildly ill. Check with your local hospital for this kind of service. Interview emergency care providers ahead of time.

I've seen parents get so angry with their children that they hit them. How can I prevent this happening to me?

If you find yourself feeling out of control with your children, make sure they are safe (in a playpen or their beds, with a relative or neighbor) and take a break from them. Have a list of different people you can call when you feel upset or overwhelmed. Your list should include someone who will probably make you laugh and someone who will empathetically understand what you're going through. Also include on your list someone who can give you good advice when you get into these states of anxiety, frustration, or fatigue. Take parenting courses and schedule regular breaks for yourself to increase your skills and patience level.

Is it really important to know about children's developmental stages? How can I find out about them?

In order to provide fair and effective discipline, it is valuable to have an idea of what children typically do at each age and stage. There are parent educators and books to explain the growth and development of children (☛ see Polland and Brazelton). However, you need to use the information only as a general guideline. It is too easy to worry if your child is not on the same schedule. Undoubtedly you'll also note "achievements." This material will give you some ideas of appropriate ways to stimulate your child.

For example, if you know that "holding on and letting go" is a stage that your 18-24-months-old child is going through, then you're not going to be surprised and upset when she suddenly pours a cup of milk on the floor, or feel she is trying to provoke you. Let your child help you clean up the milk and make sure you provide numerous opportunities for pouring in appropriate places, like the bathtub. Growth and development guidelines, used wisely, can be tremendously helpful. Make sure your child care providers have training in child development and ask them for information.

➤
If you don't tell children what they are doing that is wrong, in other words, if you aren't critical, how do you keep from creating a spoiled, obnoxious child like so many I see in action?

It is far too easy to become obnoxious ourselves when we deal with discipline situations. These are precisely the moments when we should be trying to be constructive, mature role models. Discipline situations provide opportunities to teach through our reactions and interactions. This is where we have to find the delicate balance of reinforcing what's right about the child's behavior and encouraging positive self-esteem, while finding ways to try to eradicate misbehavior. It certainly helps to read books or go to classes where you learn what to expect from children at different ages/ stages. We don't want to over- or underestimate their capabilities.

It takes time, thought, and energy to be our best selves when we face discipline situations with children. Here are some key questions that can lay a solid foundation for effective interventions.

1. What is the **goal** of discipline? We have to know what we hope to accomplish before even beginning to get there. The most basic goal of discipline is self-discipline.

2. If the goal is **self-discipline**, how can we begin to facilitate this process with children? We need to keep our goal clearly in mind and then make very conscious efforts to be effective role models. In other words, we need to make sure we are demonstrating self-discipline in how we live our own lives and in the ways we interact with our children.

3. Is discipline something we do "to" or "with" our children? If it is something we do "to" children, then how can they possibly develop self-discipline? Discipline must become a **process of interaction** with children. Both adults and children need to participate in finding constructive resolutions. Mutual respect is a cornerstone of this approach.

4. Is discipline for punishment or **for change**? When most discipline is for punishment, children tend to resent their parents and may try to perfect their skills at lying and sneaking to avoid

punishment. This process certainly doesn't encourage the growth of self-discipline. If discipline is for change, then adults must work with children to figure out consequences and future actions that are acceptable. ☛ See Rudolph Dreikurs with Vicki Soltz, *Children: The Challenge* (Hawthorne Books).

5. Are we treating children the way we hope they will treat us and each other? Our **actions need to match our verbal messages**. If we spank a child for hitting a sibling or a friend, our actions will speak louder than our words and our children will not learn to resist the urge to physically strike out at others. Whatever we say in anger and later hope children will forget, is exactly what they are bound to remember forever. We must model effective, mutual communication where positive learning and growth can take place.

Stick to a limit you set for a child; do not reward a temper tantrum by giving in to the child's demands, even if it occurs in a public place. Give children choices and responsibility whenever possible. Include children in problem solving and negotiation of family disputes. Avoid lectures and nagging; enduring the consequences gets the message across much more effectively. For example, if a child is late for dinner, the dinner is cold. If dirty clothes are not placed by the washing machine, they don't get washed.

Effective discipline is the art of learning self-control through positive guidance within limits and boundaries appropriate to the particular situation. The interactions between people both models and facilitates growth towards self-discipline. Discipline situations happen on a very regular basis. Our children mirror our emotional patterns, providing the best opportunity for growth. If we face them as a wonderful challenge for being our own best selves, then positive outcomes are likely.

What if our discipline styles as parents are different?

It would be hard to find two people anywhere who discipline the same way. Children quickly learn what kinds of reactions they can expect from each parent. You might want to take a discipline class together to formulate some areas of agreement. Buy two copies of a ☛ *P.E.T.* (*Parent Effectiveness Training*) book on discipline and read it at the same time so you can discuss it as you read. Or buy one copy and write reaction notes in the margins. To find a good parent education class, call the offices of local pediatricians. Many schools, colleges, churches, and synagogues offer them. The classes can be tremendously helpful because the two of you can spin off with topics and find where you agree and disagree. It is wise to hear a talk by an instructor before you sign up for his or her class.

How can we provide equal options for girls and boys?

To raise our children in bias-free homes, our most important contribution is to try be bias-free adults who share power, work, and access to leisure time. Here are some specific suggestions:

♦ From time to time, parents should switch household chores and parenting responsibilities. Mothers should participate in household repairs and playing ball.

♦ Fathers and/or trusted male friends and relatives should routinely participate in daily routines like bedtime rituals. (☛ See Gayle Kimball's *50/50 Parenting.*)

♦ We can give tool sets to our daughters and stuffed animals to our sons. We can give more praise to girls for doing well in math and science than for their appearance.

♦ We can use nonsexist language, as referring to mail carriers rather than mailmen, in order to expand the range of options.

♦ We can provide children's books, movies, and videos which are free of sex role stereotypes, as well as racial and religious stereotyping. Are the girls passive and dependent? Are the boys and men active and intelligent problem solvers? Are there female and male heroes? Feel free to change pronouns as you read, to include females. When biases occur, discuss them with children. Talk about why most of TV children's programming is about males.

♦ Our society is multiracial, consequently, learning and playing materials for children should reflect this reality. Are there successful people of color in the materials we share with children?

♦ We can select a mix of competent professionals when we select doctors, dentists, etc.

I'm so tired by the time I pick up my child that I can hardly get through the evening. How can I make quality time when I am out of steam?

How to create quality time with children

1. It is wise, if possible, to get the grocery shopping and other errands done before picking up your child. This avoids taking a tired child with you on errands when you have put in a long day yourself.

2. To ease your transition, sit in your car for three minutes, breathe deeply from your abdominal area (not your chest), relax your muscles, and listen to music that pleases you before you go in to pick up your child. If you can squeeze in the time, exercise before you pick up your child to release the day's tension.

3. Streamline the cooking by making enough for two days' meals at the same time; freeze half to serve on nights when you don't want to cook. Collect ideas for five-minute meals (as listed at the end of Chapter 7). Include children in food preparation.

4. Daily and evening routines at home can be turned into fun instead of chores surrounded by nagging. For example, parents and children can brush their teeth together, using their nondominant hands; it's a funny experience with guaranteed giggling and laughing.

5. Parent and child can race each other to see who can get into their pajamas first, or who can get dressed first in the morning. Wind up a music box and try to beat the music, or put on a timer and try to beat it. Make predictions about how long it will take each of you and see how accurate the predictions are.

Instead of daily routines being mundane, nagging, aggravating situations, they can become fun. Life with children is better when parents and little ones look forward to enjoying chores.

I have heard my friends asking their children, "How was your day at school?" Just about every child simply says, "Fine." How can we get children to really talk with us?

If we ask the same questions over and over again then we shouldn't be surprised when we continually get the same one-word answers back. We need to think of more interesting questions like:

Did anything funny happen in school/child care today?
What is the most interesting thing the teacher did today?
Whom did you say something nice to and how did they react?
What did you like best and least about your day?

We have to be careful not to create an interrogation format because when children are ready and want to share something they will talk on and on. ☛ See Adele Faber and Elaine Mazlish, *How to Talk So Your Children Will Listen and Listen So Your Children Will Talk* (Avon).

What are other fun things we can do together as a family?

Find out what other people you know considered fun as they were growing up. Many people remember special events like being able to pick the menu or the restaurant for their birthday dinner. Also collect ideas from magazines, books, lectures, teachers, and pediatricians. It is surprising to learn how many adults have few memories of truly fun times in their families. Life is a lot more enjoyable if we share unique good times along the way! Here are some ways to start:

♦ The night before a child's birthday, tell the story of his/her birth in age/stage appropriate ways. Children will delight in hearing about how much you wanted them and learning some of the details about their entry into the world and the first few days of their life.

♦ Have the whole family sleep outside on a warm night.

♦ Twice a year, wake up a child to have a surprise snack in the middle of the night, accompanied by a chat.

♦ If you buy a new vehicle or bike, call the family together to pick a name for it.

♦ Give cost-free gifts to each other on holidays, like a backrub, a car or bike wash, help in cleaning a room, repairing toys, baking together, a visit to the park, plan and make a meal together, or take a bus ride together.

♦ Think of someone in your community your family can help. Bake cupcakes for firefighters, plant flowers for an elderly person, or send valentines to someone who lives alone.

♦ Give each family member a list of ten qualities you really like about them.

♦ Put a surprise love note in the least expected place.

♦ Have an instant party bag ready to celebrate an achievement such as a good grade in school. Include balloons, party hats, streamers, confetti, and blowers.

♦ Put pennies under wastebaskets to be emptied.

♦ Do a "family clap" where everyone applauds the speaker who shares something he/she is proud of or a recent achievement.

♦ Cut out pictures from magazines and photographs and add words and drawings to make a family collage.

♦ Have a weekly family meeting, with rotating facilitators, followed by a fun activity or meal.

♦ Have a backward meal, with dessert first and the rest of the food second, or breakfast for dinner and vice versa.

♦ Cover a table with blankets or sheets. Eat dinner, using flashlights, under this tent.

♦ Plan a favorite friends' dinner where every family member can invite a special friend.

♦ Pick a meal where the children will try to catch even the most subtle poor table manners of their parents.

♦ Select dinner table discussion topics in advance, such as: What is one really funny thing that happened this week? If you could whisk one person out of your life this last week, who would it be and why? Share a favorite line or paragraph from a book. Tell one nice thing you did for someone this week. Everyone gives one sincere complement to everyone else at the table.

Please send your favorite family fun ideas to me, including games, traditions, and any unusual way to create meaningful family time. I am planning to write a book called *Funtastic Families* and your suggestions will be most appreciated. Write to Dr. Barbara Polland, Child Development, California State University, 18111 Nordhoff, Northridge, CA 91330.

The most important points to apply

♦ A couple's open, honest communication is a good foundation for parenting.

♦ Babies dramatically change our lives, forever.

♦ If we need or choose to work outside the home, we must take time to research and select the best child care options.

♦ Build in quality blocks of time with children.

♦ An understanding of children's growth patterns can help to provide age/stage appropriate experiences.

♦ Children learn more readily hearing what is right about them rather than what is wrong.

♦ The goal of discipline is self-discipline.

♦ Provide a variety of options for both girls and boys, creating a bias-free family life.

♦ Provide many opportunities for mutual fun.

SUGGESTED READINGS

Bettelheim, Bruno. *A Good Enough Parent.* New York: Alfred A. Knopf, 1987.

Brazelton, T. Berry. *Touchpoints.* Addison-Wesley, MA 1992.

Briggs, Dorothy Corkille. *Your Child's Self-Esteem.* New York: Doubleday, 1975.

Farber, Adele and Elaine Mazlish. *How to Talk So Your Children Will Listen and Listen So Children Will Talk.* New York: Avon, 1982.

Hochschild, Arlie. *The Second Shift.* New York: Avon Books, 1989.

Kimball, Gayle. *50/50 Parenting.* New York: Lexington, 1987.

Polland, Barbara K. *Guideposts for Growing Up.* Chicago: Standard Educational Corporation, 1991. Available only through telephone orders, 818-887-1993. *Feelings Inside You and Outloud Too.* Berkeley, CA: Celestial Arts, 1975.

ABOUT THE AUTHOR

Barbara K. Polland

BARBARA K. POLLAND

My son and daughter are my favorite teachers about parenting. For 36 years my professional work as an educator has been with children, parents, and teachers. I have had a private therapy practice for 23 years. Since 1970, I have taught at California State University, Northridge, as professor of child development and mental health specialist. I write books and create videotapes to enhance communications between parents, children, and teachers. I feel very lucky to know why I'm here on earth and, in many ways, my work, my purpose, is also my hobby.

✪Next... Parenting is enhanced by good health and the energy that accompanies it. Steps to enhancing wellness are described in the next chapter, written by a counselor/exercise instructor.

9

TAKING CARE

OF YOURSELF

SUCCESSFULLY

JUDITH EBERHART, M.S.

"I am mindful of my body's highest good: I exercise, eat, and rest accordingly. "

Chapter Goals

The goal of this chapter is to provide resources and techniques to maintain stamina, health, and vitality. Getting and keeping a job, dressing for success, maintaining healthy relationships—along with taking care of yourself financially, spiritually, mentally, and physically is a full-time job. Becoming successful in any one of these areas does not take the pressure off if we are not healthy and energetic; mistreating our bodies will take its toll.

To keep the body in good health is a duty ... otherwise we shall not be able to keep our mind strong and clear.

–Buddha

Where do I start? I don't have time to do all of the things I should to stay healthy!

Women's magazines are filled to the brim each month with advice on how to have thin thighs, eat nutritious meals on the run, and reduce stress. People fill counselors' offices, seminar halls, and wellness clinics learning how to cope with stress, feel healthy, and regulate eating habits. What do we really need to know to make the desired changes in our lives?

*Make your strategy simple

*Do what works for you

*Plan ahead

*Include regular exercise, diet, sleep, moderation, and self-forgiveness when you get off track.

Make your strategy simple.

Following a strict health regime can take most of your day—exercising, meditating, buying and preparing fresh fruits and vegetables, putting cucumbers on puffy eyes, flossing teeth, cleaning contact lenses; the list can fill books. Think like a good economist and pick the health habit that gives you the most for the time spent.

Whatever your strategy is, make sure it includes exercise.

As a counselor, when I talk with people with stress-related health problems, I ask, "Do you exercise?" Often they respond, "No, I'm too busy." Yet they must find time to go to the doctor for the muscle relaxants for their back spasms or for time off work to treat stress-related headaches and other ailments. Not all illness is related to lack of exercise, of course, but regular aerobic exercise is one of the best ways to:

♦ reduce the stress hormones in our bodies
♦ decrease intramuscular fat and increase lean muscle
♦ improve circulation
♦ lower the heart rate
♦ improve absorption and utilization of food
♦ increase energy and stamina
♦ encourage restful sleep
♦ decrease nervous tension and depression
♦ increase overall sense of well-being by releasing endorphins and enkephalins (natural opiates produced in the brain).

Regular, continuous (30 minutes) aerobic exercise is time well-spent. Plan an exercise hour 3 to 5 times a week. It could look like this—walk at lunch with a friend instead of sitting and eating, ride your exercycle or jump on your mini-trampoline for 20 minutes before your day starts, join a fitness center, or dance with an exercise video. A reader suggests that finding a fitness partner helps keep each other active.

It is important to stretch out before and after exercise, and you will also want to do some basic toning for the major body parts using hand weights for the upper body and leg lifts for the lower body. Having a healthy cardiovascular system is not enough when your back is hunched over or your arms are flabby. Here are some exercises to do for toning muscles.

Body toning

Start at 25 repetitions each or however many you can do without straining after warming up, then work up to 100 for each body part. Movements should be controlled, not flinging of the arms or legs. If any sharp pain occurs, the movement should be discontinued. ☛ Any Kathy Smith exercise video demonstrates correct positioning and movement. Consider taking lessons in the Alexander Technique to learn proper use of your body's basic movements, sitting, walking, etc. (check the telephone book's yellow pages).

Biceps (upper, front arm)

Triceps (upper, backarm)

Pectorals(chest)

Latissimus Dorsi(back)

Abductors (outer thigh)

Adductors (inner thigh)

Abdominals (tummy)

Buttocks (buns)

Drawing by Holly Etzel

What is the best exercise? How about shopping, yard work, golf, bowling, leisure walking, or housework; are these good aerobic activities?

No, sorry. Continuous, aerobic exercise makes your heart rate increase and generally makes you sweat. Generally, if your heart rate is between 20 and 30 beats for a 10-second count and you can continue to talk to a friend while you exercise, then you are exercising aerobically.

I eat on the run and I'm watching my weight; how can I eat well under these conditions?

This is where planning ahead and keeping it simple are the main keys. Don't leave home in the morning without a bottle of water and something low-caloried to munch on that you like to eat. If you hate rice cakes, that's not the answer. Toss in an apple, banana, carrots, or celery, something to tide you over. Dehydrated, instant soups are also quick fillers that can do for lunch when you are in a hurry. Other fat savers include popcorn sprayed with Tamari soy sauce or Braggs Amino Acid (found in health food stores). If you crave a piece of cheese with crackers, try mozzarella nonfat variety or feta cheese with ak-mak crackers. Nuts are high in fat and don't make good snacks if you are trying to cut down on calories. Shop with these pick-me-ups in mind.

Nutrition rules are too complicated and food labels undecipherable, so how do I keep it simple?

Think in terms of what you *can* eat. Say yes to:
♦ water (8 glasses a day)
♦ sparkling water with lemon or fruit juice
♦ fruits and vegetables
♦ whole grains and seeds
♦ brown rice, beans, whole wheat pasta
♦ vegetable oils
♦ nonfat milk and yogurt

- ♦ fresh foods, light salad dressings
- ♦ herbal teas
- ♦ nonalcoholic drinks

If it's true that we are what we eat, how come we aren't all light, new and improved?

–Iern Ball,
Good Housekeeping

➤ I have to live in the real world of junk food, fast food, social gatherings with alcohol, chips, and gooey goodies. I am not a saint. How do I stay with my health plan?

This is where moderation and forgiveness come into play. The body can overcome occasional indulgences, but not on a regular basis. Healthy habits that are followed most of the time will pay off in the long run.

➤ I would like to change some of my unhealthy habits; where do I start?

Perhaps you would like to lose weight, stop smoking, be able to compete in a race, or have more meaningful relationships. The process to follow for change is the same, no matter what area of life you want to change. First take a look at how we acquire our habits. Generally by the time we start elementary school, the manner in which we approach life has been set. We have learned from our parents what "works." For example, if your mother soothed you with milk and cookies after a bad day, you may still try to take care of daily stresses by rewards of yummy sweets or overeating to dull the pain. If it is family tradition to eat heavy, rich foods, you may learn that you don't feel "satisfied" until you have a heavy feeling in your stomach. Some of these bad habits can then become addictions and more difficult to change.

STEP ONE

It does not require great strength to do things, but it requires great strength to decide on what to do.

—Albert Hubbard

First decide exactly what you want to change in your life. Not just generally, I want to run faster, I want to lose weight, or I want to be healthier. Our mind responds to directions, but it needs **specific** goals to work towards. You must decide *how much faster* you want to run, how much weight you want to lose, or how you want to be healthier.

═══════════════ **Personal Reflection** ═══════════════

Something that I want to change about my wellness habits is:

_____

STEP TWO

Devise a program. When you make bread you don't go into the kitchen, open the cupboard, toss a little of everything into a bowl and expect it to turn out as a *bread*. No, you follow a careful, step-by-step proven plan that assures a successful loaf. The point here is that the plan must be a plan that is suited to you. For example, every diet temporarily works. Someone has lost weight on almost any diet found in print; however, not every diet is healthy or suited to your metabolism or personality.

Some diets require weighing each bit of food which may prove to be tedious. Eating lettuce and grapefruit day after day is nutritionally unsound, but too much variety may be confusing. You may like to keep your choices simple so as not to have a lot of things to think about when mealtime rolls around. Do not be discouraged when your plan doesn't seem to work. Find out what is not working and adjust it. Don't tell yourself that you can't or that you're not the type.

Charles Garfield, a psychologist, mathematician, weight lifter, and scientist with the moonshot, wrote a book describing the traits of successful people in different disciplines. He discovered that they worked for correction, not for perfection. The moonshot was off course 90 percent of the time; at no time did the scientists call off the venture because things weren't going perfectly. In fact, perfectionism is a trait that slows progress in the "analysis paralysis."

There are no failures, just lessons about what works and what doesn't and correcting what doesn't work. If you run your first 10k race and can't finish, you have learned that you need to train more and put in more time conditioning, not that you are a failure and should never attempt another 10k. If one attempt at losing weight doesn't work, then you know that what you did does not work for you, not that you can't attain your optimum weight.

Personal Reflection

My plan for change is _____
(write your steps for achieving the above goal):

STEP THREE

"If you don't know where you are going, any road will take you there."

Select your reinforcements, a way to reward yourself for success. You need to have a payoff for changing that is greater than the payoff for staying the way you are. Even though the habit you want to change is negative and harmful, there is some reason why you continue to do it. Be clear that you *are* getting some benefit or payoff from your negative behaviors. In order to change you will have to be willing to let go of the old desire in favor of a new one.

Selecting reinforcers may be an area where you will have to experiment. A reinforcement can be something that is real or imaginary. If you reward yourself with a new outfit for losing ten pounds and that motivates you, great! If you win a race and get your picture in the paper for winning an award, and that is motivating for you, fine! However, just as all programs don't work for everyone, neither do all reinforcers. An imaginary reward which you create in your mind can be just as reinforcing as something real.

Personal Reflection

My motivating reinforcers for this change are:_____

STEP FOUR

> *Even if you are on the right track, you'll get run over if you just sit there.*
>
> —Will Rogers

Select techniques to help you along the way. There are supports that can make the changes easier. Will power works, but when we become tired, stressed, disappointed, and discouraged with lack of progress, will power is overcome and the negative feelings and fatigue are victorious. This does not mean that you are doomed to failure. Remember, your efforts are not counted as failures, just lessons! Here are some power boosters that you can use for support in making a change and reducing stress.

♦ **Group support**: Any wellness activity you want to pursue is easier in a group. The most successful self-help group in the United States today is Alcoholics Anonymous (AA). It is easier to lose weight, stop smoking, run faster, do more difficult exercises, or solve a problem at work in a group of supportive individuals. Almost any activity is easier when there are others around for encouragement. When we are encouraged we get energy from others, just as when we are disapproved of we feel our energy taken away. When making a change, choose to be around people who support that change, not those who criticize, use sarcasm or negative comments. Local newspapers generally list meeting times and places of the various groups. Therapists and counseling departments should have lists of meetings for AA and Narcotic Anonymous and various other twelve-step and codependency group meetings, or look in the phone book.

If you have problems you are ready to tackle, talk with an appropriate person who can help you: a counselor, a friend, or someone trained in the area. If you are having financial problems, see a financial consultant. If you have a medical problem, see a specialist.

♦ **Visual imagery**: Our minds are very powerful tools. If we can visualize ourselves as persons with the changes we are planning to make, it is then easier to believe that we can make the changes. Many athletes use this technique. Jack Nicklaus claims that his golf game is only 10 percent involved with the actual swing. "Hitting the specific shots," says Nicklaus, "is fifty percent mental picture and forty percent setup." Many olympians now follow the lead of the Russians using three-way training for their events, including athlete, coach, and mind trainer.

Visual imagery is not only used in athletics, but businesspeople use it widely in sales and promotion. ☞ Steven Covey, in his best seller, *The 7 Habits of Highly Effective People*, writes that all things are created twice: the mental or first creation, and a physical or second creation. Take a few moments now to visualize the change you've written about for this chapter. Do this with the most vivid pictures possible, including smells, sounds, and emotions that accompany the pictures. Visualization gets better with practice.

Just what is stress anyway?

Stress is not always harmful.

We are like expensive violins. In order to play a perfect song, the strings have to be at a certain level of tension. With too much tension, the strings will break; with too little tension, the notes will sound out of tune. We are continually trying to find a balance point between too much and too little tension. The problem comes when we don't recognize that there is too much stress in our life and health suffers.

♦ **Stress** can be positive or negative.

Positive stress is called "eustress." Positive stresses could include celebrations such as Christmas or starting a new job. Negative stress is called distress. These stresses have negative feelings associated with the event. The stress response is the same, regardless of the type of stress experienced. The ability to adjust to stress is not so much the problems faced, but rather, how these problems are perceived.

Psychologist Dr. Murray Banks tells of two women he counseled. Both had recently lost their boyfriends. The similarities in their situation were striking; however, their adjustments to the same problem were radically different. Ultimately, one woman committed suicide while the other simply found a new boyfriend!

♦ Stress can be reduced or magnified by our personal habits.

-too much fat: Not only is fat high in calories, creating obesity which stresses the heart, but it is also hard to digest and contributes to gastrointestinal discomfort. Fat reduces the oxygen-carrying abilities of the red blood cells by globing onto them, reducing the body's energy level by actually suffocating the cells.

-too much caffeine: Caffeine increases the heart rate, blood pressure, and oxygen demand upon the heart. The average cup of coffee contains about 108 milligrams of caffeine. Caffeine consumption of more than 250 milligrams of caffeine per day is considered excessive and has an adverse effect upon the body. Caffeine is also found in tea, cola drinks, and chocolate.

-too much sugar: Sugar depletes vitamin B in the body and causes fatigue. The process works like this: Sugar enters the blood stream, the pancreas is alerted and dumps insulin in the blood system, the insulin metabolizes the sugar, causing low blood sugar, which causes fatigue and perhaps depression. A second harmful effect is, initially, the sugar gives energy, but because there are no vitamins in sugar, the body borrows vitamin B from other sources to metabolize the sugar. This causes a vitamin debt and the person may feel irritable, anxious, and generally nervous. Try an experiment: Cut down on your sugar consumption and notice how much better you feel!

-dieting: The average woman goes on one and 1-1/2 diets per year. Severely restricted calorie intake and diets which are not nutritionally balanced deny the body nutrients and change its chemical composition. A study at the Mayo Clinic observed a group of emotionally healthy young women who had no need to lose weight but volunteered to live together in a clinic under supervision and eat a restricted diet for an extended period of time. Before three months had passed, the women's personalities underwent startling changes. They began to quarrel endlessly with one another. They experienced unprovoked feelings of anxiety, persecution, and hostility. Some suffered nightmares; others felt extreme panic at times. These reactions were due to a lack of carbohydrates which provide energy, and a low intake of vitamins and minerals which maintain the ability of the body to handle stress, fight disease, and function normally.

Few dieters realize how seriously they may be compounding both physical and emotional problems by prolonged dieting. To lose weight, follow a nutritionally balanced program and slowly shed the pounds so that you don't cause a stress reaction of bingeing or eating junk food to feel better. Studies show that *yo-yo* diets with weight losses and gains are unhealthy.

-not enough sleep: A person can function on a few nights' sleep deficit. But after that, clarity of thinking, reaction time, poor judgement, irritability, and a host of physical reactions ultimately lower the body's ability to protect itself from disease.

-**negative thinking:** Worry, guilt, anxiety, and any kind of negative thinking create stress. When a person is connected to a biofeedback machine or a lie detector (polygraph), the machine immediately reflects a negative thought (such as a lie) even though the person may say something to the contrary. This is the same way the body responds to a physical stress. The response may not be visible to someone else, but the body has registered a reaction. Think about people you know who are always complaining, who worry about everything, and who have a negative outlook on life. Do they have lots of colds, bodily complaints, or some kind of illness? Perhaps they seem healthy now, but something is brewing for their future!

You can't afford the luxury of a negative thought.

—John Roger and Peter McWilliams

Which are the most effective stress reduction techniques?

Successful relaxation techniques include meditation, autogenic training, progressive relaxation, and the use of biofeedback equipment.

Meditation has been popularized by Maharishi Mahesh Yogi's teaching of transcendental meditation. Researchers have found that during meditation people experience a lowering of metabolic rate, respiratory rate, pulse rate, oxygen consumption, and blood pressure. This state is the opposite of the physiological condition that occurs in reaction to stress. Dr. Herbert Benson, a Harvard heart specialist, suggests that a similar technique is just as effective in creating the relaxation response, and involves the following steps:

♦ Sit quietly in a comfortable position

♦ Close your eyes

♦ Relax all your muscles deeply

♦ Breathe through your nose and say the word *one* each time you breathe out

♦ Do this for 20 minutes maintaining a passive attitude; that is, don't try to bring about the desired reaction.

Autogenic Training was developed by Dr. H. H. Shultz, a German psychiatrist. The method involves self-hypnosis using imagery and suggested feelings of heaviness and warmth in the limbs. Autogenic training has been found to result in decreased respiratory and heart rates, decreased muscle tension, and an increase in alpha brain waves (a relaxed, meditative state).

The following is a typical instruction for autogenic training:

Sitting with your hands resting on your thighs (not touching each other), back straight against the chair, head hanging loosely forward, and feet flat on the floor, close your eyes. Imagine you've just come from a long walk and you're very tired. Your legs weigh themselves down. Now they are feeling very warm. Just relax them, but feel how heavy and warm they are. Enjoying this feeling? Retain it.

Repeat these instructions several times using specific limbs, then generalize the heaviness to all limbs and visualize a peaceful scene at the same time until you begin to feel relaxed. The exercise can be done a second time focusing on the warmth in your extremities. This exercise is designed to increase peripheral blood flow and relax blood vessels. Repeat, "My heartbeat is calm and regular," and "my solar plexus is warm." The final overall calming exercise is the repetition of the words, "My forehead is cool." These instructions could be read to you or played on a tape recorder while you visualize them.

Progressive relaxation is a process developed by Dr. Edmund Jacobson which requires the participant to tense and then relax muscles in the body in order to learn to recognize tenseness and to learn to relax during periods of stress. It is called progressive because it starts with muscles in one part of the body and progresses to all other parts. Try this in bed tonight before you fall asleep. Tighten the muscles in your feet, then relax; tighten the legs, then relax, and work all the way up to the top of your head. Before you reach your head, you may be fast asleep!

Biofeedback training uses a machine that *feeds back* information about your body through a dial and corresponding sound. The machine can pick up electrical impulses, temperature, and moisture through electrodes attached to the body. All of these are indicators of the stress response. The machine itself does not produce the relaxed state; its function is to enable the subject to recognize and control his or her own response. One of the advantages of biofeedback training over some of the other techniques is the speed with which the participant learns the relaxation response. A disadvantage is that it involves the use of sophisticated, expensive equipment only accessible in a psychologist's office or a clinic.

While handling a maximum amount of stress, if you add one more activity, something has to give. So, don't start a diet when you are moving, ending a relationship, or undergoing some other emotional or physical trauma. Reducing stress in your life allows your mind to focus on a new pattern and adjust to it. It is like letting a pot which has food cooked hard on the bottom soak overnight. The next morning the food is easily scrubbed off. Becoming more relaxed allows the new thought patterns to soak in and replace old ones.

Other quick tension reducers include:

♦ drinking herbal teas, such as camomile or mint

♦ taking a hot shower or a warm bubble bath

♦ lying down with your eyes closed for ten minutes (research shows that often this is as good as a nap)

♦ taking five deep breaths from your abdominal area (try that now!)

♦ stretching

♦ doing something different for ten minutes

♦ listening to relaxing music

♦ having a massage

♦ having a good, hearty laugh, and changing your mind by:

— riding the horse in the direction that it is going. In other words, accept that's the way it is: I didn't get the job, my lover doesn't want to commit to me, I didn't get the promotion; I can't change that but I can learn from it and move on. Yes, there will be disappointment and pain. The sooner you grieve the loss and move on, the faster you move through the pain.

Change your thoughts and you
change your world.

–Norman Vincent Peale

— Giving in once in awhile is another version of acceptance. We can tell ourselves: The house doesn't always have to be as clean as I would prefer, I can let them have their (ridiculous) point of view, I don't always have to be right and it doesn't mean that I have lost. ☛Steven Covey in *The 7 Habits of Highly Successful People* (Simon & Schuster) lists a win/win attitude as a key habit, the belief that there is enough to go around so that everyone can win.

— Remind yourself you do not have to do everything, be everything, save everyone, experience everything, and send holiday cards to everyone.

Being a success in the world and a success in your wellness program can be at odds. In order to get the job or the promotion, you have to be the best at what you do and hustle double-time to let people know you're competent. If this attitude is exhausting you to the point of frequent colds, accidents, or worse, the solution may not be as simplistic as drinking some camomile tea and having a few good laughs. These self-destructive patterns should be carefully examined and looked at with a competent therapist or support group.

Other examples of stresses beyond self-help would be if a person is married to an alcoholic. Meditation and exercise may help to minimize the stresses in the family, but it does not deal with the codependent relationship and how the spouse supports the drinking spouse. This is a much deeper problem and needs to be addressed in therapy or counseling.

We experience anxiety perhaps because of a busy schedule, drinking too much coffee, being in the wrong job for our skills and interests, or not sleeping nights due to eating the wrong foods or drinking late at night. It is important not to deal with stress through a cookbook formula, i.e., here are five causes of stress and six ways to reduce it. Instead, stress management is a process that leads people through self-exploratory steps to get to the root of their individual stress and develop effective ways of dealing with it. This usually involves getting unbiased help and instruction.

Caution

Remember the title of this chapter is "Taking Care of Yourself Successfully," not "perfectly." The anguish over five or ten pounds, the personal insecurities which fuel the billions of dollars the cosmetic industry earns each year by manipulating our self-doubts, and the pain of thinking we should be somewhere else doing something else are not productive.

An excellent affirmation is **I am always at the right place at the right time, doing the right thing.** This thought counters destructive ideas, such as "If only I had" (a different job, clearer skin, a better relationship, nicer boss, more time, were more organized, weren't so codependent, or made more money). Learn the lesson of the present situation and then move on. The job of taking care of yourself is not life itself, but the foundation to go out and be as healthy as you can be while doing life.

> *Do something, and when you've done something and it works—*
> *do it some more and if it doesn't work—do something else.*
> –Franklin Delano Roosevelt
> 1932 Baltimore Address

The most important points to apply

Lack of information is not the problem. *Doing* something to change the direction you are going or loving yourself the way you are is the challenge:

♦ start small
♦ commit to reachable goals
♦ do it and reward yourself
♦ get help

Include in your daily routine:

♦ exercising
♦ eating a lowfat, balanced diet
♦ making decisions by asking, What is best for my highest good?
♦ getting enough rest
♦ drinking a lot of water
♦ taking regular, relaxing moments for yourself.

> *Try? There is no try. There is only do or not do.*
> –Yoda, *Empire Strikes Back*

SUGGESTED READINGS

There are not only shelves of books on self-improvement but entire stores specializing in this literature. If you have a particular issue or concern, pick up a book on the topic, join a group focusing on the problem, or see a healed therapist (one who has worked on his or her own issues).

Nutritional Healing

One type of resource book that I recommend you have on hand is a reference book for home remedies for healing. The book I use currently is *Prescription for Nutritional Healing* by James F. Balch and Phyllis A. Balch (New York: Avery Publishing Group, 1990). This is a practical A-Z reference to drug-free remedies using vitamins, minerals, herbs, and food supplements. Even those who are free from disorders will benefit from this book, because advice is given on how to achieve optimum health, build the immune system, and increase energy levels. Written by a medical doctor and a certified nutritionist, the book blends the latest scientific research with traditional nonsurgical treatments. This is not intended as a replacement for appropriate medical investigation and treatment.

For Women

The New Our Bodies, Ourselves, by and for women, was revised in 1992. This book was written by the Boston Women's Health Book Collective, published by Simon & Schuster, New York. This is an excellent resource book, including chapters on taking care of ourselves, relationships and sexuality, controlling our fertility, childbearing, growing older, common and uncommon health and medical problems, and women and the medical system.

Mental Healing

Another time-honored book, *Anatomy of an Illness,* by Norman Cousins, was written in 1979. This book is basic for discussing how every person must accept a certain measure of responsibility for his or her own recovery from disease or disability.

The Feeling Good Handbook was written by David Burns, M.D., in 1990. This book provides step-by-step exercises to help cope with the full range of everyday problems such as self-defeating attitudes, procrastination, fears and phobias. There is also an up-to-date section on commonly prescribed psychiatric drugs and anxiety disorders such as agoraphobia and obsessive-compulsive disorder.

The Addictive Personality by Craig Nakken, published by Harper & Row in 1988, is an easy-to-read book explaining compulsions and the addictive process. Nakken uncovers the common denominator of all addictions and describes how, over time, an addictive personality develops and how society pushes people toward addiction.

Humor

Every library should have a few good laughs and a paperback you can toss in your bag for a pick-me-up. Three of my favorites include:

It Was on Fire When I Lay Down on It by Robert Fulghum, also author of *All I Really Need to Know I Learned in Kindergarten,* published by Ivy Books, 1988; and *The 637 Best Things Anybody Ever Said,* arranged by Robert Byrne, and published by Fawcett Crest in l982.

Anything written by Ashleigh Brilliant, including *I May Not Be Totally Perfect, But Parts of Me Are Excellent,* published by Woodbridge Press in 1979.

Weight Management

Habits Not Diets by James Ferguson, M.D., published by Bull Publishing in 1988.

Fit or Fat and *Target Diet,* by Covert Bailey and published by Houghton Mifflin. *Target Diet* was written ten years after *Fit or Fat* and is the best for the latest references.

Stress Management

Any book or tape by Donald Tubesing, who has written about stress management for 20 years. Dr. Tubesing has developed his own publishing and marketing company for stress management materials.

An easy-to-use book is *Kicking Your Stress Habits,* a do-it-yourself guide for coping with stress, also authored by Donald Tubesing and published by Whole Person Associates in 1981. Although the book is old, it still holds up as one of the best.

Another excellent text is *Stress Management for Wellness,* by Walt Schafer, Fort Worth: Harcourt Brace Jovanovich, 1992.

Healthy Problem Solving

The 7 Habits of Highly Effective People by Stephen Covey, published by Simon & Schuster in 1990, presents a holistic, integrated, principle-centered approach for solving personal and professional problems.

Spiritual Health

Days of Healing, Days of Joy by Earnie Larsen and Carol Larsen Hegarty, published by Hazelden Foundation in l987.

Meditations for Women Who Do Too Much by Anne Wilson Schaef, Ph.D., published by Harper & Row in l990.

Both contain daily quotes and uplifting thoughts. *Meditations* has quotations of women from different ages, cultures, disciplines, and perspectives. Each day's thought is one page and takes only moments to read—a few moments to be uplifted and redirected.

ABOUT THE AUTHOR

Judith Eberhart

JUDITH EBERHART, M. S.

I am a licensed marriage, family, and child counselor, an associate professor at Palomar College, and dean of graduate studies at California College for Health Science. I have taught personal development courses in stress management, weight management, assertive training, relationships, success, staff development workshops for industry and education and am my own best guinea pig for behavioral change. Additionally, I developed the curriculum for the master's degree in Community Health Administration and Wellnesss Promotion at California College for Health Science. I have maintained my sanity and reduced my own stresses by teaching aerobic exercise for 20 years. My wish for you is stated best by John Luther: "Learn from the mistakes of others—you can never live long enough to make them all yourself."

✪Next... The well-being of our bodies is affected by our emotional habit patterns, our ways of responding to challenges and how we approach achieving our goals. Principles of positive thinking—how to harness the power of the mind—are discussed in the following chapter, written by the minister of a New Thought church.

10

"I know that the power of my Mind is immense. I consciously direct that power within me for a greater experience of good in all areas of my life now."

USING THE POWER OF YOUR MIND FOR SUCCESS

FRANCIS MICHAEL LEE

This chapter discusses how to successfully use our most powerful, but often underutilized tool—the Mind. William James observed, "The greatest discovery of my generation is that human beings, by changing the inner attitudes of their minds, can change the outer aspects of their lives."

The Mind is like a garden. It can be consciously cultivated or left without care and direction to grow wild. Either way, cared for or abandoned, the garden will grow something: weeds or beautiful flowers or nourishing food. You, as the gardener, decide what seeds are planted and what harvest to reap. It is up to each one to tend the garden of her or his Mind. Psychologists remind us that most of us use only about 10 percent of the Mind's capacity. Let's take a look at this tool called the Mind by seeing how we can start using the other 90 percent. The three categories discussed in this chapter are

-the Mechanics of Mind,
-the Techniques,
-the Applications.

The Mechanics of the Mind

What do you mean by the Power of Mind?

The Power of Mind is creative, it is without limit, and it works through every one of us all the time. Whether or not we happen to be conscious of this, whether or not we believe that this power exists in us, it is constantly out-picturing the sum of our beliefs in our daily experiences. You can call it whatever you want—the Universe, the Source, the Power, the Presence, the Force, Divine Law, God—whatever works for you. Many people aren't comfortable with the word *God* because of their upbringing. So if you choose not to use that particular word, that's fine. The Power doesn't care what the heck it's called.

How do I access the Mind and its Power?

It's not something to be accessed. It's something we are. Let me tell you a story. Once there was a fish looking for water. It searched for a great, wise fish guru to lead it to the water. It finally found one guru and asked, "Oh wise one, where is the water?" The wise fish responded, "It is all around you. It is in you. It is what you are." The fish thought briefly, and then continued its search.

The idea is that this Power, this Presence, has always been and always will be expressed in and through everything that exists. This is wonderful news because this includes human beings. As human beings, we are unique in that we have the ability to be conscious of self—our self. We can be aware of the fact that this Power exists within and once that is discovered, we can use this Power consciously for our good. The Presence operates as an unconditional, impersonal, and dependable force.

That sounds interesting, but abstract. Can you tell me what I can do to apply this principle?

Look at your world, look at nature, and watch how the laws of nature work. If you do, you will find that each quality mentioned above is reflected in the laws of nature. For example, I see the law of electricity. I know that if I go over to an outlet, there is an inherent power in that outlet and it is sitting and waiting for me to give it something to do. Electricity doesn't care whether I give it direction or not. It exists in its fullness as potential until directed. I also recognize that electricity is only limited by my application, by what I plug into it. I can plug in a lamp with a 30-watt bulb or a 500-watt bulb. It doesn't care what is asked of it. If it's a really hot day and I decide to plug in a heater, the power is not going to tell me, no fool! you don't want heat, you want to be cooled off! It just responds to whatever direction is given.

If I work with the law of electricity, it becomes my servant. If I stick my finger in the outlet, it will zap me and I'll have a curly hairdo. Or I'll be dead. And it doesn't matter if I'm a 2-year-old kid, or a 100-year-old-woman, a Moslem, a Jew, a Christian, black or white; it is no respecter of persons.

That's the same thing with the law of gravity. If I'm going down the stairs and I trip and lose my balance, the law of gravity makes sure that I get to the bottom of those stairs quicker than if I had used the steps. Now I don't get angry at the steps and I don't get angry at the law of gravity, but what I do is recognize that there is a law at work here, and if I cooperate with it, it becomes my servant. What humans have done is to discover laws/principles that have always existed and use them. All the principles in physics, such as gravity or electricity,

252

have always been in existence as principles. Humans did not create them: We just discovered their existence and use them.

You speak of laws and principles. Is there any one law or principle regarding this Power of Mind that I can apply to make a difference in my life?

The secret to success in life is to understand this one law: It is done unto you as you believe; not as you wish or want, but as you believe. All the great philosophers and sages of history: Jesus, Buddha, Plato, and Emerson, to name a few, both Eastern and Western; and all the wise books: the Bible, the Koran, the Bhagavad-Gita, and the Upanishads proclaim this edict. As a person thinks, so she or he is. Literally, our Mind is an incredibly powerful tool that manifests in our world what we truly believe. The inner creates the outer. Most of us are not aware of this so we end up being at effect of our world, rather than being cause to our world and director of our life.

So, are you saying whatever I want, I can have?

No, I'm saying whatever you truly believe and embody you can experience. There's a big difference between want or desire and embodying the consciousness of a thing or a condition as a done fact. Intellectually, we can say we want all sorts of things. It's not what one thinks, not at the level of intellect, but what one really believes, way down deep inside.

For example, you can say you choose to have a new car. Let's say you want a fancy, convertible sports car. You work with the principles mentioned thus far and, after all is said and done, you end up with a Volkswagen Beetle. What happened? You demonstrated at the level of your consciousness, not your intellectual desire. It's not that you're being punished or that the principle didn't work. It worked perfectly by reflecting your true belief about what you believe you can have as a car. This applies to all aspects of your life.

Our mind has two aspects: the conscious and the subconscious, or what we'll call the subjective. The conscious aspect is what you are experiencing now, in your awake state. The subjective aspect is the creative mechanism and the storehouse of your embodied beliefs, opinions, and attitudes. The subjective receives your conscious thoughts. It takes your thoughts and turns them into life experiences. What you think exists at the conscious level. What you really believe exists at the subjective level. You have embodied the consciousness of a particular idea when it has moved from being an intellectual idea to a deeply held, conviction-filled, subjective belief.

Oh great, so how do I find what I truly believe?

To find what you truly believe, down in your gut, all you have to do is look out into your world. Your world always mirrors back your true belief about any particular area of your life. If you want to find out what you really believe about money, take a look at your money right now. You can apply this concept to all areas of your life. Is your life a friendly, supportive, loving experience, or an adversarial, mediocre, conflict-filled experience? Your answer is right in front of you: It is your life staring back at you.

Personal Reflections

1. Playing with the idea that your world reflects your beliefs, describe what an impartial observer would conclude are your beliefs about:
   a. prosperity
   b. health
   c. relationships
   d. creative self-expression.

2. Do you disagree or agree with the idea that you are the director of your life? Explain. Provide other explanations you've heard for how our lives unfold (fate, karma, luck, chance, sin, salvation, and so on) and what you think about them.

3. Can you think of examples of how your beliefs have generated action in your life? Are there beliefs standing in your way?

4. Make a list of wonderful events in your life, the high points. Next to the event, write what you did or thought to generate it.

You state all of this so matter-of-factly, but is life that simple?

I never said life was simple. I agree, it's not. This Mind that is within us can only work through us, through the law or principle. These principles in and of themselves are very simple, but living them and experiencing them is not a guarantee of simplicity because it takes much courage to be responsible. It takes a lot of discipline to be aware of your thoughts and tendencies and a lot of courage to acknowledge, "I create the good and the bad in my life." It's very easy to get lots of support in the world as a victim who does not have to take responsibility. But, do you want agreement or do you want to be happy? Do you want to be a victim or be at cause in your world? You have the choice.

Using the idea of a movie theater and the film projector, let's imagine the film projector is you. The film is your belief system. The Light that is shining through the projector and through the film is that Unconditional Presence and Power. What is shown on the screen is the result of your belief system. Now, if you are watching the movie of your life and you don't like what's playing on the screen, what do you need to do? Jump up and try to mess with the screen? No! You need to put in some new film! The Light that shines through the projector does not care what's playing. Its job is to shine Light. No matter what film is being played through the projector—drama, comedy, thriller, suspense, tragedy—the Light shines through them all.

Remember the idea that Universal Law is impersonal and unconditional? You are the casting director; you cast all the characters in your play of life. So if you are aware enough to see that in your world it's really your movie, you have the ability to stop the film and make new choices and choose new cast members and new beliefs so that you can have a different experience on the screen of life. Whatever challenge is put in front of you is for you. You can find good out of every experience and be blessed by the opportunity for growth. You can do this consciously, by saying, "This too is good, this too is for me, and I declare that I receive the blessings from this now."

You are no longer at the effect of any person, place, situation, or condition in your world. You are at choice, knowing that your belief creates your experience. When you find yourself in an experience that you don't like or a life pattern that does not serve you any longer, you can change your mind and change your belief to change your experience. Therefore, you are empowered in your world and you are not a victim.

SUGGESTED READINGS:

Deepak Chopra. *Unconditional Life—Mastering the Forces That Shape Personal Reality.* New York: Bantam, 1991.
Wayne Dyer. *You'll See It When You Believe It.* New York: Avon Books, 1990.
Louise L. Hay. *The Power Within You.* Carson,CA: Hay House, 1991.
Ernest Holmes. *Living the Science of Mind.* Marina del Rey, CA: DeVorss, 1991.
Joseph Murphy. *The Power of Your Subconscious Mind.* New York: Prentice Hall, 1988.

Techniques

What are specific techniques and practices that can change my belief systems?

First, accept the idea that all thought is creative.

Your thoughts create your experience. Take responsibility for everything in your life as being the result of your beliefs– all the good and all the bad. It's easy to accept the good or the positive as a result of your beliefs; however, it is difficult to accept that what we call bad or negative is also a result of our thinking. Remember one of those lab stories where a student practically blows himself up? The student thinks he is doing everything correctly, but the result shows otherwise. He uses principles of chemistry incorrectly and this action set up a natural result—disaster.

Second, become aware of your thinking.

Start listening to the way you think. Literally. What are your tendencies of thought? Start listening to the way you converse with your friends. What opinions and attitudes are you taking and defending? Take a look at the things that you are reading and what you're talking about. What are you paying attention to in your life? Is what you're thinking or saying something that you want to experience?

Ask yourself, Do I really want to experience the results of this line of thinking or attitude? If you do, great. If you don't, perhaps that's something to change. Write your responses to these questions in your journal if there are changes you would like to make in your life.

Third, is the principle that what you praise increases, and what you damn persists.

Praise what you have right now. I don't care how little it is. It's very difficult to have more in your life when you're not grateful for what you presently have. The idea is that everything in your world right now is here because you attracted it. Yes, everything. I know that might be tough to accept, but work with me here. Once you acknowledge that what is in your life is your creation, you are then free to change your mind and create something new to take its place.

If you are doing the opposite, whining and moaning about this concern or that concern, all you are doing is keeping it around by giving it attention. Each of the different experiences in your life are like so many fires. Which fires are you continuing to fuel with your attention? If you have a big fire in your life called lack of money, are you constantly throwing gas on it with your attention by complaining about it? It doesn't matter what kind of *fire* you have, if you want a different experience, stop paying attention to it in the old way. Turn away from it to build a new one. Remember, it is done unto you as you believe. Work on building a new belief, not feeding an old, worn-out one. You are always at choice.

For example, I had a job that I enjoyed very much, but I had to work 60-plus hours a week to make ends meet. After working for this company about a month, I was assigned to a particular project that involved about an hour's drive through the countryside. At first I was not happy with all the driving time and getting up so early. However, as I continued on this project, I changed my attitude. I got to see the sunrise every morning and the country scenery was beautiful. I began to look forward to the drive every day because it became to me precious, contemplative quiet time. I spoke my gratefulness and praised my job out loud while driving. I praised what I had—sincerely.

I approached the manager for a raise, as working all those hours was getting old and I felt that I was performing consistently at a high level. However, company policy stated that no raises were possible until one had completed the probationary and review period. I was disappointed but continued on with my contemplative drives. I continued to be grateful and praise my job. A week later, I received a phone call from a manager of a company in the same industry. She had been told by the company president to contact me, although I had never met him.

When I met with her, she asked me about salary. I added $200 to what I was earning and asked for that as my monthly salary based on a 40-hour work week. The manager accepted. I was making more money than before and working 20 hours a week less. They also paid for further schooling and offered a much better pension and medical plan. I had never thought of going to another company in the same industry. I had not prepared resumes and sent them out. I just praised and was grateful for what I had. My good came to me. List what you are grateful for now, in your journal.

Les Hait, a trainer for Neuro Linguistic Programming, suggests the following seven additional techniques for changing our beliefs. (NLP is a process of mind reorganization to recondition old stimulus response patterns so that we can have more effective and rewarding lives.)

Use Counter-Examples

We customarily support our beliefs about ourselves with examples from our past that support the *truth* of the belief. For example, at the time of Columbus, most of Europe believed that monsters lived in the Atlantic Ocean, but Columbus and his followers believed that India, symbolizing adventure and prosperity, lay to the west. A more contemporary example might be someone with a belief that he or she is socially clumsy. This belief functions as a continually renewed reminder to behave awkwardly in social situations. If, however, we were to recall situations where we acted with grace, humor, poise, and power, and begin to reflect on these counter-examples, then we would create some doubt about the certainty of the old belief. Because beliefs are simply generalizations about ourselves accompanied with feelings of certainty, the antidote for a feeling of certainty is a feeling of doubt. With enough doubt the old belief fades away, and our new empowering feeling of certainty comes to the foreground. We could then visualize in the future handling a variety of challenging social situations with grace and comfort, based on our new belief.

Make the new belief part of your enlarged identity. As an example, if I say I am a drug addict, then that is part of my identity. I will always be susceptible to acting consistently with my own definition of my identity as a drug addict. If I think, I am a person who has learned the hard way never to use drugs, then the message I send to myself is entirely different. It is much more likely I will never use drugs, with the second identity.

Identify Values Violations

We can contrast an unwanted belief with our highest values. If we believe that there is a Higher Consciousness at the center of all things working for the good of all, yet we harbor negative attack thoughts toward ourselves, then we are violating our own values. Becoming fully aware of the massive violation of our own spiritual values is very helpful in inducing change in beliefs of unworthiness. We would never treat someone else the way we treat ourselves. Why be that harsh to ourselves?

Contrast a Painful Past and a Positive Future

We need to ask what it will cost us to continue to live with the old belief. What will it cost our families? Our friends? Our self-esteem? As we experience the pain of the old belief, we can look at the benefits of the new empowering belief. Reinforce the new belief regularly: Praise or acknowledge yourself for applying it.

Focus

If we focus on what we want, we are much more likely to get it than if we focus on a dread of what we don't want. Most of us tend to focus on the latter. It's like a fastball pitcher at a key moment in the game. If she thinks about not pitching a high pitch, she is focusing on the negative. Far better is to focus on what she does want, say a strong, low pitch, and visualize doing that well. (This technique is also important in giving instructions to children and coworkers.)

We also focus by having clear and written goals; otherwise, how will we know where we want to head? Emotion is important, too, because if we suppress our passion, we crush the juice out of our lives. When emotion is transmitted throughout our body, then the unconscious mind recognizes that this is an important topic and helps to accomplish the goal. If we draw out our feelings, longings, and caring, then we will be propelled toward what we want with enthusiasm and fire, calling up the power of our inner resources.

Make a Commitment

We can announce our new beliefs to ourselves and perhaps our friends or family. We can make a public commitment to the new belief that will challenge us to be consistent to the new commitment.

Observe Role Models

We can learn from people who overcame their own limiting beliefs to move ahead. How did they do it? Also, we can role-play and imagine handling events consistently with new beliefs.

Seek the Assistance of Others

We can call on others to help us with our belief changes. We can keep track of how we are doing, and regularly report to others on our progress.

Are there other resources I can use to tap this Power of Mind?

Bookstores/Libraries

Major book stores and libraries have sections regarding self-realization, self-awareness, philosophy, metaphysics, meditation, etc. The good news is out in a big way. Check out church and synagogue libraries and book stores. I am most familiar with Religious Science International, United Church of Religious Science and Unity which have monthly magazines available for subscription, with useful articles and daily meditations.

Affirmations

Webster's definition of affirm is "to assert positively; to tell with confidence; to declare." An affirmation is simply a statement of Truth repeated over and over again until it becomes part of one's feeling and thinking. It is a specific, positive statement, usually spoken or written in the present tense, expressing a particular condition and/or experience. You can use affirmations to assist yourself in creating a new belief about a current situation that you would like changed, or to bring into your experience something totally new. An affirmation is listed at the beginning of each of the chapters in this book. Post an affirmation on your bathroom mirror and see how you feel about it.

Meditation

The Power, the Presence we've been talking about, does not know past and does not know future. It only knows the ever-present now. For you to get a sense of what this Presence really is, you need to meet It on Its terms, fully in the here and-now. Meditation is a tool that helps to quiet your thoughts so that you can experience the present moment in a deeper way.

A fairly standard example of meditation is to put aside time, preferably the same time every day without extraneous input from TV or radio, kids screaming, phone calls, etc. The basic idea is to create a quiet space. Meditation assists to keep our mind where our bodies are. So often in this fast, techno-microwave age, the body is driving the car, washing the dishes, supposedly listening to a conversation, while the mind is off thinking about relationship problems, or the checkbook that didn't balance, or my boss the jerk, etc.

Have a spot for your meditation area—maybe a special chair that's very comfortable. Make that time of day and that place sacred. Set aside that time of day and be there. What comes next is up to you and the results of your research. It may be closing your eyes and listening to soothing music. It could be the repetition of a particular phrase, an affirmation. It might be just listening to yourself breathing. It might be reading something that is meaningful to you. It might also be sitting quietly in a park, imagining the beach or a forest, and being present amidst the beauty of nature. Meditation is not necessarily closed eyes and crossed legs.

Some people sit down and don't know what to do. Their mind may be thinking I've got taxes to do and different projects and the boss wants me to have this report and on and on. This is *the committee* hard at work. If there's someone on your committee who says, "You know, this is really stupid and you've got much better things to do and everything about this meditation stuff is a bunch of hooey," just acknowledge each of those ideas and say, "Thanks for sharing, but please shut up, I'm not interested right now." One-by-one, quiet down the committee.

There are many helpful cassette tapes on the market. The tape might be strictly instrumental music—a flute, violin, or harp, peaceful music that assists one in just being in the now. There are also guided meditations where the narrator leads you through the meditation. These can be calming and a great help for the person just discovering meditation. This is a personal exploration and, if you look, you will find a style that works for you. This can take time. The first format you come to may not be the one for you. Do some research, as there is not any right or wrong way to meditate, only the way that works for you.

Groups

I will be optimistic for a moment and assume you understand that you no longer are a victim in life and that you can consciously make a difference in what you experience in life. This concept may get agreement from your present circle of friends. Good. You already have a network of like-minded people. If not, it's important to have people in your life who can support and assist you in this new adventure of self-discovery. There are various support groups available in nearly every city. To find what is available in your area, check out these sources: libraries, health food stores, adult education courses, YWCA/YMCA, religious groups, alternative newspapers, or women's/men's groups. When you start looking, you will attract what you need.

SUGGESTED READINGS

Jack and Cornelia Addington. *The Joy of Meditation*, Marina del Rey, CA: DeVorss, 1979.
Shakti Gawain. *Creative Visualization*. Berkeley,CA: Whatever Pub., 1978.
Joel Goldsmith. *The Art of Meditation*. San Francisco: Harper & Row, 1990.
Stuart Wilde. *Affirmations*. Taos, NM: White Dove International, 1988.
Lawrence LeShan. *How to Meditate*. New York: Bantam, 1984.

Application

How can I apply the principles you describe? I believe you can take everything that goes on in your life and put it into four categories:

-prosperity,
-relationships,
-health
-self-expression.

If you take a look at any possible problem or any human

scenario, it will fit into one or more of these four aspects.

Prosperity/Career

Your experience of money is based on your sense of self-worth, your self-esteem. The Universe doesn't know the difference between $10 and $10 million. You do, however. You filter the unlimited generosity of the Universe through your level of self-worth and acceptance. Do you have room in your life for more money? I bet you do. But it takes your cooperation with the Power of Mind to open yourself up to this possibility.

Here's an exercise to expand your previous boundaries of acceptance. Start by saying yes and thank you. When you're offered something positive, accept it! Say yes and thank you. Do not editorialize, do not explain, accept it. Circulate it if you can't use it, but start accepting what is being offered to you! Start paying attention daily to all the times that you are offered things and observe your usual responses. Many times it is probably no. Often this is a result of training and conditioning. This exercise includes saying yes and thank you to intangibles such as compliments. Someone offers a compliment about your clothes, your car, your hair, and you say; "What! This old thing?" "Yeah, it's an alright car but I want a new one." "Well, my hair desser still hasn't gotten the color right." Practice accepting the little things and it will be easier to receive the bigger things.

Regarding career and jobs, do not accept as truth any statement that you don't want to experience. It doesn't matter if the world says it's a bad job market or the economy is in a slump right now. If you accept that statement, you have taken on someone else's belief system. If you embody it and agree with that, it will be your experience. On the other hand, you can take what somebody says, acknowledge it, and say, "Thank you for sharing, but that's not my truth."

The outlet accepts whatever is plugged into it. You can plug into the outlet the appliance called perfect job. Say, "I know the right job is out there for me. The idea that there isn't is a belief that I no longer hold true. I know that my talent is valuable and there is a great job for me: It's a win-win situation and I am compensated wonderfully for it." Hold on to this belief and you will experience the result of it. The Universe, the Presence, can only give us what we are willing to receive.

Start recreating your belief system in the now as if you already have the job. Use your imagination! What does this job look like?

What does it feel like? "This office is so neat—they've got gourmet coffees...it always smells so good when I get there in the morning..." Start letting your imagination build a picture and feelings that will assist you in actually having a picture of your desired experience. Think what a delight this job is and what a great addition you are to your new company. Get into a feeling of expectation that this job is already here now, rather than any feeling of desperation. The feeling of desperation and "I don't have" is literally building a belief system of scarcity.

Remember, the formula for experience is: thought plus feeling equals the experience. Visualize and imagine. Build on that idea until you really feel that you have the job and you are knowing that at any minute someone is going to say, "Yes, it's right here."

SUGGESTED READINGS

Adelaid Bry. *Visualization Directing.* New York: Harper Collins, 1979.

Jerry Gillies. *Moneylove.* New York: Warner Books, 1988.

Napolean Hill. *Think and Grow Rich.* Northbrook, IL: Napolean Hill Foundation, 1989.

Catherine Ponder. *Dynamic Laws of Prosperity.* Marina del Rey: DeVorss, 1985.

Arthur G. Thomas. *Abundance Is Your Right.* Redondo Beach, CA: Los Arboles, 1992.

Stuart Wilde. *The Trick to Money is Having Some.* Taos, NM: White Dove International, 1989.

Relationships

The most important thing about relationships is to be in right relationship with yourself. Can you say, "Exactly as I am, I am okay, I am fulfilled on my own, I am an intelligent, wonderful, loving being, and on my own I am enough"? When you really believe and embody that idea, then you are at a very healthy place and can *choose* to *share* yourself with another person, rather than needing someone else to fill up some void in your life and make you whole. When you are whole within yourself, you bring something wonderful into the relationship to share—yourself.

One whole person plus one whole person equals one powerful and healthy relationship. One half person plus one half person equals one sick relationship. If necessary, be willing to be alone for awhile to develop, nurture, and find out about you. This is a precious investment in yourself that will have great rewards.

I highly recommend doing some serious reading regarding gender. In recent years the women's movement and the men's movement have highlighted basic and important differences between men and women. The understanding of our individual sex, our psyche, and these differences are, I believe, of paramount importance to the success of contemporary relationships. There are probably men's, women's, and couples' groups meeting in your area now to explore.

SUGGESTED READINGS

Robert Bly. *Iron John*, Reading, MA: Addison-Wesley, 1990.
Jean Shinoda Bolen. *Goddesses in Everywoman*. New York: Harper Collins, 1985. *Gods in Everyman*. New York: Harper Collins, 1990.
Warren Farrell. *Why Men Are the Way They Are*. New York: Berkeley, 1988.
G. Hendricks and K. Hendricks. *Conscious Loving*. New York: Bantam Books, 1990.
Susan Jeffers. *Opening our Hearts to Men*. New York: Fawcett, 1990.
Linda S. Leolard. *The Wounded Woman*. Athens,Ohio: Swallow Press, 1982.
Robin Norwood. *Women Who Love Too Much*. New York: Pocket Books, 1989.
Hugh and Gayle Prather. *A Book For Couples*. New York: Doubleday, 1988.

Health

The body is wonderful because it tells us clearly what is going on with us. Your body reflects your belief systems. All bodily ills, all dis-ease are effects, not causes. Recognize once again that your thought is creative. The body will express your thoughts. If your body is expressing sickness or dis-ease, that ill health is a messenger letting you know that at some level you have embodied some belief, fear, or resentment that is now expressing in your body. To heal the body, heal the mind. Thoughts created the experience. New thoughts can create a new experience. Listen to your body and what it is saying.

Here's an example. I had a client who had a very strained relationship with her father. Her father was coming to visit and she was very nervous and anxious. She had been doing a lot of inner personal healing and some of that included her father. She knew it was time to communicate some of her insights and that frightened her. She was to see him on a Saturday. When I saw her the following Monday she whispered a barely discernible hello. She was just coming from the doctor's office for treatment of a bad case of laryngitis. I couldn't help laughing. "When," I asked, "did you get this?" "Friday night," she responded with a small, guilty smile.

It's mighty tough to communicate when you can't talk. She was so fearful of what she had to say, that her body perfectly reflected her state of mind. She saw very clearly she had created the laryngitis. When she got clear that her intention was to communicate with her father, that what she felt was valuable and important, the laryngitis went away.

SUGGESTED READINGS

Frederick Bailes. *Your Mind Can Heal You.* Marina del Rey, CA: DeVorss, 1975.

Deepak Chopra. *Quantum Healing.* New York: Bantam, 1990.

Creating Health. Boston: Houghton Mifflin, 1991.

Louise L. Hay. *You Can Heal Your Life.* Santa Monica,CA: Hay House, 1988.

Bill Moyers. *Healing and the Mind.* New York: Doubleday, 1993.

(Video and audio-tapes can be obtained by phoning 1-800-633-1999.)

Self-Expression.

Self-expression is that avenue by which you get to express your individuality. It's important that you know what is unique about you and that sharing that uniqueness will give you great fulfillment. Recognize that you are a very special person, that there is absolutely nobody like you on the planet. Because there is no one here like you; there is no one that can share this particular expression as well and as uniquely as you can. For some people it's the environment, politics, making punch rugs, cooking, working with kids, working with senior citizens, or artistic endeavors. The possibilities are endless. Your self-expression may be your career and job. It is what you love to do. Your expression is your gift to the world. Find out what that is and give it.

What do you think we are here for?

We are here to experience the fullness of life. We are totally acceptable to the Universe exactly as we are. What we need to do to have a greater experience of life is to become aware of our perceptions, our beliefs, and change them if necessary. The only price we need to pay in life is paid by the coin called *attention*.

As long as you can stay aware and look out into your world and see what's going on, you can judge your perceptions and your beliefs. That is not judging yourself. Please make this important distinction. Judge your belief, not yourself. Do not beat yourself for what is going on in your life. Be kind and gentle with yourself. The *junk* that you experience in your life is the result of erroneous beliefs which can be changed. You, your unique essence, are the perfect expression of the Presence, the Power, now.

The most important points to apply

◆ There is a power for good in the Universe and you can use it.

◆ This power works through impersonal, unconditional, dependable, provable principles.

◆ What you experience in your life is a result, not a cause.

◆ Take responsibility for everything in your life.

◆ All thought is creative.

◆ Thought + feeling = experience.

◆ Become aware of your thinking.

◆ Discover what you truly believe.

◆ Judge your perceptions, not yourself. Be kind to yourself.

◆ Be grateful for what you currently have in your life and know there is more.

◆ Through the power of your mind you can be aware of your beliefs, change your beliefs, and change your life.

> *Mind is the Master-Power that moulds and makes,*
> *And Man is Mind, and evermore he takes,*
> *The tool of Thought, and, shaping what he wills,*
> *Brings forth a thousand joys, a thousand ills:*
> *He thinks in secret, and it comes to pass:*
> *Environment is but his looking-glass.*

—James Allen

SUGGESTED READINGS

Robert Heinlein. *Stranger in a Strange Land.* New York: Putnam, 1961.

Fynn. *Mister God, This is Anna.* New York: Ballantine Books, 1982.

Emma Curtiss Hopkins. *High Mysticism.* Marina del Rey: DeVorss, 1987.

Kellog Albran. *The Profit.* Los Angeles: Price, Stern, Sloan, 1978.

Joseph Campbell. *The Power of Myth.* New York: Doubleday, 1988.

LES HAIT'S SUGGESTED READINGS

James Allen. *As a Man Thinketh*. White Plains, NY: Peter Pauper Press.

Bandler, Gordon and Lebeau. *Know How: Guided Programs for Inventing Your Own Best Future*. Moab, Utah: Real People Press, 1985.

Robert Dilts. *Changing Belief Systems with NLP.* Cupertino, CA: Meta Publications, 1990.

Dilts, Hallbom and Smith. *Beliefs, Pathways to Health and Well Being*. Portland, Oregon: Metamorphous Press.

Tad James and Wyatt Woodsmall. *Time Line Therapy and the Basis of Personality*. Cupertino, CA: Meta Publications, 1988.

Norman Vincent Peale. *The Power of Positive Thinking*. New York: Ballentine Books, 1952. *The Power of the Plus Factor.* New York: Fawcett Crest, 1987.

Catherine Ponder. *The Dynamic Laws of Healing*. Marina del Rey, CA:DeVorss, 1966.

Anthony Robbins. *Awaken the Giant Within*. New York: Summit Books, 1991.

David Schwartz. *The Magic of Thinking Big*. New York: Simon and Schuster, 1959. *The Magic of Getting What You Want*. New York: Berkeley Books, 1983.

Martin Seligman. *Learned Optimism*. New York: Alfred A. Knopf, 1991.

ABOUT THE AUTHOR

FRANCIS MICHAEL LEE

I am the Minister of the Paradise Church of Religious Science, A Center For Positive Living, Paradise, California. I've been on the spiritual path since my early teens and have studied the Science of Mind philosophy for the last ten years. I also draw from a variety of life experiences including jobs as an business owner, salesperson, and training coordinator for company in the environmental business in Hawaii.

✪Next... Knowing how to be the director of one's drama, rather than the reactor, is probably the most important skill for achieving our goals. How to define where we want to head and decision-making techniques are provided in the final chapter. The author is a psychologist.

11

"I creatively channel my talents and interests into a lifecareer that allows me to grow and change in a meaningful and positive manner."

SUCCESSFUL

LIFE

PLANNING

JACQUELINE R. SHEEHAN, PH.D.

This chapter overturns common barriers to effective life planning such as lack of training in decision making, lack of self-knowledge, burdens of old emotional baggage, and rigid family roles. By involving you in proactive measures, such as the Family Genogram, Philosophy of Life, and the Five-Year Plan, you will empower yourselves with the tools of a well-constructed approach to life planning. As the last chapter in this book, the focus is on your future choices.

What will happen when I grow up?

Nearly all of your relatives and friends ask, "What are you going to do?" You may really know the answer. Or you may have developed a stock answer to fend off the curious. After all, adults have asked, "What do you want to be when you grow up?" since you were in kindergarten. Adolescents and young adults alike find the prospect of making a do-or-die decision about one's career to be overwhelming. And no wonder.

There is a common belief that your career is somewhere outside yourself and your mission is to locate it, seemingly without a map. This is indeed a frightening assignment. It may appear that others know exactly what they plan to do, where they plan to live, with whom, and what their retirement income will be in 40 years. It is likely that all of the above are illusions, held in place by a culture that has been oddly fatalistic about career planning and life planning. By fatalistic, I mean the perception that the forces that determine your life are entirely outside your control and thus, you should accept what you get.

It is not uncommon for people in our culture to believe that once you "find a career," you will remain in the same career for the rest of your life. Following this line of thought, it may also be believed that changing careers in midlife is an act of failure. These self-limiting beliefs are, in fact, quite far from reality. The average person now can expect to change careers at least six times in his or her lifetime.

Anne Miller-Tiedeman coined the term *lifecareer*, in her refreshing approach to career development. Miller-Tiedeman explains lifecareer as everything we do in life. Jobs, occupations, and professions may come and go. Your means of livelihood is only one piece of the puzzle, not the entire picture. Other aspects of your lifecareer may include your family, choice of friends, hobbies, spirituality, creativity, recreational activities, or contributions to the community. Life, and all that we put into it, is our career.

Begin now to think of your life as a career. Part of your life is finding meaningful work that fits with your personality, your interests, your needs, your learned skills, the skills you want to learn, your values, and your goals. All of these things are within you, not outside of you. To fully understand yourself and your lifecareer requires considerable effort on your part and a willingness to be flexible, tolerate ambiguity at times, and to accept change as a constant variable. When the idea of occupation fits into your life as a career, it becomes increasingly clear that all choices encountered in life (geographic moves, choice of a partner, the choice to have children or not to have children) can be approached in a more holistic manner. The first step is increased self-knowledge.

How do I identify my personal philosophy?

The development of your personal philosophy will be a critical tool for planning in all aspects of your life. Your personal philosophy includes such areas as your values in relationships, personal heroes, skills that you find satisfying, concepts that changed your perception in some significant way, spiritual values, and long-term goals. In brief, your personal philosophy is your own manifesto, your inventory of yourself.

Self-knowledge requires a form of close scrutiny that may be unfamiliar to many as we are simply not accustomed to clarifying our beliefs. The act of outlining your personal philosophy can be a time-consuming project. But think how long your lifecareer will be. We can expect to live to our seventies and eighties. It would seem foolish to live such a long time without taking the time to conceptualize your own personal philosophy of life.

To begin your journey into your personal philosophy, imagine you had exactly one week to live. Priorities tend to become more clear to us if we picture ourselves on the edge. Many of us have experienced or heard of people who gained amazing clarity about their values, the important things in life, after a close brush with death or after the death of a loved one. For the purpose of this exercise, please imagine that your time here has been radically abbreviated.

Answer the following questions as fully as possible. Keep in mind that your answers may change over time. You may find it helpful to complete this with a friend, perhaps keeping some responses just for yourself. The purpose of this exercise is to clarify your values, interests, skills, and goals as a rational basis for decision making.

=========== **Personal Reflections** ===========

Questions to answer to develop your personal philosophy:

HEROES

1. List three people whom you regard as heroes in your life. These may be people in your family, people from work or school, or public figures whom you have never met. Make sure one is the same sex as you.

2. What do you admire most about your heroes?

3. How did they affect your life or change your behavior?

4. In what way are you like your heroes?

5. What quality would you most like to possess that is present in your heroes?

6. What would have to change for you to possess that quality?

INTELLECT

7. List the three most pivotal classes that you took in college. These are the classes that were important to you in some deep and meaningful way. List the three most pivotal ideas that you formed while in college. These were ideas that prompted an internal change of a meaningful nature.

8. What is important to you about these classes or ideas?

9. How have these concepts changed your life?

SKILLS

10. What skills have you learned that you find most satisfying?

11. What skills do you want to learn?

12. What would it require for you to learn those particular skills?

13. Before you die, what skill do you most want to learn?

PAST EXPERIENCES

14. List three peak experiences for you. These may be in the area of occupation, personal accomplishments, relationships, recreation, etc.

15. What is it about the peak experiences that stand out for you? Look for overlapping characteristics.

RELATIONSHIPS

16. List the three most important qualities that you value in friendships of any sort, whether they are romantic or simply good friends.

17. If you were to design your own family, list the top three values of your family. Describe a typical day for your ideal family.

18. What are you willing to do to create these values in a family?

SPIRITUALITY

19. Pretend that you are confronted with an alien from Mars and it asks you the following question: "What is the purpose of human life?"

20. Your Martian friend inquires further: "What is your life purpose?"

21. What does spirit or soul mean to you?

ASPIRATIONS

22. On the last day of your life, what three things would you hope to be most proud of? These could be personal accomplishments, social changes, political improvements, or goals of any sort.

23. What would you regret most deeply if you did not do it in your lifetime?

24. What is the first step you would need to take to reach this goal?

25. How would you like to make a difference in your community?

Here is a brief example of what I experienced in the process of self-knowledge by writing my personal philosophy. I graduated from college and worked for several years as a recreational therapist in a rural area. I had talents and learned skills in many areas, such as photography, freelance writing, and social activism, aside from my work in recreational therapy. My greatest fear was that I would make the wrong choice and then be trapped for life. So I avoided making a commitment.

My work in recreational therapy was somewhat rewarding but the future opportunities looked limited. In fact, I had the nagging feeling that I wanted to expand into other occupational areas, but I did not know where to begin. The funding for my job ended, leaving me suddenly unemployed. Not long after, I experienced a life-threatening, medical emergency, an ectopic pregnancy. During my six-week recovery, I was shocked by the close brush with death and made a vow to examine my life and to make an all-out effort to focus my energies into a purposeful goal. Once I had established a life plan, my intention was to pursue it with gusto. I gave myself six months to formulate my plan.

After writing my personal philosophy, I discovered that my heroes were people who took a strong stand on social issues, who tried to make the world a better place in some meaningful way, who loved their work so much that it hardly seemed like work, and who were willing to take it to the limit. When asked to put it on paper, I discovered that my most pivotal classes in college were psychology and cultural anthropology. My most satisfying experience was a brief job working with inner city youth.

The personal philosophy that I struggled with turned out to be the catalytic force that led to my decision to return to graduate school to pursue a doctoral degree in psychology. Within six months of my surgery, I had made my decision. Within one year, I was enrolled as a doctoral student. My clarity of vision made my experience at graduate school more of a pleasure than the agonized experience I witnessed in many of my classmates.

How do I know what I really want to do, apart from my family's expectations?

You are, in part, a product of your environment and a large determinant of your environment is your family. Some of your most important role models for life planning may have been your parents. How did your parents choose their current careers? How did they negotiate the responsibilities of raising a family and occupational choice? What were the dreams of your parents at age 20, 25, 30, and 40? What would they do differently in hindsight? How were their paths similar to and different from their own parents? You may want to interview your parents to find the answers to some of these questions.

It is important to develop an awareness and understanding of how your family has influenced your approach to life planning, so that you can consciously decide what you want to continue and what you want to do differently. To get a better understanding of family influence in life planning, it is helpful to construct an occupational genogram of your family for three generations. A genogram is a picture of one's

Genogram Guidelines

1. gender   male – □   female – ○

2. marriage connections
   significant relationships

3. separations or divorces

4. children   male – ■   female – ●

   father   mother
   marriage
   male child   female child

5. deaths   b. 1935 d.1992

6. Put in other important data, such as, occupations, major family events (geographical moves, etc.), and indicate who you are closest to emotionally

278

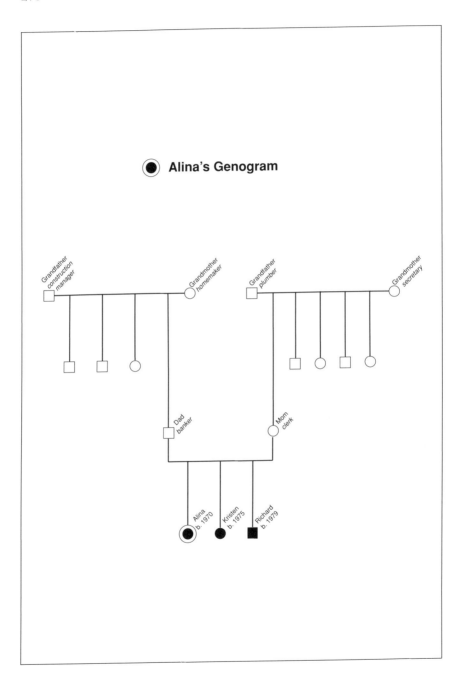

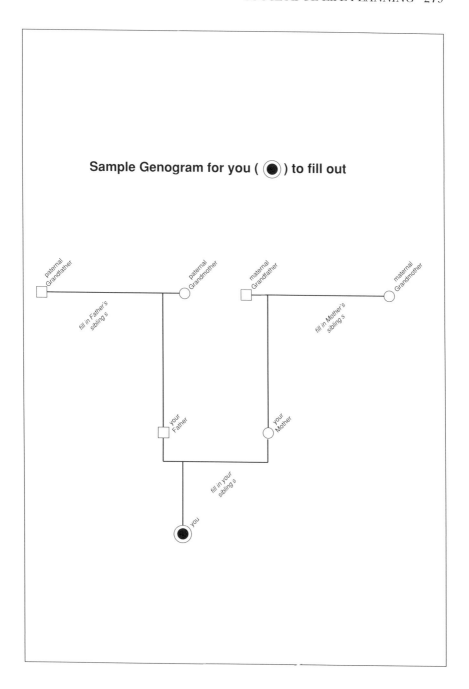

Sample Genogram for you (●) to fill out

family that displays birth order, marriages, separations, divorces, and other significant events and occupations. My clients have consistently found genograms to be surprisingly illuminating.

Family beliefs or processes tend to repeat themselves. What happens in one generation is likely to reappear in subsequent generations. "But I'm not at all like my parents, certainly not like my grandparents," you protest. You may be surprised by the unexpected ways in which family patterns repeat themselves in decision making.

Family genograms are a variation on the old theme of family trees. Your goal is to diagram your present generation, your parents' and your grandparents'. Generally accepted symbols for diagramming families are illustrated on page 277.

What Alina discovered after mapping out her family's genogram was that out of 20 cousins, she was the only one who was in college. At the time that Alina constructed her genogram, she had one more semester left before graduation. All of the aunts and uncles on her maternal side married quite young and had children at a young age. Gender roles were very traditional on the maternal side in terms of occupations and family roles. On her paternal side, her grandfather, a successful general contractor, was an alcoholic and a gambler. However, when not giving in to his addictive impulses, he was a meticulous planner.

Her paternal grandmother was one of the strongest influences in Alina's life. She had strong spiritual and ethical beliefs and had imparted these values to her granddaughter. What made Alina and her immediate family much more functional than other branches of their family had a lot to do with their ability to be proactive in their life planning. When Alina tried to track down the source of such a positive trait, she began to see that her father was the recipient of the best life planning skills from his parents.

Alina used the best of these skills when faced with major life planning decisions, and in fact, she is an excellent example of someone who has integrated the concept of lifecareer. Alina faced two decisions at the time she constructed her genogram. The first was where should she get her master's degree and second, should she and her boyfriend of three years live together before getting married?

By looking at the genogram, Alina could see that her decision to get a master's degree and to cohabitate with her boyfriend would make her increasingly different from her extended family. The two major components that Alina found to be important in decision making were spirituality (the influence of her paternal grand-mother) and logically examining the long-term picture (the influence of her father and paternal grandfather).

Alina realized that there were predominant myths in her extended family that women should marry right after high school, have children immediately, and tolerate alcoholism in their husbands. However, in her own nuclear family, her parents valued the intelligence and growing autonomy of their three children and no one in her immediate family tolerated alcohol. Alina determined that she could accept being the most *different* person in her extended family, particularly since she was prepared by anticipating such an event through the genogram. She also felt confident, after thorough contemplation, that her choice of a master's degree was an excellent long-term investment for her. Likewise, her decision to live with her boyfriend fit in with her personal sense of ethics.

In Alina's example, her primary task was to understand how her family played a part in influencing her career and relationship choices. For other people, it may be especially important to understand how established skills may transfer to other areas.

What are my transferable skills?

It is not uncommon for students to graduate with a particular degree and believe (or be told by their families) that the only job that they can get must be directly related to their major. Take a hard look at your major area and begin listing the skills that you have learned academically. For example, if you graduate with a degree in English, you probably have a good liberal arts background that most large corporations value. You have skills in written and spoken communication, as well as a broad scope of general knowledge. Write down your history of jobs, internships, volunteer work, or co-op work experiences you have had, and list the skills you learned.

Brad graduated with a degree in liberal arts, with several years' experience as a resident adviser in a large residential hall at a state college. When he began listing the skills that he had acquired in his job, he found that they could transfer to many situations other than dormitory life. The skills included: crisis intervention, organizational skills, management skills, motivational speaking, hiring and firing personnel, long range planning, training workshops, and impressive time management. Brad was hired by a large corporation to provide ongoing training to new hires across the country. If you had asked Brad five years ago what he was going to be when he was an adult, it is unlikely he would have said, "assistant director of training and education for a large corporation." It took Brad several months of self-evaluation and more than a few anxious interviews before he found an employer who recognized his diverse talents.

In Brad's example, it was important that he and his future employer were able to understand the transferability of his skills, education, and experience. When you have a clear understanding of how your skills transfer, it will become easier for you to present yourself as a versatile person and you will be in a better position to make lifecareer decisions.

What is the best way to make effective decisions?

Before embarking on decision making, it is a good idea to understand how you got to your present situation. For example, let's look for a moment at how you picked your major. Many people feel that they simply "fell" into their present academic major or career choice by being at the right place at the right time, and some report that their career just "happened" to them. But even the act of refusing to make a decision is a decision. Likewise, people report that great things happen to them unexpectedly, when closer examination reveals that they have prepared themselves for prosperous opportunities. Here is a quick and easy way to graphically portray the influences in your decision making over your lifetime.

A lifeline is one way of looking at influences in your life that affected your decision making. In this case we will be looking at how you decided on your present academic major or your present career. We could just as easily apply the lifeline to decisions about relationships or other major life choices.

Personal Reflections

Begin by drawing a horizontal line across a page. On the left end is your birth and at the right end is your present age, as in the example of a lifeline on the next page. In between, begin to mark places where important influences affected you.

Positive Image of School	Influence of Teacher	Choice of Poli Sci	
5	11	18	25

For instance, one young woman noted that at age five, she was the only one out of five siblings who was not in school. She remembered thinking that school must be a glorious place to be and she could not wait to get there. Another influence was her sixth grade teacher who was a dynamo and encouraged her in science and political thought. Yet another influence was the death of a parent and her fear of poverty. Finally, she noted that in general, she had made her choice of a college major (political science) based on what other important people in her life had told her she was good at, rather than by making a more comprehensive assessment of herself. By seeing the graphic portrayal of the importance of the opinions of others, she was able to put more emphasis on her personal needs.

Decision making is a learned skill, not unlike learning computer programming. What keeps so many of us from actively learning decision making is that there is always an element of risk. According to ☞ Serge Kahili King, author of *Urban Shaman*, what keeps many people from making decisions is the fear of making the wrong decision and having things turn out unhappily because of it. Unfortunately, this fear can be so paralyzing for some people that they will decide not to decide, which places them in the even riskier position of passively accepting whatever choices other people may toss their way.

You can reduce some of the negative outcomes of risk by learning models of more systematic decision making. Anne Miller-Tiedeman notes that not only does decision making parallel developmental stages (for example, you use a different style of decision making at age five than you do at age 21), but personality affects the way people approach decision making (☞ see Kiersey and Bates). For this reason, I give several systems for you to use.

Decision making is, for the most part, a process of choosing between several options. The greatest fear that most people have is choosing the wrong option and losing out on a once-in-a-lifetime opportunity. It is unlikely that your choice will be as far-reaching as that, although most important choices feel crucial at the time. Most decision-making systems are variations on the old system of listing the negatives and positives of a potential option. System One uses weighted advantages and disadvantages.

—————————— **Personal Reflections** ——————————

SYSTEM ONE: WEIGHTED OPTIONS

List below as many options as occur to you for a specific decision you are considering. Under each option list the weighted advantages and disadvantages. Weight the options in the following manner.

3 = very important
2 = somewhat important
1 = of limited importance

OPTION ONE _____

ADVANTAGES WEIGHT	DISADVANTAGES WEIGHT
_____ 1_____	_____ 1_____
_____ 2_____	_____ 2_____
_____ 3_____	_____ 3_____
total_____	total_____

Continue with the next option, giving numerical values to the advantages and disadvantages. You may find that you are considering more than one option in your decision making. For example, you may be considering taking a job that you would love that offers little money but great experience, taking a job that you are much less interested in that offers financial security, or studying abroad for one year with the hope of generating better career prospects. Some people find that options become more manageable when they get them on paper and particularly when they are assigned numerical value.

SYSTEM TWO: MULTIPLE CRITERIA RANKING

You will have a unique set of criteria that will be most important to you in your choice of options. Look at the following example of a young man, Juan, choosing a medical specialty.

Criteria	Options		
	General Medicine	Pediatrics	Internal
Greatest love	3	2	1
Best schedule	1	2	3
Financial return	1	2	3
Opinion of family	3	1	2
Contribution to others	3	2	1
Total:	11	9	10

In this example, you can see that the decision is still very close. What was helpful was that Juan saw how important his family's opinion was in his choice.

You can use this ranking system for other purposes as well. In relationships, you can rank your preference on a 1 to 10 scale, with the person with the strongest preference making the decision, such as what movie to see. The idea for each system is the same. It requires that you list your options and assign a numerical value to a consequence, advantage, or criteria. The very act of outlining your major influences affecting an option may be all the help that you need at times.

How can I obtain my goals?

When embarking on a life transition, whether it be a job after graduation, a new project, a new relationship, or other venture, it is important to focus your energy on making it work. If you focus your mental energies on the fear of failure, you are depriving yourself of the fuel for success.

When I was first learning to cross-country ski, I would do quite well until I would come to steep downhill areas, which invariably had trees at the bottom of sharp turns. Looking down the hill, I would concentrate unwaveringly on the tree or the sharp turn, ignoring the wide trail that would permit even a beginning skier to maneuver. Without exception, when I focused on the problem, I would fall. When I focused on the tree, I would be drawn to it like a magnet. When I finally began to focus on the wide swath of trail available to me, the tree and the sharp turn seemed to simply blend in with the whole.

Spend 10 minutes two times a day picturing an end result that you desire. Picture what you might be wearing, notice any people who would be around you, sounds, colors, smells, and most importantly, notice how it feels to be in the imagined goal. A reader comments, "This seems so dreamy to me," but, in fact, thoughts are very powerful, as ☞ explained in Bill Moyer's *Healing and the Mind* (Doubleday).

By now, you have done some of the hardest work in life planning. The hardest work that you will ever have to do in life planning is the decision-making part. Now you can start to put into physical reality all of the crystallized ideas that you have worked on in various ways. The action part merely takes persistence. Everyday, do some activity that takes you closer to your goal. It might be a phone call, an interview, research, a spiritual insight, or more tenderness to yourself or others, but it must be SOME DAILY ACTION.

The following worksheet allows you to organize your plan of action into a time frame, starting with increments of five years, one year, one month, one week, and one day. It is possible to use the worksheet for any aspect of your lifecareer, such as goals in the areas of relationships, education, recreation, spiritual aspirations, or occupation.

―――――――――――― **Personal Reflections** ――――――――――――

THINGS I WANT OR NEED TO DO IN THE NEXT FIVE YEARS
Goals should be meaningful, specific, and achievable.
THINGS I CAN DO WITHIN THE NEXT YEAR
For each goal that you want to accomplish in the next five years, list those things that you can do this year towards accomplishing each goal. Repeat this exercise with each of your five-year goals, eliminating those that cannot be pursued this year.

PICK ONE GOAL FROM THOSE THAT YOU WISH TO ACHIEVE THIS YEAR
Toward that goal:
What can I do this month? (List five steps.)
What can I do this week? (List five steps.)
What can I do tomorrow? (List five steps.)
What can I do today? (List five steps.)

Are you still waiting for some specific goal or event to take place in your life before you can be happy, satisfied, or accepted? Think for a moment about how you would be different if you had reached your goal. More specifically, Marsha Sinetar, an organizational psychologist, suggests that you ask yourself how you would live on a day-to-day basis if you respected yourself, others, and your life's purpose. Begin. Begin to live as if your lifecareer was in action. Begin to admire yourself for taking action. Begin.

A reader, Kelly Lynn Baylor, shares her experiences with putting the planning process into action. We conclude with her thoughts, as she wrote them.

I was once a successful businesswoman with my own home and a comfortable life. I developed a neuro-muscular condition that left me a functional quadriplegic, with a neck brace, often unable to speak. I lost everything I owned because of medical bills and my inability to work. I have rebuilt my life and raised a wonderful son in the process. I now walk without the assistance of any devices and talk fluently. I enjoy being a full-time student. My goal is to get my Ph.D. in clinical psychology and specialize in treating the victims of abuse.

Sometimes in spite of our best efforts and planning, life can be unfair. Sudden tragedies can occur and life can deal us a difficult hand of cards to play. If that happens, it is important to realize you still have choices; you can decide how to play your hand. You can give in to the tragedy or you can set new goals, develop new visions, and work toward a brighter future.

If you find that your life is not turning out as planned, here are some steps I've found effective.

◆ First, have the courage to look at your circumstances and see them for what they are. Only by understanding exactly where you are can you plot a new course and work toward a new future.

◆ Next, develop a new vision of your future. Set your sights high and let your new vision fill you with passion, as it will sustain you in the struggle to reach your goal.

◆ Make a list of all the steps necessary to achieve your new goal. Even if your ultimate goal seems unachieveable, keep in mind that the impossible can be achieved. Keep your list where you can mark off the steps as you achieve them.

◆ Allow yourself to frequently daydream and use active imagery. Picture living your ultimate goal.

◆ Realize that just planning a new future is not enough. You have to be willing to work hard to achieve it. Don't listen to those around you who tell you it can't be done. The surest way to fail is to stop trying, so grit your teeth and keep trying.

◆ Make a list of what has gone right in your life. Train yourself to look for the good: The hardest struggles seem easier if you focus on what went right each day.

◆ Finally, allow yourself to feel the thrill of every achievement, no matter how small. You are a winner, so seize the moment and feel like one. Celebrate your victories in life and you will see that what you once perceived as tragedy is an opportunity to grow and feel the richness of life, as is true for me.

The most important points to apply

◆ Your lifecareer encompasses all aspects of your life; your occupation fits within the larger picture of your lifecareer.

◆ Your personal philosophy will be your guide to your lifecareer. Each person's personal philosophy is a work in progress, continually being edited as you change and grow.

◆ The influence that parents and family members have on our occupational choices is rarely acknowledged. Take time to see what messages may have been handed down to you about occupations, values, self-esteem, and so forth. Evaluate what you want to retain.

◆ Genograms can illuminate the influence of family dynamics for you. Constructing your family genogram will point out not only the trouble spots, but also the strengths of your family influence. When you have a clear understanding of how your skills transfer from one occupation to another, it will be easier for you to present yourself as a versatile person who can adapt to a changing workplace.

◆ The art of decision making is a learned skill that takes practice. As with all skills, you will improve as you practice. Practice a decision-making system that works for you and use it in all areas of your life.

◆ A lifeline is one way of looking at influences in your life that affect your decision making. By looking at the graphic portrayal of critical incidents in your life, you will gain a greater understanding about how you make decisions.

◆ Spend time each day picturing the end result of what you want. Make the image as real as possible by picturing how it would feel to experience the desired goal. Focus on the future success of your goal, not the possible failure.

◆ Begin to take action. Insight, reflection, and imagery are important parts of the equation but they will amount to nothing if you procrastinate. Do something each day that will bring you closer to your desired goal.

◆ Develop a plan for five years, one year, one month, and each day. This is your personal map for life planning.

SUGGESTED READINGS

Richard Bolles. *The 1990 What Color is Your Parachute?* Berkeley, CA: Ten Speed Press, 1990.

D. Keirsey, & M. Bates, *Please Understand Me.* Del Mar, CA: Gnosology Books Ltd., 1984.

Serge Kahili King. *Urban Shaman.* New York: Simon & Schuster, 1990.

Anne Miller-Tiedeman. *How Not to Make it...And Succeed.* Vista, CA: Lifecareer Foundation, 1989.

Marsha Sinetar. *Do What You Love, The Money Will Follow.* Mahwah, NJ: Paulist Press, 1987.

ABOUT THE AUTHOR

JACQUELINE R. SHEEHAN

I am a psychologist at the counseling center of California State University, Chico. I also teach part-time in the Psychology Department and am currently working on research about dreams of incest survivors. I live with my husband and daughter in Chico. Understanding that life planning is a skill that can be learned has been one of the most empowering forces in my life. I hope that life-planning skills can be passed on to all of you.

Final Thoughts

Now you have an overview of key information you need to determine and achieve your goals. Update your journal periodically, notice how your responses to "personal reflections" change, and remind yourself of your real priorities and values. We wish you joy, love, growth, and generosity as you create your life plan. Write to the panel of authors to share your experiences.

Please tell your friends about *Everything You Need to Know to Succeed After College*. We happen to have an order form right here! Two other books and videotapes by the editor are also available.

Order Form

Send me _____ copies of *Success* at $14.95 each
Send me _____ copies of *The 50/50 Marriage* at $14.95 each
Send me _____ copies of *50/50 Parenting* at $9.95 each

Videos on *Dual-Earner Families, Parenting,* and *Men's Changing Roles* are $40; each is 30 minutes long and in color.

SubTotal $_____
Add 7.25 % sales tax (California residents only) $_____
Add $2 for handling and mailing. $2.00

Total $_____

Send your check or money order and/or your comments to:
Equality Press, 42 Ranchita Way, Suite 4, Chico, CA 95928.

Where should send your order?

Name_____

Street address _____

City_____ State _____ Zip_____

Thank you!